D0076947

Dostoevsky and
The Age of Intensity

By the same author

Nightmare Culture

ALEX de JONGE

Dostoevsky and
The Age of Intensity

The novel is the form of
absolute sinfulness

J. G. Fichte

St. Martin's Press · New York

CONTENTS

Isn't it time we paused to wonder why the nineteenth century, with its glorification of humanism, freedom, and the rights of man, led straight to the twentieth, which has not only surpassed all previous ages in its crimes against humanity but has managed, into the bargain, to prepare the means for total destruction of life on Earth?

Nadezhda Mandelstam

INTRODUCTION

> Alexandre Dumas père taught me much
> more about the living reality of the
> age of Louis XIII and Louis XIV than
> the history textbooks. The genuine
> creator has a mysterious intuition
> of the concrete and particular truth
> which historians, sociologists and
> ideologues do not have.
>
> EUGÈNE IONESCO

There has never been a shortage of books about Dostoevsky. In recent years not only have we had remarkable studies in close reading, such as Dr Richard Peace's *Dostoevsky*,[1] we have also had studies of particular aspects of his thought: for example, an alleged preoccupation with the scientific possibility of raising the dead (as in Robert Lord's *Dostoevsky Essays and Perspectives*[2]). There have been more ambitious works that cast him in the part of the Aeschylus of modern times. But the combination of studies based on close reading and the enthusiastic celebration of 'Dostoevsky and the human spirit' by no means exhausts the possibilities.

Rather than investigate the obscurer corners of the work, or consider it *sub specie aeternitatis*, we shall use a more obvious, but perhaps no less important approach: a study of Dostoevsky as an artist who was supremely representative of his age. Not until Proust will we find another novelist who reflects his own time so clearly. Dostoevsky echoes the issues, traumas and psychological stresses of his epoch with an insight and a breadth of vision which are virtually unique. Proust alone is his equal.

The suggestion that Proust, a Jew, a homosexual, an invalid and a snob, could make a significant contribution to social history may surprise. No less surprising is the contention that Dostoevsky, a Russian whose education had not steeped him in the humanities, a man of mediocre birth who spent his formative years in a Siberian penal settlement, and who spoke appalling French, should have caught the spirit of nineteenth-century Europe more perfectly than a Flaubert or a Zola.

Proust and Dostoevsky paint portraits of their times that have little

1

enough to do with conventional realism. They lack the bravura descriptive set-pieces that feature in the great realist novels of the age like so many Frith *Derby Days*. They do not share that fascination with the trivia of everyday life that we find in Balzac or Dickens. Unlike the so-called realists, neither author is concerned with the depiction of everyday life as such. Instead Dostoevsky in particular probes into the deep-structure of his age. He does not seek realistic representation, he depicts the psyche of his world. He writes not the history of the nineteenth century, but its mythology.

The world of myth is unlike the real world in that it is free of all contingency: uncluttered by the overlay of happenstance which is the supreme distinctive feature of everyday life. In the real world, as in the world of the realistic novel, nothing ever runs quite true to form. *Tak v zhizni ne byvaet* – it's not like that in real life – was the ultimate condemnation for Chekhov, perhaps the greatest realist of them all. The complete antithesis of Dostoevsky, his work offers a perfect rendering of the fragmented and inconsequential texture of reality—the context in which everything is adulterated. In contrast, the world of myth is the world of pure, uncut values and events. It is always larger than life because it never defers to chance or contingency.

Although Dostoevsky's novels are apparently set in the Russia of his time, this should deceive no one. His Russia, like Gogol's, is a dream world, a Russia of the mind. In their actions and attitudes its inhabitants act out the desires and ambitions – dreams of murder, Godhead and child-rape—that, in reality, remain safely embedded in the dream-life of society. Dostoevsky does not portray the world of nineteenth-century reality; he reveals the myths upon which that reality is founded.

It is this 'portraiture at one remove' that accounts for Dostoevsky's oblique approach. It is an obliqueness which he shares with Proust. For ethnic, and for other reasons, both authors were to one side of the main currents of European culture. It is this status of outsider which seems to have conferred upon them the detachment which enabled them to go beyond reality and find the world of myth.

Dostoevsky was aware that, as a Russian, he had a uniquely privileged view of European culture. In *The Adolescent* the cosmopolitan Versilov describes the Russian gentleman as the keeper of the European conscience. Russia alone was sufficiently detached from the parish-pump vicissitudes of European history to be able to transcend purely nationalistic considerations and think of Europe as a whole. Russia alone could achieve a generality of vision.

This view of Russia is motivated by Dostoevsky's somewhat peculiar sense of his nation's historic mission, but it helps to explain the extraordinary nature of his own achievement. It was precisely his own situation on the fringe of Europe which permitted him to understand it.

Dostoevsky was anything but a cosmopolitan. He was an unashamed patriot of the most orthodox and, finally, jingoistic kind. He despised foreigners and foreign culture. He was much too unsophisticated for Europe. Yet for all his naïvety, his chauvinism, his sentimental affection for his cultural grass-roots, he provides a unique account of the traumas and dislocations which civilisation had wrought upon the psyche of nineteenth-century man.

As a chronicler of contemporary trauma and malaise, Dostoevsky's only rival is Baudelaire. That the two writers have much in common is a truism. But only the superficial aspects of the relationship have been brought out. They share much more than an interest in the poetics of the city and the *goûts particuliers* of the sado-masochist. There is a profound resemblance in the patterns of views and values that lie at the very heart of their respective creative impulses, and from which their whole work is to be derived.

Such a relationship is much more important than 'influence', the superficial pattern of echo and interaction the study of which gives comparative literature a bad name. On this level the authors have enough in common to fill a short, nugatory article. It is below the surface that the real relationship exists. It is not the works themselves that resemble each other; nothing could be further apart than *Les Fleurs du Mal* and the sprawling *Brothers Karamazov*. Rather, it is as if the two writers have identical assumptions, begin from the same set of premises – and this is not to say that they arrive at the same conclusions. Neither work renders the other redundant in any sense, but one's insight into each author is tremendously enriched by reference to the other.

That Dostoevsky's work should bear any such relationship to that of Baudelaire is itself a confirmation of his claim to the title of historian of the nineteenth-century psyche. Baudelaire was supremely aware of the rôle of the artist as the 'Painter of modern life', the depictor of the mythic elements that subtend contemporary reality. Both by temperament and by circumstance he was well equipped to write the mythology of his age. His talent for sympathetic response reacted with equal strength to poetry, painting, music, and the poetry of city life. His capacity to extract quintessences and turn mud into gold was not confined to his poetry; it permeated every word that he wrote.

Baudelaire was favoured by circumstance as much as by temperament. He lived at the spiritual centre of nineteenth-century culture. It is not for nothing that the German writer Walter Benjamin, perhaps his greatest critic, describes Paris as the 'Capital of the Nineteenth Century', and sees the Second Empire as its golden age.

Yet despite the fact that he was so well equipped to express the spirit of his times, Baudelaire's rendering, however accurate and intense,

3

is narrower, more stilted and partisan than that of Dostoevsky. As a 'mythographer' the Russian includes and goes beyond the Frenchman's achievement. We shall finally learn more about the age that has engendered and shaped our own by examining a series of obscure events occurring in the tenements of St Petersburg, or in even more unlikely places such as the town of Skotoprigonevsk, than we will from any of Baudelaire's penetrating studies of life in Haussmann's Paris.

Both writers stand at the centre of their age. They straddle the nineteenth century, and their work captures a crucial phase in the development of the modern consciousness.

One may or may not accept the Marxist view that consciousness is determined by economic factors alone. But this does not invalidate the most important contribution of Marxist and neo-Marxist criticism, namely the assertion that consciousness has a history. Thus the historian of ideas Michel Foucault has shown that the consciousness of sixteenth-century man is as different from our own as his attire. Of course there are similarities, but there are also vital differences. Baudelaire and Dostoevsky echo a stage in the history of the European consciousness when the similarities between our own time and the past begin to outweigh the differences. Their work articulates and clarifies the impact upon the psyche of European man of the most radical series of transformations in his culture since the fall of the Roman Empire. They portray characters subject to stresses and anxieties that were utterly foreign to their immediate ancestors, but which are all too familiar to us.

They both describe a very particular form of ontological unease. Where eighteenth-century man had an essentially stable, integrated world-view, built on stereotypes of harmony, permanence and whole meanings, his universe supported by the comforting argument from design and the figure of the divine clock-maker, the characters of Baudelaire and Dostoevsky are in the process of losing that sense of cosmic and indeed social wholeness. They trace the erosion of a sense of metaphysical order and well-being, the loss of the feeling that 'all's well with the world'. The psychological consequence of that process of erosion was a fundamental change in the nature of man's attitude to his *Umwelt*. Nineteenth-century man gradually lost the belief that his actions were ultimately supported by some metaphysical set of values: the belief that such actions could in some non-specific, but vitally important sense have meaning. The world of nineteenth-century reality, the age of steam and rigged elections, the physical manifestation of his cultural heritage, tended to reduce his confidence in that culture, and indeed in the very possibility of the constructive and the valuable.

This turning away from a world-view founded on a sense of whole meanings and universals makes for the emergence of a particular syndrome, which is perhaps the supreme distinctive feature of the modern age: the syndrome of intensity.

In compensation for his loss of a framework of values and beliefs, and the sense of metaphysical well-being that went with them, modern man turns to sensation, to intensity of experience, as a process that is self-justifying. Strong feeling comes to act as a substitute for meaning. The ever-increasing importance that modern artists attach to intensity of response, at the expense of all other aesthetic values such as meaning, formal harmony, or anything else that smacks of Platonic universals, is the direct manifestation of the growing importance attached to intensity of experience in the modern age. It features in virtually every aspect of our culture, accounting for what might otherwise appear to be inexplicable aberrations: the compulsive and wasteful acquisitiveness of the consumer culture, the self-destructive habits of the aggressive motorist, the even greater self-destruction of the middle-class drug addict. We live in an age in which intensity of experience overrides all other considerations.

Baudelaire and Dostoevsky, in their various ways, both sense the increasing importance of the intensity drive. As artists they are aware of a deterioration in the quality of contemporary consciousness; an erosion of values, an impoverishment of the inner resources and an increasing capacity for addiction of every description. As creative artists, as opposed to sociologists, they both describe and explain this change. Dostoevsky's account, in particular, is intuitive rather than analytic. He senses what is going wrong, without ever being quite able to isolate the disease. Yet his work, read properly, which is to say with the understanding afforded us by hindsight, provides the most penetrating and comprehensive account of the steady disintegration of European culture, and foretells the coming of an age of terror, of Rimbaud's *temps des assassins*.

It is on this aspect of Dostoevsky's work that we shall be concentrating, not only because to consider his work in terms of its treatment of the intensity syndrome is to illuminate every word he ever wrote, but because, seen in that light, his work makes a definitive comment upon his age, an age not so very unlike our own.

5

PART ONE

Baudelaire and the Romantic Heritage

CHAPTER ONE

La Douceur de Vivre

In order to understand the issues raised by Baudelaire and Dostoevsky, we require a historical perspective. Their work may only be understood by seeing it in terms of what had come before, since both writers stand at a cultural watershed. They had both been young enough to have had contact with Romanticism, but Romanticism remained a part of their youth. They freed themselves from its rhetoric, if not from it, essential concerns; their mature work points forward rather than backs and is closer in feel to our own age.

However, there is a greater measure of continuity between Romanticism and the modern age than might appear at first sight. The Romantics were the first generation to face certain problems that have been confronting Western man ever since.

It is a commonplace of histories of Romanticism that meaningful generalisation about the movement is not possible. As early as Musset's entertaining discussion in the letters of Dupuis and Cotonet, it emerges that a Romantic author may always be found to refute the suggestion that any single feature constitutes the *sine qua non* of the movement.

More recent historians such as H. G. Schenk, Lilian Furst and Henri Peyre, have all subscribed, more or less, to the thesis that a unified view of Romanticism as a European phenomenon is not possible – there are only Romanticisms.

But to settle for this discrete approach is surely an admission of defeat. Our intuition informs us that, although the historian may be obliged, for good order's sake, to speak of a series of independent movements, those movements have so much in common that any account that seeks to be intuitively satisfying must put them together. The cultural historian is too easily deterred by the fact that his various Romanticisms possess mutually contradictory features. It is only in the world of set theory that all members of all classes have constant features justifying their class-membership. Cultural classifications can make do with more flexible parameters. That there may not be any one essential and universal property manifested by every Romantic movement should not prevent us from forming a view of Romanticism as such.

Form such a view we must, if we are to understand the nature of the problems facing Dostoevsky and his response to them. The Romantics were the first generation to meet situations which have faced us ever since, but which did not, on the whole, face the men of Enlightenment.

9

Their responses were accordingly both fresh and naïve, compared with later attitudes. A summary examination of their reactions to problems which we have come to take for granted, and which Dostoevsky reluctantly came to face, can do much to illuminate both his time and our own.

The re-creation of the nineteenth-century world-view calls for little more than the removal of a few layers of dirt from the portrait. We all know, more or less, what it looks like. Cleaning only brings out the detail. By comparison, the re-creation of eighteenth-century man calls not for a restorer but an archaeologist, so remote does that world seem.

No doubt, Dostoevsky, who mocked the Russian socialists for their attempts to bring about reform in their own country according to the history of Parisian revolutionary movements, would be the first to complain of a study of his work which begins in eighteenth-century France. The only defence offered of the approach is that it works: it provides a way of bringing out precisely what it was that was new about Romanticism, and this will in turn clarify the main concerns of both Baudelaire and Dostoevsky.

The reader who distrusts cultural panoramas – and such panoramas are notoriously unscholarly – may care to regard the rest of this chapter not as history, but as a historical model designed to illuminate his view of Dostoevsky.

Talleyrand's suggestion that it was necessary to have lived under the *ancien régime* to have known *la douceur de vivre* is no doubt an unreliable guide to the quality of life in the late eighteenth century. But it is important in one respect: it points to a sense of rupture, a solution of continuity between the old order and the new. In truth the Restoration had restored nothing, and the world of the *ancien régime* was gone for ever. As a political fact this is a commonplace, but it was no less true in other respects. The picture that we may infer of eighteenth-century man differs radically from that of his Romantic successor.

Perhaps the most striking point of difference is man's relationship to his society. Eighteenth-century man was much more closely integrated into his social group, had a greater sense of social unity. This is reflected in an infinity of ways: for example, in the writer's view of his rôle. Authors such as Diderot and Voltaire saw themselves as figures serving a public, writing essentially for their readers. It was in so far as they served those readers that they felt justified professionally. With the outstanding exception of Rousseau, eighteenth-century authors were not primarily motivated by the need to express themselves. Indeed the notion of self-expression, of writing for yourself, was to become an important feature of the new aesthetic of Romanticism; in contrast with the eighteenth-century view of the man of letters as a public figure fulfilling a social rôle.

That eighteenth-century man had a more developed awareness of the part he played in the community emerges in the, to us, disastrous concern of the age with civic duty, as reflected, for example, in the *drame bourgeois*. This emphasises man's obligations, not to the gods, the throne, or even his woman, but to his fellow citizens and members of the merchant community. The concern with public morality, man's duty to discharge the obligations of his middle-class status, are reflected in virtually every work written in the latter half of the century, from *Le Paysan perverti* to *La Nouvelle Héloïse*. This concern with the public and the collective aspects of experience is a far cry from the romantic concern with themes of individualism and alienation. Indeed one of the very rare individuals of eighteenth-century literature, Rameau's nephew, is presented by Diderot as a tragi-comic sport of nature; his very existence is a challenge to established order. If he cannot be suppressed, then he must be disregarded. His individualism may have been unnervingly well portrayed, but one feels that Diderot was dismayed by his own creation. Certainly he neither admired him nor considered him in any sense typical.

Our conception of individualism was non-existent in that age, because there was a greater belief in social harmony and integration – whether or not such harmony really existed is another matter – than we can conceive of. As de Tocqueville writes in *L'Ancien Régime*:

Nos pères n'avaient pas ce mot d'*individualisme*, que nous avons forgé pour notre usage, parce que de leur temps il n'y avait pas, en effet, d'individu qui n'appartînt pas à un groupe et qui pût se considérer absolument seul . . .[1]

The eighteenth-century idea of happiness confirms the virtual non-existence of the concept of the individual. In no sense does it seem to have been based upon that plenitude achieved in splendid isolation to which the Romantics aspired. Happiness, too, was a collective enterprise. Thus, in his monumental study on *L'idée du bonheur au 18-ème siècle*,[2] Robert Mauzi cites countless examples of how happiness was sought through the group, the tightly knit community. Witness one Watelet, whom Marmontel described as the man of his age who had best arranged his life. He had the good sense to confine himself to a 'société bénévole, un petit monde clos et choisi'.[3] Similarly d'Holbach feels that he can only fulfil himself through the execution of his social rôle, however corrupt his society may be.[4]

Significantly, this vision of a stable and integrated community as an image of happiness is, on one occasion at least, specifically offered as a reflection of a higher order. Mauzi cites an article, 'Indépendance', which suggests that everything in the universe is related. Echoing the order of a cosmos which links the smallest portions of nature to one

11

another, the order of the social universe sets each member in a vast ensemble.[5]

The sense of harmony which underlies such attitudes may be seen to function in various ways. For example, one of Diderot's justifications for morals suggests that pleasure is good, virtue gives pleasure, therefore virtue is good. Ignoring the weakness of the argument, its association of pleasure with one's duties towards others points to a great compatibility between codes of public behaviour and private impulse. If virtue makes you happy, then all happiness becomes a virtue: 'Ils sont trop heureux, ils ne peuvent être coupables,' quotes Mauzi, who continues, 'L'évidence du plaisir devient le critère moral de l'acte.'[6]

To suggest that the world-view of that age was based on a sense of peace, harmony and stability is not of course to suggest that it was a golden age of universal happiness. The very fact of the Revolution makes such a view absurd. Moreover, the slightest acquaintance with the economic history of the eighteenth century will remind one that it knew periods of dreadful distress and famine. It is not suggested that eighteenth-century man saw harmony all around him. The rôle played by harmony and a sense of being integrated is more delicate. They form the warp and woof of his world-picture. It is in terms of harmony and stability that he thinks. These notions form his mental codes. Thus, in the following passage from Blondel's *Loisirs philosophiques*, we find inequality preferred to disorder, suggesting that social order and harmony were the first requirements of the age:

> . . . de ce que dans les sociétés civiles, toutes sortes d'états sont nécessaires pour y maintenir une dépendance continuelle les uns des autres, sans laquelle les sociétés tomberaient dans une anarchie qui en causeraient la perte, il s'ensuit qu'il doit y avoir des hommes faits pour servir les autres, et que si ces hommes . . . viennent à découvrir l'horrible néant, dans lequel ils sont plongés, ils détesteront infailliblement la vie, chercheront à sortir par la mort ou la fuite de cet état de misère, et détruiront ainsi l'harmonie de la société . . .[7]

Harmony is clearly preferred to social justice. Perhaps the most telling illustration of the all-important rôle of harmony is the fact that, for all the dissent, the expressions of dissatisfaction with the *status quo* in which the age abounds, revolution as such was inconceivable. Revolutions were essentially palace revolts that only happened in harems; they had nothing to do with Europe. The idea of a French Revolution was literally unthinkable. De Tocqueville makes it clear that no one anticipated revolution because:

> . . . la notion même d'une révolution violente était absente de l'esprit de nos pères. On ne la discutait pas, on ne l'avait pas conçue.[8]

It was necessary for the fabric of the régime to fall apart of its own accord. No one pushed it, because it occurred to no one to do so. We can only form ideas on the basis of our own experience, or the experience available to us. To the inheritors of a tradition of political continuity that appeared to reach back to Charlemagne, the idea of radical political transformation was unthinkable. However urgently the reformer of 1780 might press his case, that case was always made out in terms of re-jigging the *status quo*.

That instability and change were something of a conceptual impossibility is confirmed by the apparent absence of a sense of time in the eighteenth century. This emerges in a number of ways. In the first place there is no sense of evolution in the arts. The Neo-Classical aesthetic, based upon the principle of the imitation of the ancients, the perpetual re-creation of their works, was essentially an aesthetic of timelessness. Even the bourgeois aesthetics of Diderot, based on the realistic representation of everyday life, did not acknowledge the possibility that its patterns might change. Political systems were equally based on the principle of stability. Montesquieu's division of societies into monarchy, republic and despotism was expressed through a code of stable states. It conceded that no republic was likely to remain one indefinitely, but the concession was incidental. The notion of evolution, or indeed devolution, played no real part in his thought. He seems to have believed in the real possibility of final and enduring solutions.

The lack of a sense of time is also reflected in the eighteenth-century novel. We have been accustomed by nineteenth-century novels to regard the hero's evolution through time as the definitive novel form: the final appearance of Frédéric Moreau in resigned middle age, the eventual self-discovery of Proust, and, later, Orlando's union with her destiny in time present, are moments that seem to express the very essence of the novel. But pre-nineteenth-century novels do not develop along a temporal axis. Instead, they move their characters through space. Hence the vital part played in their narrative by the journey.

The journey is a device of extraordinary importance in pre-nineteenth-century literature. Thus the seventeenth-century notion of love is expressed spatially, on *la carte du tendre*. Indeed the whole construction of the *roman précieux* is the illustration of the comforting proposition that journeys end in lovers' meetings. The journey is used to develop the narrative of *Pilgrim's Progress*, as it is of *Candide*. Change is envisaged spatially, as the picaresque character moves across the face of a varied but otherwise unchanging earth. Change is rendered through spatial displacement because temporal development was much harder to conceive. The temporal dynamic was to be an essential component in the new culture-pattern of Romanticism.

It may be alleged that this picture of a world-view of unchanging peace and stability is at variance with the facts. It takes no account of discontent, of the enormous numbers of pamphlets sniping at the government, or indeed of the more serious if less widely read works of the *Philosophes*. More important is the charge that it fails to handle Voltaire's anguish at the Seven Years' War and the Lisbon earthquake. But it was precisely because the mental attitudes of the age expressed themselves in terms of a balanced and organised universe, a sort of cosmic Rolls Royce, that events such as the earthquake made such a disturbing impact upon Voltaire, whereas they would scarcely disturb his twentieth-century equivalent. Similarly the enormous output of radical literature was only permitted because no one believed that it meant anything. It was, as de Tocqueville points out, an age in which anyone could say anything, because words could never hurt or threaten the stability of the state. We hear much more about censorship under the Restoration, for the Bourbons had by then acquired a developed sense of the precarious impermanence of political institutions.

It was not, I suspect, the conventional stereotypes of the *ancien régime* – the world of Boucher, Fragonard and Crébillon *fils* – to which Talleyrand looked back with such nostalgia. Rather, it was to a more tenuous and metaphysical sense of well-being, a well-being founded on stability, on the feeling that one formed a small but not utterly insignificant part of a design to which everyone made their contribution. It was essentially a world which contained meanings, truths; in which everyone knew their place and believed in it. There was no hint of any ontological insecurity, of *Angst* in the face of existential absurdity, which might threaten that universe of plenitude and whole meanings. It was not necessarily an age of universal happiness, but it was an age in which most people knew who and where they were, an age of fixed parameters. It is with a nostalgia echoing Talleyrand that Chateaubriand, in his *Memoires d'outre-tombe*, describes an England which appeared unaffected by those changes which had made France a less stable and agreeable place:

> Il n'y avait qu'un peuple. Cette classe jalouse appelée bourgeoisie en France, qui commence à naître en Angleterre, n'existait pas; rien ne l'interposait entre les riches propriétaires et les hommes occupés de leur industrie. Tout n'était pas encore machine dans les professions manufacturières, folies dans les rangs privilégiés.[9]

CHAPTER TWO

Romantic Agony

Where the eighteenth century was founded on a stable world-picture, that offered by Romanticism is one of cultural collapse. It is impossible to overestimate the impact of the French Revolution and the ensuing twenty-five years of war upon the contemporary European consciousness. We are accustomed to violent cultural transformations, insecurity has become part of our way of life. But to the generation that experienced the Revolution and the Napoleonic wars, the effect of a sudden, totally unforeseen transformation of an entire continent must have been utterly traumatic. Where we have developed stereotypes of upheaval through which to handle further vicissitudes of fortune – the assassination of yet another Kennedy would not find us unprepared – that generation knew nothing but stability and security. They were totally unready for what was to happen to them.

Chateaubriand is a typical victim of the disintegration of the old order. He experienced a particularly violent transition from security to rootless destitution. A young Breton nobleman, brought up on his family estates, he must have supposed when he was presented at court and had his first taste of the royal hunt in the forest of Fontainebleau that the new life into which he had been launched was just beginning. The year was 1788.

After fighting in the counter-revolutionary armies and undergoing great physical hardship, he ended up in London, penniless, with scarcely a shirt to his back. The movement from riches to rags must have seemed both total and irreversible. One thing at least must have been clear: that henceforward to build on a sense of stability, to trust in the future, however inevitable that future might appear, was folly.

The factor that unifies the various European Romanticisms, and which forms their underlying constant, is this sense of fundamental insecurity. Romanticism is the reflection of cultural collapse. Its themes either reflect or derive from the sudden and violent realisation that what had seemed to earlier generations a permanent and stable political and social reality was no longer to be trusted. You could no longer be certain of anything—your wealth, your nationality, or, especially, the likelihood of dying in your bed.

The immediate and obvious consequence of this sense of insecurity was the development of Romantic individualism. It has been suggested that whereas most philosophies seek to avoid solipsism, which is

15

regarded as a blind alley arrived at by default, the Romantics positively cultivated it. They did so because they found themselves in a world in which the self alone seemed to offer a measure of certainty – although, ironically enough, the deeper they entered into themselves, the more the self became open to doubt. The obsessive egoism of René, his sense that the world was stale and unprofitable, could never match the intensity of his self-awareness; his aspirations to apotheosis, bear witness to the new self-consciousness. René's self-concern, just as much as the *égotisme* of Stendhal's characters or Pechorin's introspection, reflects a new individualism: a sense of opposition of the self to the rest of a world from which one feels traumatically cut off. For, along with the new self-interest and self-reliance that was Romantic individualism, are to be found the themes of alienation and estrangement from reality. The romantic protagonist is by definition estranged. Apart from his world he is *El Desdichado* – the disinherited. His condition is recognised by Hegel, who, in his *Vorlesungen über die Aesthetik*, suggests that the only form of modern tragedy possible would portray the conflict between the individual and society: a conflict in which he was inevitably doomed. As opposed to feeling a part of an integrated and organic whole, man had come to think and dream of himself as alone in an essentially hostile world. What in Rousseau was the paranoiac persecution mania of one untypical individual had, by force of historical circumstance, become the emotional mode of a whole generation.

The most important single theme of Romanticism, the root cause of individualism and alienation, is that of the degraded present. In its reflection of cultural collapse Romantic literature offers the most unflattering picture of its reality. Where reality was joyfully embraced by the Enlightenment, for which the values of this world were quite sufficient, Romanticism rejects its reality out of hand.

The rejection is amplified and encouraged by a second revolution. Although it is the sudden encounter with political instability that is primarily responsible for the major cultural shift of Romanticism, there is a secondary cause which takes on increasing importance in the course of the century: the industrial and commercial revolution. Its effects may have been less immediately dramatic than the impact of war and revolution proper, but they were perhaps more lasting and more profound.

If the vast proportion of the themes of nineteenth-century literature reflect a need to escape from an intolerable here and now, it is reasonable to acknowledge the contribution made by the development of industry and finance to rendering that here and now intolerable.

In its attitudes towards industry, Romanticism is again in contrast with the Enlightenment. The eighteenth-century attitude to industrial work was positive – but then the typical worker of that age was a craftsman rather than a millhand. Images of craftsmanship abound. There are the *planches* with their drawings of lathes and drilling machines, which Diderot supplied as a supplement to the *Encyclopédie*. There is Louis XVI's skill as a locksmith, the lathe of Andrey Bolkonsky's father. Eighteenth-century writers tend to refer to work in terms of a glowing enthusiasm. Peasants remain characters from pastoral. Their rôle in the literature of the age is to be contrasted with *les grands* who are deemed to be 'less happy', and represent idleness.[1] An equally glowing picture of work is painted in D'Estaing's poem 'Le Plaisir':

> L'artisan désséché par le feu qu'il allume
> Qui fait plier le fer et fait gémir l'enclume;
> Le laboureur tardif armé d'un aiguillon
> S'appuyant sur le soc pour ouvrir un sillon;
> Le manoeuvre englouti dans le sein de la terre
> Qui cherche des métaux ou détache la pierre;
> L'auteur dont le travail est l'effet du besoin . . .
> Les tableaux différents de mille états divers
> Offrirent à mes yeux par un juste partage
> Du plaisir en tout temps et de goûts à tout âge.[2]

The spectacle of work is proposed as a source of pleasure. Moreover, there is no suggestion that some forms of work are more agreeable than others. There is no discrimination, for example, between manual work and the work of the author.

The image of work as pastoral does not survive the industrial revolution. It will be recalled that Chateaubriand harked back to a golden age in England before the division of labour. Indeed, it would appear that the transition which large numbers of persons were obliged to undergo, from an agricultural life working by the sun to an industrial life working by the clock, was extraordinarily painful.

The consequent transformation in the literary attitude towards work did not come overnight. The Romantic artist could not, on the whole, be said to be over-concerned with the plight of the proletariat. Yet there was a growing consciousness of the social cost of industrialisation. It is interesting to see Robert Owen, in 1815, describe the disintegration of what had once been an organic community:

The general diffusion of manufactures . . . generates a new character in its inhabitants; and as this character is formed upon a principle quite unfavourable to individual or general happiness . . .

All ties between employer and employed are frittered down to the consideration of what immediate gain each can derive from the other. The employer regards the employed as mere instruments of gain, while these acquire a gross ferocity of character . . .[3]

The degrading effects of industrial work were subsequently to form the point of departure for both Ruskin and William Morris. They were above all concerned with the damage it did to the psyche:

> It is verily this degradation of the operative into a machine, which, more than any other evil of the times, is leading the mass of the nation everywhere into vain, incoherent, destructive struggling for a freedom of which they cannot explain the nature to themselves.[4]

William Morris actually looked to art as a means of transforming the nature of work, and restoring it to the non-alienating activity that the Romantics (Marx among them) chose to consider it in the pre-industrial era:

> The cause of Art is the cause of the people . . . One day we shall win back art, that is to say the pleasure of life; win back Art again to our daily labour . . .[5]

and on another occasion:

> The aim of art is to destroy the curse of labour by making work the pleasurable satisfaction of our impulse towards energy.[6]

Although these lines were written by Morris they could equally well have been written by Charles Fourier. The founding principle of his new communities was that work should be made a pleasure. He developed his system to the most extraordinary lengths in order to seek some balance between pleasure and work. Fourier's system, his view of work, was not the result of idle speculation; it had been learnt the hard way by a lifetime in commerce.

It has always seemed something more than a coincidence that this new image of work, created by the industrial revolution, should occur at the same time that a revolution took place in the attitude towards artistic work, which was transformed into something quite different in kind from all other forms of activity.

The Enlightenment had made little or no distinction between artist and artisan. The writer was essentially a man of letters, professional or dilettante; not a frenzied vessel of inspiration. In *The Mirror and the Lamp* M. H. Abrams has given the definitive account of the transition from one view of art to the other. Among the series of oppositions which he establishes between the two aesthetics, we find that where the eighteenth century saw art as imitative – the mirror – the nineteenth saw it as creative – the lamp. Where the eighteenth-century artist was a part of his society, his successor was apart from it. More important for our immediate thesis, where the eighteenth century used mechanical models to describe creativity, the nineteenth used organic ones based on biological images such as plant growth. In the meantime, mechanical terms became pejorative. Carlyle was to write:

> Not the external and physical alone is now managed by machinery, but the internal and spiritual also . . . Men are grown mechanical in head and in heart as well as in hand.[7]

The upgrading, indeed the exaltation of artistic work as a self-justifying activity of supreme value is, in part at least, the consequence of the downgrading of other forms of work. The repetitive and degrading activity of the industrial wage-slave destroys the image of work as pastoral. It has become an infernal activity. In compensation, the culture creates a positive antithesis – creative work, which is viewed as having all the value which has gone from other kinds of work. On the Saussurian principle that meaning implies choice and *vice versa*, the apotheosis of creative work serves to bring out the meaning of industrial work; the relationship being of course reciprocal. Each one comes to imply its opposite. When the eighteenth century held a positive view of work as such, artistic work enjoyed no outstanding distinction, but was a skill among others. It was the downgrading or destruction of most other skills that was responsible for its promotion.

The birth of the industrial society does not simply mean dark satanic mills, it also implies dark satanic financiers. One of the most important elements of Stendhal's fiction is a group that might be termed the 'party of reality' – hard-faced persons of commonsense such as M. de Renal, M. de Valenod, Lucien Leuwen's minister and indeed the entire political machine of the July Monarchy. Balzac depicts the same characters from a different angle, admiring his Nucingens and Gobsecks for the sheer scale of their success as the new power élite. Even in Stendhal's world these votaries of the pecuniary ethic always win in the end, even though they may be governed by motives so base that they are laughable. Stendhal's heroes have their being in a world that is basically absurd, but it is a world in which the party of reality goes on forever. These gentlemen are by no means peculiar to the works of Balzac and Stendhal. We find them in Hugo's poetry as the voters who brought Napoleon III to power. One of their more distinguished members keeps a pharmacy in Yonville. Surviving both Emma Bovary and her husband, his services to the cause are eventually recognised by a decoration. The unspeakable Luzhin of *Crime and Punishment* is another party member.

More important perhaps than individual studies of this kind of 'new man' is the rôle played by the party of reality in de Tocqueville's *L'Ancien Régime*. His picture of the social climate of the old order is of an age in which there was a strange kind of liberty of spirit and a concomitant belief that there was more to life than the accumulation of *phynance*. His study invites a perpetual comparison with the values of his own age, in which the party of reality, headed by Napoleon *le Petit*, reigned unopposed. He makes the contrast directly in the following immortal lines:

> Les hommes du dix-huitième siècle ne connaissaient guère cette espèce de passion du bien-être qui est comme la mère de la servitude, passion molle, et pourtant tenace et inaltérable, qui se mêle volontiers et, pour ainsi dire, s'entrelace à plusieurs vertus privées, à l'amour de la famille, à la régularité des moeurs, au respect des croyances religieuses, et même à la pratique tiède et assidue du culte établi, qui permet l'honnêteté et défend l'héroisme, et excelle à faire des hommes rangés et de lâches citoyens. Ils étaient meilleurs et pires.
>
> Les Français d'alors aimaient la joie et adoraient le plaisir; ils étaient peut-être plus déréglés dans leurs habitudes et plus désordonnés dans leurs passions et dans leurs idées que ceux d'aujourd'hui; mais ils ignoraient ce sensualisme tempéré et décent que nous voyons. Dans les hautes classes, on s'occupait bien plus à orner sa vie qu'à la rendre commode, à s'illustrer qu'à s'enrichir. Dans les moyennes même, on ne se laissait jamais absorber tout entier dans la recherche du bien-être; souvent on en abandonnait la poursuite pour courir après des jouissances plus délicates et plus hautes; partout on plaçait, en dehors de l'argent, quelque autre bien.[8]

De Tocqueville sets up an opposition between 'then' and 'now' which, whatever it may tell us about the eighteenth century, has more to say about his own time. It describes the moral consequences of the industrial and political revolutions which had won pride of place for the pecuniary ethic, creating an age in which Guizot's *Enrichissez-vous* could be a political slogan.

The immediate consequence of the emergence of the commercial and industrial society was the rise of the modern city. The theme of urban life takes on an ever-increasing importance in the literature of the age. Balzac, Dickens, Baudelaire, Zola and, of course, Dostoevsky are its greatest exponents. Essentially, the city is the place in which the consequences of the industrial revolution are endured to the full. Even essentially pre-industrial images of the city, such as Pushkin's *Queen of Spades*, treat it in terms of loneliness, isolation and despair. From Pushkin and Gogol to Dostoevsky, the city is the very embodiment of alienation.

In his treatment of urban themes in Baudelaire, the critic Walter Benjamin very properly concentrates on the phenomenon of the crowd. The crowd captured Baudelaire's imagination, as it did that of Poe, Hugo, Hoffmann and Dostoevsky. It is the perfect expression of the social consequences of city life: an agglomeration of people with nothing to unite them except a coincidental presence in the same place at the same time. It embodies the experience of the city since it combines anonymity, isolation and a total lack of privacy. The essence of alienation, the crowd conveys perfectly the sense of disruption, the lack of ties, the loss of any sense of community, which are the distinctive features of urban life as portrayed in the literature of the age.

Urban misery as such plays a direct and important part in Romantic and post-Romantic literature. It also makes another, no less important, contribution. We saw that changing attitudes towards work resulted in a downgrading of the mechanical and corresponding promotion of the organic image of creativity. The mechanical/organic opposition also features in the subject matter of Romantic literature. The organic side of the opposition is filled by the vitally important concept of nature.

The rôle of nature in Romantic art can only be fully understood when it is seen to form part of a binary contrast, set in opposition to the degraded life of contemporary human society. It forms part of a nature/culture contrast in the full sense of that expression, representing everything that vile man is not.

Just as Romantic theories of creativity were generated by the antithesis of industrial work, so the Romantic image of nature is created by the industrial revolution and urban expansion. That kind of nature had played no greater part in the literature of the Enlightenment than had theories of creativity. It is essentially part of the divided, fragmented world of the Romantic and industrial age. It was the deterioration in the quality of community life that was directly responsible for the existence of its antithesis in literature.

Accordingly, it is no coincidence that it is England, the most developed industrial nation, that also produced the greatest poets of nature, and indeed the most evolved corpus of Romantic literary theory. Both Romantic poetry and the *Biographia Literaria* are ultimately the outcome of industrial development. It was the mills that created the Romantic attitude to nature. Meaning implies choice, and if nature has meaning it is in so far as it stands in opposition to a counterpart. It is the new industrial environment which imparts to the Romantic image of nature that desperate edge of poignancy which renders it the denial of culture – as opposed to its emblematic complement as it is in the lyric poetry of the Elizabethans and the *Pléiade*.

That the Romantic image of nature was an escape, a rejection of the cultural environment, is expressed, cryptically, by Georg Lukács in *The Theory of the Novel*:

Estrangement from nature, the first nature, the modern sentimental attitude towards nature, is only a projection of man's experience of his self-made environment as a prison instead of a parental home.

When the structures made by man for man are really adequate to man, they are his necessary and native home; and he does not know the nostalgia that posits and experiences nature as the object of its own seeking and finding. The first nature as a set of laws for pure cognition, nature as the bringer of comfort to pure feeling, is nothing other than the historico-philosophical objectification of man's alienation from his own constructs.[9]

Everything we have seen so far about the Romantic movement relates to the notion of the 'degraded present'. The acknowledgement that 'the structures made by man for man' were not 'really adequate to man' constitutes the essential motivation of Romanticism. The notion of binary contrast, of nature being advanced against the industrial city, was seen to explain and link together apparently independent aspects of the Romantic culture pattern. The theme of the degraded present operates in the same way, on a much larger scale. It is against a sense of a hostile, alien and valueless reality that Romanticism mounts its various strategies of escape. It is the reality of the Romantic age that inspires some of the richest and most ambitious attempts to deny reality that the West has known.

It is this attitude to reality, coupled with the knowledge that escape is finally impossible, that the party of reality is invincible, which creates Romantic despair. Romantic attitudes are regularly expressed in the language of disillusion: 'Wir suchen überall das Unbedingte und finden nur Dinge,' writes Novalis.[10]

Romanticism is essentially a literature of lost illusions. Chateaubriand, Byron, Novalis, Hölderlin, Stendhal, Balzac, Lermontov, all treat the theme in one way or another. This must not be viewed as the discovery of a hitherto untapped vein of literary material. It is the direct reflection of a new type of society: one in which illusions were lost. Because society is unable to provide satisfaction, otherwise reasonable ambitions and expectations of happiness are redefined as – illusions. The point is made by Nodier, who justifies a flight into fantasy by proposing as a suitable author of a *conte fantastique*:

> ... un autre fou ... un homme sensible et triste qui n'est pas dénué d'esprit ni de génie, mais qu'une expérience amère des sottes vanités du monde a lentement dégoûté de tout le positif de la vie réelle, et *qui se console volontiers de ses illusions perdues dans les illusions de la vie imaginaire.*[11]

The point of departure for Romanticism's flight into fantasy is its acknowledgement of reality's shortcomings. Thus, for Hoffmann the intervention of the 'spiritual principle' through dreams is evidence of the existence of another world, a place of total harmony from which we are banished.[12]

The positive side of Romantic literature seeks to escape our world and reach or recreate the world of harmony. Hence the great importance of nostalgia and the theme of a golden age. This can take the form of a longing for childhood innocence: 'Je me suis conservé enfant par dédain d'être homme,' writes Nodier;[13] and Jean Paul is another writer who gives pride of place to an image of childhood as escape.[14] Alternatively, escape may be sought in the past. This accounts for the rise of the historical novel, and, even more, for the attempt to resurrect the values of a bygone age of spiritual harmony through Gothic revival. Indeed revivalist Gothic architecture shows that Romantic nostalgia and the longing for something better than contemporary reality extend well beyond mere literary conventions. Yet another instance of a real attempt to recreate the world of harmony is the Fourierist blueprint for Harmony on Earth. His *phalanstères* were intended as practical propositions, and indeed attempts were made to put his theories into practice.

To revert to the purely literary plane, Rousseau proposes the need to escape from reality as the very mainspring of his creative drive; as, for example, in his introduction to *Julie* which describes him inventing the characters he was unable to find in reality. In the same mood he writes in *Confessions*:

Si je veux peindre le printemps il faut que je sois en hiver; si je veux décrire un beau paysage il faut que je sois dans les rues, et j'ai dit cent fois que si jamais j'étais mis à la Bastille je ferais le tableau de la liberté.[15]

Rousseau still expresses his association of imagination and escapism in the spatial code of the eighteenth century. By the time of the German *Frühromantiker* the aspiration has grown more ambitious, aiming at passage into another world, or even at eternity itself. Thus, in their terminology, Ec-stacy transports us from our normal condition and restores us to a second existence; it is an escape to a higher reality.[16]

Escape from reality is regularly expressed as an escape from time. The rediscovery of time is one of the most important characteristics in which Romanticism differs from the Enlightenment. It is surely to the political upheaval of 1789–1815 that the rediscovery should be ascribed – to the traumatic discovery of change. The process manifests itself on various levels. Nationalism, both political and cultural, itself a consequence of the revolution (see C. Hayes' *The Historical Evolution of Modern Nationalism*), and the disintegration of the European community of the Enlightenment, were reflected in an increasing interest in cultural grass-roots, as opposed to the timeless culture of the ancients.

23

Chateaubriand's *Le génie du christianisme*, Scott's historical romances, Mme de Staël's interest in Germanic folklore, all point to a rediscovery of historic themes, and this presupposes the rediscovery of history, change, and ultimately of time itself.

The phenomenon is curiously well reflected in linguistic theory. Classical linguistic study had been largely concerned with normative grammar. It sought to perfect the written language as an instrument of expression. Its efforts were ultimately underpinned by the stereotypes of Classical Latin, and, to a lesser extent, of Greek. Linguistics reflected the timeless values of Neo-Classicism. In direct contrast, Romantic linguistics was concerned with the origins and history of language, and was descriptive as opposed to normative. The turn of the century witnessed the beginnings of the great schools of historical philology. In their attempt to trace modern European languages back, eventually to an Indo-European prototype, and in their concern with the study of linguistic change, diachronicity, they may be seen to be derived from a shift in the pattern of consciousness, a shift that had come to acknowledge the importance of change and dynamic development through time.

Time comes to play no less important a part on the personal level of imaginative experience. From Rousseau on, it serves to remind man of his impermanence. It negates his achievements by measuring them against the fact of his mortality. Although this new concern with transience is in part the reflection of the experience of change, it is also an indirect consequence of man's loss of his sense of community and of the development of the corresponding theme of individualism. Since Romantic man trusts only in his self, he is bound by the restrictions of his own mortality. It is this that creates the Romantic anguish in the face of time.

The greatest exponent of this anguish is Baudelaire. But he is the inheritor, in this respect, of a rich lyric tradition. Some of the most anthologised poems of Romanticism are longings for timelessness: Lamartine's 'Le Lac' and Hugo's 'Tristesse d'Olympio'. The need to escape is regularly expressed as the need to escape from time, and passing time becomes the very signature of reality.

Thus Romantic artists look on artistic creation as the negation of time. Blake writes:

I have written this Poem from immediate Dictation, twelve or sometimes twenty or thirty lines at a time, without premeditation and even against my Will; the Time it has taken in writing was thus rendered Non Existent, and an immense Poem exists which seems to be the Labour of a Long Life all produc'd without Labour or Study.[17]

For Shelley, too, poetry is essentially timeless. The history of poets is, as Abrams points out:

> . . . a history essentially without change; for according to this outlook, the poetry of every age, so far as it is truly poetry and not its simulacrum, reapproximates the same unaltering pattern. In Shelley's essay therefore, all the greatest single poems lose their particular locations in time and place, lose even their identity, and are viewed as though they were fundamentally simultaneous and interconvertible since a poet participates in the eternal and the one; as far as relate to his conceptions, time and place are not.[18]

German Romanticism has similar preoccupations. Its greatest chronicler, Albert Béguin, sums its aspirations up as follows:

> Ainsi la poésie serait une réponse, la seule réponse possible, à l'angoisse élémentaire de la création enfermé dans l'existence temporelle.[19]

The preoccupation forms the central notion with which Novalis planned to end *Heinrich von Ofterdingen*. The notes he left describe his 'blessed company' destroying the rule of the seasons, as they speed towards Youth, finally to Old Age, to the Past at the same time as the Future. His hero-poet was to achieve his final triumph in the abolition of time and the corresponding accession to eternity.

Romanticism operates through a code of antithetical pairings – nature/culture, individual/society, past/present, reality/timelessness. The most important opposition of all includes within it the notion of opposition itself. Both structurally and thematically it is a pairing of crucial importance, opposing on the one hand dualism and the divided self to unity and synthesis.

Dualism and internal division are fundamental to the Romantic malaise. They are as much the signature of Romanticism as the sense of secure unity, derived from fitting neatly and properly into a great chain of being and meaning, was characteristic of the eighteenth century (as, for instance, in Pope's *Essay on Man*). Virtually every important writer of the Romantic age treats of the divided self: Faust, René, Julien Sorel, Lorenzaccio, Don Juan, Pechorin, Onegin, variously reflect internal contradiction, being at odds with oneself. The sense of being disunited is a key characteristic of the age. It is usually associated with self-disgust and disgust at the world at large. This disgusted sense of schizoid division is perhaps the most important of all Romanticism's reflections of its sense of the inadequacies of its reality. It provides the motivation for the most serious and ambitious of all the aspirations of Romanticism: the restoration of unity, harmony and synthesis.

It is the desire to recreate synthesis and organic unity in a world which was felt to have lost them which makes Romanticism something more than a literature of escape. The longing for totality and unity of experience, set against a world of division, is its most important legacy. The *Gesamtkuntswerk* of Wagner, the aesthetics of symbolism, the aspirations of the surrealists towards what André Breton termed *le point central*, all partake of the Romantic ambition.

The desire for unity lies at the very centre of the aesthetics of Coleridge. By his term the 'esemplastic imagination' he understood 'a bringing together and a combining'. It viewed the imagination as:

> an instrument with which to achieve unity within the universe, to bring disparate elements together in a coherent shape.[20]

A. W. Schlegel sees the quest for harmony quite specifically as an escape from a world of duality and discord:

> The Greek idea of humanity was a perfect concord and balance of all forces, natural harmony. The moderns, on the other hand, have become conscious of an inner dualism which precludes such an ideal; hence they strive in their poetry to reconcile and force together the two worlds between which we are torn: the spiritual and the sensual.[21]

It is in similar terms that Abrams views the Romantic quest for unity:

> an attempt to overcome the sense of man's alienation from the world by healing the cleavage between subject and object, between the vital, purposeful, value-full world of private experience and the dead postulated world of extension, quantity and motion.[22]

Béguin also sees the history of Romanticism as a striving for an organic unity. The same aspiration, joined with a sense of loss, an awareness of the degraded present, is eloquently expressed, in more immediately political terms, in the writing of a certain Jean-Georges Farcy. A casualty of the attack on the Louvre in the July Revolution, he expresses his sense of the loss of an organic community spirit as follows:

> Dans l'antiquité chaque individu était membre vivant d'une cité vivante . . . Aujourd'hui, c'est tout le contraire . . . L'image de la patrie ne se trouve ni dans le temple, ni dans le gymnase, ni dans le camp . . . L'idée de gouvernement est devenue de plus en plus mesquine . . . Il n'y a plus là ni monarchie, ni aristocratie, ni démocratie même. Il y a individualisme, et . . . égoisme. Par intérêt pour le libre développement de l'individu, le forcerons-nous de s'avancer seul dans la vie, quand l'indifférence absolue donne à son esprit des vertiges . . .[23]

The longing for unity, a sense of the world as a divided and alienating place, is equally reflected in the philosophy of Hegel, and in the more mystical aspects of Marxism. It forms the core of Fourier's work, and accounts for the whole Utopian bias of Romantic political thought.

It is important to our understanding of Dostoevsky that we should see the Romantic striving for unity as evidence of Romanticism's sense of cultural collapse and disruption. It was *against* a general sense of collapse, of loss of meanings and values, that the Romantics advanced their dream of synthesis. The unsatisfactory and unstable nature of their reality motivated attempts to build an earthly paradise of the imagination. Romanticism, the most powerful assertion of idealism and denial of reality that Western culture has seen since the Renaissance, was the product of that very reality which it sought to deny.

Dissatisfaction with the present is the point of departure for the Romantic hero in his contact with his reality. Against that dissatisfaction he sets certain expectations. Adolphe hopes that sexual involvement will cure him of his boredom, and so he manufactures it. René is less specific about the cure for his ills; his very vagueness is a telling symptom. His creator has provided a penetrating analysis of Romantic dissatisfaction in which he suggests that emptiness and disillusion are the distinctive features of his generation. He ascribes this 'vague des passions' – in which *vague* might best be rendered by 'void'—to the fact that

> le grand nombre d'exemples qu'on a sous les yeux, la multitude des livres qui traitent de l'homme et de ses sentiments rendent habile sans expérience. On est détrompé sans avoir joui; il reste encore des désirs, et l'on n'a plus d'illusions. L'imagination est riche, abondante et merveilleuse; l'existence pauvre, sèche et désenchantée. On habite avec un coeur plein un monde vide, et sans avoir usé de rien on est désabusé de tout.[24]

Chateaubriand describes the plight of a generation out of phase with its society, that feels that the world can offer it nothing, but which, paradoxically, expects a measure of fulfilment as part of its birthright. It is this set of attitudes which creates the most important literary theme of the age: the theme of the quest.

Le Rouge et le Noir is a characteristic example. At the outset Julien Sorel has certain precise preconceptions, other less clear expectations. He embarks upon a career, in the course of which he learns that fulfilment of preconceived ideas will always disappoint; reality invariably falls short of expectation. The discovery of this painful truth lies at the very heart of the quest, for this takes place in a world which, by definition, is unable to meet the demands which the searcher makes of it: once again 'Wir suchen überall das Unbedingte und finden nur Dinge.'[25] The realisation that this is so may make characters – Sorel is finally able to realise himself, in prison. Alternatively, it may destroy them – Mme Bovary—or else the hero reconciles himself to living in an imperfect world, abandons hope and settles down to wait for death – Frédéric Moreau in *L'Education sentimentale*.

In the novels of quest, which are essentially novels of education, the hero has to learn to come to terms with a world which can only disappoint. This theme of a coming to terms reflects the unwilling acceptance of the world of nineteenth-century civilisation, positivism and the pecuniary ethic, on the part of the inheritors of the first wave of Romanticism. The party of reality is accepted in resignation, the acceptance being echoed in that irony which permeates the novels of Stendhal and Flaubert, to be brought to a climax and transcended in the work of Proust. This irony is reflected in a tension between the world of dream and the world of reality, a tension which Lukács associates with time. It is this that, for him, constitutes the essence of the nineteenth-century novel:

> The greatest discrepancy between idea and reality is time: the process of time as duration. The most profound and most humiliating impotence of subjectivity consists not so much in its hopeless struggle against the lack of idea in social forms and their human representatives, as in the fact that it cannot resist the sluggish yet constant progress of time; that it must slip down, slowly yet inevitably, from the peaks it has laboriously scaled; that time . . . gradually robs subjectivity of all its possessions and imperceptibly forces alien contents onto it. That is why only the novel, the literary form of the transcendent homelessness of the idea, includes real time . . . among its constitutive principles.[26]

The theme of the quest for values, for Lukács' 'idea', reflects the cultural turmoil of the age. The world of stable whole meanings and values had vanished, and as a result each generation found it necessary to redefine and rediscover its values for itself. It is this perpetual reappraisal which is responsible for the existence of another aspect of the theme of the quest, namely the concept of authenticity of experience. Stendhal, Gogol, Goncharov, Dostoevsky, finally even Nietzsche and Gide, all handle the theme of authentic as opposed to empty, false, living. The preoccupation derives directly from the enduring need to re-examine one's values in the light of shifting patterns of experience. To live by a false set of values is to enjoy a living death, to be a zombie. The persistence of the *Bildungsroman* throughout the last century and, with authors such as Hesse, well into the present one, is proof of the survival of the need. So rapid has been the rate of cultural transformation that each generation felt it necessary to rebuild its value-systems; at no stage has there been a sufficient degree of stability and continuity to make cultural transmission possible. Each generation had to acquire its own stereotypes, and this accounts for the enduring relevance of the *Bildungsroman* and its concomitant theme of a restless quest for meaning in a world that was considered essentially meaningless and absurd.

The experience of its absurdity brings with it a condition of irritated dissatisfaction which makes serenity or repose impossible. This irritation, *spleen*, *ennui*, *hype* or *khandra* is the characteristic condition of the age. It is as if the state of dissatisfaction had been interiorised, compressed into a condition of a vague, sub-conceptual irritation, that colours all thought and action without itself taking form. At its most acute, in a Musset or a Lermontov, it makes for the blackest despair, a condition in which all possibility of happiness seems for ever lost, and the only hope is oblivion.

The malaise creates a mode of consciousness, rather than a state of mind, colouring an outlook in such a way that it becomes impossible placidly to accept the here and now. This fundamental sense of ontological unease lies at the heart of the more desperate aspects of the literature of the age, introducing the supremely important notion of escape at any price.

Heroes of Romanticism such as Pechorin, Lorenzaccio, and, in a sense, Onegin, whatever their differences, seem to move along parallel axes. They are unsettled by definition. Out of place, unable to reconcile themselves to that fact, they are disgruntled misfits. Onegin is too much the product of his age to be able to fit into the essentially pre-nineteenth-century pattern of Russian country life. Pechorin, understandably, finds life in a garrison town in the Caucasus equally intolerable. Superficially the case of Lorenzaccio is different; he is both appalled and fascinated by the moral corruption of the Florence of the Medicis. But, in each of these cases, the character in question is driven by boredom and his sense of being a misfit to extreme action. In each case, action ends in death. Onegin's disenchantment comes to a head at the Larins' ball. He grows enraged with boredom, embarrassment and irritation. He begins something which he sees through to the bitter end, lacking the maturity to abandon it, and kills Lensky as a result. Pechorin's case is comparable. He too fights an unnecessary duel, which he enters into through sheer perversity. He arranges matters in such a way that, provided he survives the first shot, he cannot fail to kill his man. He does so in a mood of blind, seething rage and outrage. Lorenzaccio is in a situation in which he realises that the assassination he had planned would be pointless. Nevertheless, he persists, knowing that the only consequence will be his own death.

There is nothing else to do, and in his situation it is better to do anything than to do nothing.

The characters share a common feature. They gravitate between inactive boredom and potentially disastrous actions to which they are driven by a certain sense of metaphysical spite. They risk everything in their effort to jerk themselves out of their inertia, regardless of the consequences to themselves or to others.

The key to their characters is disenchantment with their *status quo*. Ultimately, the widespread existence of the literary figure of the misfit is a reflection on nineteenth-century society. There have always been misfits – Molière's Alceste, Don Quixote, Rameau's nephew – but in the past they were offered as freaks; the freak has now become the heroic rebel without a cause.

The Romantic misfit has a need to alleviate his sense of empty disgust and boredom, a need which creates a new category of behaviour. This brings together into the same class actions which would traditionally have been classified quite differently: it is the category of the palliative. Love, murder, drugs, drink, sex, danger, pain, art, all form part of a single paradigm. They all offer more or less adequate means of alleviation, and the characters of Romantic fiction turn to them with the same expectation of relief. This new category introduces a notion which is crucial to the understanding of both Baudelaire and Dostoevsky and, indeed, of the entire post-Romantic world-picture: the notion of *intensity*.

Intensity of experience is the most important concept developed by Romantic culture. Intensity is resorted to as the supreme palliative that will distract from that sense of bored disgust which becomes high Romanticism's stock response to the new world of industrial and mercantile reality. Hence its heroes who will stop at nothing in their search for relief from boredom. Their sole concern is that their actions should be intense enough to distract them from their *ennui de vivre*.

The concern with intensity of experience and its moral consequences is reflected in the extravagance of Romanticism. In his *Confessions d'un enfant du siècle* Musset specifically derives his love of excess of every kind from the need to escape reality. Any means of escape is acceptable regardless of the cost. The concern with sheer intensity is reflected in what has come to be known as the 'Romantic Agony'. The Romantic involvement in a rhetoric of Gothic intensity extends from *Sturm und Drang* down to Surrealism, as does its concomitant feature, an aesthetic of surprise for the sake of surprise. From its origins in the Gothic novel, the frisson of horror is seen as an aesthetically self-justifying response. No excess, no rhetorical extravagance is spared in the effort to achieve it. The phenomenon of Gothic, of black Romanticism, is the reflection of a concern with intensity of experience as such.

The literature of the Romantic agony is content to reach its public on the level of sheer sensation. Response is the sole concern. There is no interest in verisimilitude, characterisation or intellectual appeal. The reader is reduced to his nerves and reflexes, the sole criterion being 'Does it make the hair stand on end?' Intensity-oriented art must, by definition, lack verisimilitude, since it is the creation of a culture from which intensity is absent. Intensity and verisimilitude are incompatible.

Along with the Gothic excesses of the Romantic agony we witness the emergence of another parallel phenomenon, the dandy. The late Dr Starkie described dandies as persons who 'tried to escape from the pervading sense of futility and from the growing materialism of their age'.[27] They create for themselves a style which is an ironic rejection of the values of their world. It is founded upon extravagance and conspicuous consumption, in a society regulated by penny-wise prudence and commonsense. Dandyism and the Gothic are both rejections of an age in which the party of reality triumphed over Bourbon and republican alike, to create a political *juste-milieu*.

The growing importance of the intensity aesthetic is reinforced by another phenomenon; the birth of the popular press. In the 1830s both France and England saw the emergence of cheap newspapers relying more on advertising than on subscription revenue, which increased their circulation by publishing serialised works of fiction.

The popular press became an important cultural force almost overnight. The consequences for fiction would be considerable – for Dostoevsky as much as for anybody. The new popular novel gave a vastly extended currency to the rhetoric of intensity. Its authors had other concerns, it is true. Eugène Sue introduced numerous chapters of humanitarian and reformist polemic into his works. But the overriding concern was to make the reader obey the injunction 'And now read on . . .'. The appeal of the popular novel was founded in intensity. It sought to excite at all costs, and did not pay much deference to the reality principle.

The anti-intellectual quality of both the Romantic agony and the popular novel, the abdication of high seriousness in favour of sensationalism, suggests an increasing need for a distractive palliative. Indeed the abandon of verisimilitude and of high seriousness is a reflection on the age. It points to a sense of despair, a belief that high seriousness was no longer possible because the age was rotten.

Romantic culture reflects a failure in the relationship between the individual and his society. In the age of steam and rigged elections, in which the new rich got richer and the new poor got their first taste of massive urban misery in industrial slums, the artist used his art as an escape – into history, nature, timelessness or the creative process itself.

It is the age of dissatisfaction, of an increasing sense of inadequacy and discontent. Discontent is, of course, reinforced by the new mobility of the nineteenth century. In a stable society in which neither advancement nor decline are easy, one may anticipate a corresponding freedom from discontent. But in an age which looks to Napoleon for a yardstick of possible achievement, and which, at the same time, feels that *carrières ouvertes aux talents* were a thing of the immediate past, the capacity for restlessness, discontent and personal impotence could have known no bounds. After the immensely fluid situations of the Napoleonic era, Europe had embarked upon several generations of peace-time soldiering, and all the frustration and disenchantment which that involved.

Small wonder that the age felt such a need for distraction, for escape at any price, that it should have expressed itself in a language of division, alienation and the irreconcilable antithesis of dream and reality. The age presented itself as a time in which no one could get what they wanted, a time of perpetual stressed tension between the real and the ideal. It is these factors that are the main characteristics of Romanticism. But they remain characteristic of European culture to the present day. Simply, the Romantics were the first generation to have to face them as the signature of their everyday life, as opposed to its occasional aspect.

Their response to discontent, instability and disillusion was extreme in its search for compensations and surrogates, for, in Baudelaire's expression, *paradis artificiels*. So rapid had been the transformation of European culture from the old order of monarchy to the new order of bankerdom, that the Romantics experienced that transformation with a peculiar degree of sensitivity. They had no defensive stereotypes to blunt their responses. It is this that accounts for the strength and delicacy of the Romantic reaction, and also for its obscurity. For all their emphasis upon expression, the Romantics remained inarticulate when it came to expressing and analysing the relationship between their own values and the new civilisation which had created them. It may seem unfair to charge a generation that fled from reason, in view of the world which reason had made, with a lack of conceptual clarity. Yet both Baudelaire and Dostoevsky were to prove that such clarity was in no way incompatible with the rejection of mercantile commonsense. It remained for them to make explicit the relationship between the new reality and the response initiated by Romanticism. It was they who would reveal the almost irreparable damage that nineteenth-century civilisation had wrought upon the hearts and minds of its people.

CHAPTER THREE

Baudelaire

> Celui-là sera le peintre, le vrai peintre
> qui saura arracher à la vie actuelle son côté épique,
> et nous fair voire et comprendre . . . combien
> nous sommes grands et poétiques dans nos cravates
> et nos bottes vernies.[1]

With this magnificent sentence Baudelaire defines the function of the modern artist. He required him to express the spirit of his age through his creative imagination; to shape its mythology.

He only arrived at his complete formulation of this view of the artist's function relatively late in life, in his essay on Constantin Guys, *Le Peintre de la vie moderne*. In earlier years he had suggested that it was Delacroix who successfully depicted his era. Now Delacroix was, in essence, the last great painter to use the conventions of academic art, the last of the great tradition. Consequently, his aesthetic values were ultimately founded in universals and whole meanings. He drew on cultural tradition for his subject matter. Although he may have rendered the feeling-tone of Romanticism through his tortuous forms and exuberant colour, his iconography was essentially traditional.

Baudelaire's shift of emphasis to Guys suggests that he had sensed the end of the academic tradition. The mid-nineteenth-century artist seeking to capture his age must draw for his subject matter upon everyday life. Traditional rhetoric was no longer adequate to render the contemporary mood. Modern art must be both less formal and more directly a mirror of its age.

The tacit recognition that the academic tradition, founded on high seriousness and whole meanings, had become a dead letter, is important to Baudelaire's own work, more important still to the history of aesthetic conventions. It reflects the disappearance of agreed canons of taste and the rise of aesthetic individualism, anticipating the series of informal aesthetics which were to dominate the arts to the present day. More important for our immediate purposes, the realisation that the painter of modern life must employ informal conventions, only to transcend them, is a *de facto* recognition of the aesthetics of Dostoevsky, and the uses to which he would put the popular novel.

Art then, for Baudelaire, is something much more than self-expression. He sought to capture the psychological climate of his age.

Although his art derives at least in part from personal experience, its value resides in its capacity to transcend the personal. *Les Fleurs du Mal* is not a work of confessional literature.

Baudelaire regarded his age as a time in which the essential concerns of Romanticism were still crucial. In this respect he saw through immediate trends in artistic fashion, which considered Romanticism a dead letter, a thing of earlier decades. Baudelaire described Romanticism as 'art moderne', and saw it as the aesthetic rendering of the spirit of the nineteenth century:

> . . . chaque siècle ayant possédé l'expression de sa beauté et de sa morale . . . Si l'on veut entendre par romantisme l'expression la plus récente et la plus moderne de la beauté . . .[2]

His awareness of the enduring relevance of the concerns of Romantic art confirms our contention that Romanticism was merely the first wave in a movement which has not yet worked itself out, reflecting the essentially uneasy relationship which modern man forms with his culture. Baudelaire's own work is precisely a reflection of this relationship. *Les Fleurs du Mal* is the critical account of a response to an age which the poet describes as 'un monde où l'action n'est pas la soeur du rêve'.[3] This is the most important phrase that Baudelaire ever wrote. It explains the motivation of Romanticism in a nutshell, providing a succinct analysis of nineteenth-century man's world-view – a view as relevant to Lermontov or Dostoevsky as it is to Baudelaire. It stresses the point that man's aspirations cannot be satisfied in the world in which he finds himself. It articulates the opposition between *is* and *might be* which is crucial to an understanding of the age. The conviction which Baudelaire expresses, and which forms the theme of the concluding poem of *Les Fleurs du Mal*, namely that reality can never meet the demands we make of it, is *the* point of departure for the art of the nineteenth century.

Dissatisfaction with the given reality forms the bedrock of *Les Fleurs du Mal*. It expresses itself as *ennui* or *spleen*: that state of mind in which nothing has value, nothing seems possible, and the sheer fact of existence is experienced in all its naked horror. The condition derives from that restless dissatisfaction which Baudelaire sees as the mood of his times. It is a fundamental ontological dissatisfaction which motivates that feverish quest for experience that, in 'Le Voyage', concludes his account of the human condition, providing his most complete rendering of the theme of man's perpetual questing restlessness.

Baudelarian dissatisfaction combines the eternal and the contingent. Human nature is presented as perpetually dissatisfied. Man is a fallen creature tainted by hereditary guilt, torn by conflicting aspirations to good and evil. Internal division is a human universal:

Il y a dans tout homme, à toute heure, deux postulations simultanées, l'une vers Dieu, l'autre vers Satan. L'invocation a Dieu, ou spiritualité, est un désir de monter en grade; celle de Satan, ou animalité, est une joie de descendre.[4]

The view perpetuates the Romantic tradition of the divided self. But along with his suggestion that division is a human universal, Baudelaire suggests that the nineteenth century had done much to compound that universal restlessness which was the heritage of the fall.

Baudelaire saw his age as a time of decadence, a time without values beyond the pecuniary ethic. Like Dostoevsky, he singled out the decline in a sense of the spiritual as the dominant characteristic of the age. Once society lost sight of spiritual considerations, its sole motivation became the principle of profitability, set in the theoretical framework of utilitarianism – the intellectual apotheosis of mercantile commonsense.

It was the loss of any sense of spirituality, hence also of an awareness of guilt and hence of human dignity, that Baudelaire singled out to define the essence of his epoch. Technology and hysteria were both no more than epiphenomena:

Théorie de la vraie civilisation
Elle n'est pas dans le gaz, ni dans la vapeur, ni dans les tables tournantes, elle est dans la diminution des traces du péché originel.

Peuples nomades, pasteurs, chasseurs, agricoles et même anthropophages, *tous* peuvent être supérieurs, par l'énergie, par la dignité personnelles, à nos races d'Occident.[5]

In the following passage, which is very close in its thought to Dostoevsky, he prophesies the collapse of his society. The prognostication is based on the decline in values and whole meanings, the correspondingly increasing importance of the pecuniary ethic, the disintegration of the family, the disappearance of a religious sense and a universal trivialisation—all themes treated by Dostoevsky in his *Diary of a Writer*—

Le monde va finir. La seule raison pour laquelle il pourrait durer, c'est qu'il existe. Que cette raison est faible, comparée à toutes celles qui annoncent le contraire, particulièrement à celle-ci: qu'est-ce que le monde a désormais à faire sous le ciel? – Car, en supposant qu'il continuât à exister matériellement, serait-ce une existence digne de ce nom . . . La mécanique nous aura tellement américanisés, le progrès aura si bien atrophié en nous toute la partie spirituelle, que rien parmi les rêveries sanguinaires, sacrilèges, ou anti-naturelles des utopistes ne pourra être comparé à ses résultats positifs. Je demande à tout homme qui pense de me montrer ce qui subsiste de la vie. De la religion, je crois inutile d'en parler, et d'en chercher les restes . . . La propriété avait disparu virtuellement avec la suppression du droit d'aînesse; mais le temps viendra où l'humanité comme un ogre vengeur, arrachera leur dernier morceau à ceux qui croient avoir hérité légitimement des révolutions . . .

. . . ce n'est pas particulièrement par des institutions politiques que se manifestera la ruine universelle, ou le progrès universel . . . Ce sera par l'avilissement des coeurs. Ai-je besoin de dire que le peu qui restera de politique se débattra péniblement dans les étreintes de l'animalité générale, et que les gouvernants seront forcés, pour se maintenir et se créér un fantôme d'ordre, de recourir à des moyens qui feraient frissonner notre humanité actuelle, pourtant si endurcie? – Alors, le fils fuira la famille, non pas à dix-huit ans, mais à douze, émancipé par sa précocité gloutonne; il la fuira, non pas pour chercher des aventures héroïques, non pas pour délivrer une beauté prisonnière dans une tour, non pas pour immortaliser un galetas par des sublimes pensées, mais pour fondre un commerce, pour s'enrichir, et pour fair concurrence à son infâme papa . . . Alors, ce qui ressemblera à la vertu, que dis-je, tout ce qui ne sera pas l'ardeur vers Plutus, sera réputé un immense ridicule. La justice . . . fera interdire les citoyens qui ne sauraient faire fortune. Ton épouse, ô Bourgeois! ta chaste moitié dont la légitimité fait pour toi la poésie, introduisant dans la légalité une infamie irréprochable, gardienne vigilante et amoureuse de ton coffre-fort, ne sera plus que l'idéal parfait de la femme entretenue. Ta fille, avec une nubilité enfantine rêvera dans son berceau, qu'elle se vend un million. Et toi-même, ô Bourgeois – moins poète encore, que tu n'es aujourd'hui – tu n'y trouveras rien à redire, tu ne regretteras rien. Car il y a des choses dans l'homme, qui se fortifient et prospèrent à mesure que d'autres se délicatisent et s'amoindrissent, et, grâce au progrès de ces temps, il ne te restera de tes entrailles que des viscères![6]

The poet looks to the day when money and the utilitarian ethic will reign supreme. He links that vision with egalitarianism, fair shares for all, and an inconceivable degree of political terror, with a general coarsening of the ethical palate. In their various ways, both Baudelaire and, as we shall see, Dostoevsky anticipated the terrorism and sheer animality that would play such an important part in the history of Europe for the next century.

Les Fleurs du Mal, in its first edition, was a somewhat abstract work. 'Spleen et Idéal', the account of the lapse into intensity was presented as the fate of Everyman. The focus is greatly altered in the second edition, which narrows the context of the work by inserting immediately after 'Spleen et Ideal' the section entitled 'Tableaux Parisiens'.

This situates the account of spiritual degradation in a specific location: Benjamin's capital of the nineteenth century. Baudelaire paints a picture of city life which proposes it as the cause of man's despairing attempt to escape into intensity. The 'Tableaux' are pictures of the world 'où l'action n'est pas la soeur du rêve'.

Baudelaire's view of the city is very close to Dostoevsky's. For each writer it is the point of departure for his account of the flight into intensity. For it is modern life, as represented by the city, which instigates it. Both authors see the city as the home of the homeless loser. The similarity of treatment and attitude, the choice of an identical point of departure for their particular accounts of the age of intensity, is very striking. That the two artists should react alike to the impact of their cultural environments – different in so many superficial respects – suggests that their work isolates the essential common characteristics of the nineteenth-century experience: characteristics that are responsible for rendering that age the age of intensity. Small wonder that they should have paid particular attention to the quality of city life, for it is the development of the industrial city that is the single most important aspect of the cultural transformation of the age.

The opening poem of 'Tableaux Parisiens' sets the tone in which the city will be treated. It is a source of negative inspiration, its title 'Paysage' being ironic. The poem is described as an eclogue, but it is an eclogue of the city, a townscape of steeples and factory chimneys. The landscape is essentially a wintry scene from which the poet seeks to escape into the warmth and springtime of his imagination. This flight from reality is one of Baudelaire's essential themes, and the particular respect in which he perpetuates the concerns of Romanticism.

The series of portraits that come next confirms his negative attitude to the city. They form a whole paradigm of urban misery, including major poems such as 'Les Sept Vieillards', 'Les Petites Vieilles'. These powerful evocations of urban dereliction, of the pariahs of civilisation, combine savagery and pathos. The poet spares neither subject nor reader in his presentation of the horrors of old age.

Baudelaire uses a code, in these poems, which will prove of utmost importance to Dostoevsky's treatment of the city: the code of 'urban Gothic'.[7] This is a convention widely used in the earlier part of the century to portray city life. Historically it is created by the transformation of the Gothic novel into the pseudo-realistic *roman d'aventures* set in the 'human jungle' of the city underworld. Descriptive passages were written in a tone designed to communicate melodramatic intensity. Writers such as Balzac and Sue, both of whom began their careers as authors of purely Gothic works, used the rhetoric of intensity to describe the Paris underworld. They emphasise intensity as an intrinsic aesthetic value. It is this that dictates their treatment of the city. Sordid reality is described, not because it is sordid, but because it is exotic; an appropriate setting to the strange events which, as Sue puts it in the opening paragraph of *Les Mystères de Paris*, are

> as far removed from civilisation as the savage people so well des-
> cribed by [Fenimore] Cooper; only the barbarians of whom we
> speak live among us, and around us; we can elbow them if we
> venture into the dens where they assemble to plot murder and
> robbery, and to divide among themselves the spoils of their victims. [8]

The intensity-directed treatment of squalor, which brings out a quality of strangeness bordering upon the supernatural, builds a bridge between romantic fantasy and the new realism. Thus it is just this use of urban Gothic which informs the greatest humanitarian tract of the age, *Les Misérables*. The work appeals through a language of sentimental intensity, in such scenes as the final confrontation between Jean Valjean and Javert, or the hallucinatory episode in which Valjean carries the wounded Marius through the sewers of Paris.

This is the convention employed by Baudelaire in 'Les Septs Vieillards'. The poem is set in:

> Fourmillante cité, cité pleine de rêves,
> Où le spectre en plein jour raccroche le passant!
> Les mystères partout coulent comme des sèves
> Dans les canaux étroits du colosse puissant. [9]

The city is clothed in an atmosphere of myth and hallucination which brings the poet to the edge of vertigo:

> Vainement ma raison voulait prendre la barre;
> La tempête en jouant déroutait ses efforts,
> Et mon âme dansait, dansait, vieille gabarre
> Sans mâts, sur une mer monstrueuse et sans bords! [10]

It is characteristic of the convention that it blends horror with pathos. 'Les Petites Vieilles' is a case in point:

> Dans les plis sinueux des vieilles capitales,
> Où tout, même l'horreur, tourne aux enchantements,
> Je guette, obéissant à mes humeurs fatales,
> Des êtres singuliers, décrépits et charmants.

But this Gothic line is tempered by a note of sentiment:

> Ah! que j'en ai suivi de ces petites vieilles!
> Une, entre autres, à l'heure où le soleil tombant
> Ensanglante le ciel de blessures vermeilles,
> Pensive, s'asseyait à l'écart sur un banc. [11]

Baudelaire's concern with the city is developed by the prose poetry of 'Le Spleen de Paris'. Using informal conventions and realistic subject matter it creates the iconography of an urban civilisation. His low-key rhetoric portrays scenes and attitudes typical of urban culture. It would seem that he had come to understand with an increasing clarity that it was the city that was ultimately responsible for the spiritual void, the exasperated despair, which he had described in his verse.

In order to do justice to this theme, and to the sense of a waste land that he was developing, Baudelaire abandoned the rhetoric of verse and high Romanticism. This would appear to be at least partly because verse, finally, reflected eternal and unchanging aesthetic values, themselves founded in those very whole meanings and universals which Baudelaire felt to be in the process of dissolution. Verse reflected high seriousness and a concern with the sublime, whereas Baudelaire was attempting to portray a world in which the sublime was no longer possible, and man settled instead for intensity.

Thus one of his most significant prose poems is entitled 'Perte d'Auréole'. It describes a poet attempting to cross a busy street. In his efforts to avoid the traffic his halo slips and falls into the mud. Where Baudelaire had once written of Paris, 'Tu m'as donné ta boue et j'en ai fait de l'or', the mud of Paris now holds his golden halo fast. The language of the sublime can no longer cope with a world in which there is no sublimity left; hence the choice of the flat low-key idiom of the poem in prose.

Dostoevsky's work confirms the suggestion that the new urban culture invited this kind of 'infernal' treatment; a convention free from the connotations of high art. His novels also reject the forms of high literature – the well-wrought novels of analysis à la Turgenev or Constant. They use the codes of the *feuilleton*, its tension, its melodrama, its unashamed use and abuse of surprise. The conventions of high literature are inappropriate to the depiction of the age of intensity, because the quality of life in the nineteenth-century city was such that it could never be handled by forms evolved in the depiction of moral beauty, whole meanings and high seriousness.

Baudelaire's prose poetry portrays society's losers, characters such as 'Le Vieux Saltimbanque', an acrobat too old to perform his tricks, or 'Un Cheval de Race', the superb evocation of a raddled old Edith Piaf figure, with all the dignity and nobility of time's ravages about her. The city also contains its freaks: Mme Bistouri is one of the poet's strangest creations. If the chief effect of modern civilisation was the pathological distortion of the personality – and this is the central contention of both Baudelaire and Dostoevsky – then Mme Bistouri embodies the spirit of her age. She is a whore who has a sexual obsession with surgeons. She longs for them to visit her with their instruments and gowns, preferably somewhat bloodstained. The poet concludes his portrait as follows:

> Quelles bizarreries ne trouve-t-on pas dans une grande ville, quand on sait se promener et regarder? La vie fourmille de monstres innocents. – Seigneur, mon Dieu! . . . ayez pitié des fous et des folles! O Créateur! peut-il exister des monstres aux yeux de Celui-là seul qui sait pourqoui ils existent, comment ils *se seront faits* et comment ils auraient pu *ne pas se faire*.[12]

The *monstre innocent* is the archetypal creation of the urban environment and its monstrous psychic dislocations.

To sum up: for Baudelaire as for Dostoevsky the city is a root cause of contemporary trauma and spiritual loss. It is treated in the language of isolation and abandon – witness 'Le Cygne', the greatest of all the 'Tableaux Parisiens', it is a superb daydream about loss, set firmly in the middle of Haussmann's Paris. The city stands in antithesis to the sense of organic community which shaped the mood of the preceding age. Urban culture has become the perfect medium to render Romantic preoccupations with loneliness and alienation. It is the place in which it is appropriate for such feelings to be felt.

Baudelaire captures the quality of urban experience once and for all in 'Une Passante' – very much the work of a painter of modern life. It transmutes a casual incident into the definitive icon of urban experience. It describes a fleeting exchange of glances with a woman dressed in mourning, as the poet passes her in the crowd: a momentary flare of understanding which can never be pursued. This brief encounter is the perfect expression of the joyless anonymity and isolation of the city. It occurs in a crowd, the agglomeration of isolated individuals with no trace of a binding unity. It combines physical proximity with a total spiritual isolation, creating a context in which genuine human contact is by definition impossible.

Along with his evocation of the external qualities of his world, the poet is equally concerned with inner experience, with *ennui*. It is a mood of spiritual dispersal which saps the will, negating everything except for a belief in *ennui* itself. All forms of meaningful activity become impossible and man is left with nothing but his sense of time's passing.

The mood is crucial to *Les Fleurs du Mal*. It is consequent upon man's loss of a sense of whole meanings, and had come to form the base element of the contemporary experience. The point is made in the preface, which describes man's loss of his sense of spirituality, so that he has become capable of any crime or transgression – were he not dominated by the apathetic inertia of the *monstre délicat* of *ennui*.

Baudelaire suggests that man will try to jerk himself out of this listless apathy at literally any price. The need to escape is at the very centre of his account of human behaviour. So great is man's sense of ill-being that he is prepared to clutch at any straw in the search for a palliative, regardless of the consequences for body or immortal soul.

Les Fleurs du Mal describes the gradual lapse into intensity and self-destructive escapism of a hero who was born a poet. Baudelaire makes it very clear that at his 'birth' his character has through his art, a grasp on spirituality, high seriousness, whole meanings. His art provides him with a means of unifying the apparently dispersed and haphazard experience of reality. It shows him that it is subtended with a meaningful pattern of *correspondances* which permit him to find in it 'une ténébreuse et profonde unité', pointing to a nobler and purer world of values.

Unfortunately, very early on the hero loses his faith in the religion of art, and hence his grasp upon whole meanings. Poems such as 'La Muse Malade', 'La Muse Vénale' trace his gradual loss of inspiration. Initial confidence is eroded by an increasing sense of despair.

At this point a choice is made, one crucial both to the book and to the age. The poet elects to pursue first aesthetic and then erotic beauty, regardless of the moral consequences. Thus beauty is gradually converted into a source of sensation.

Baudelaire was profoundly aware of the moral ambiguity of beauty, as was Dostoevsky. He understood that the statement 'all that is good is beautiful' could not be reversed. Beauty could be diabolic as well as divine. But so great was the hero's need for alleviation that any kind of beauty came to serve. The point is made in the following lines from 'Hymne à la Beauté':

> Que tu viennes du ciel ou de l'enfer, qu'importe,
> O Beauté! monstre énorme, effrayant, ingénu!
> Si ton oeil, ton souris, ton pied, m'ouvrent la porte
> D'un Infini que j'aime et n'ai jamais connu?
>
> De Satan ou de Dieu, qu'importe? Ange ou Sirène,
> Qu'importe, si tu rends, – fée aux yeux de velours,
> Rhythme, parfum, lueur, ô mon unique reine! –
> L'univers moins hideux et les instants moins lourds?[13]

The stanzas reflect the need to distract oneself at all costs. The inability to face up to the frightfulness of the universe, to shoulder one's discontent, lies at the very heart of the problem. As Baudelaire puts it:

> . . . tout homme qui n'accepte pas les conditions de la vie, vend son âme.[14]

To yield to the temptation to seek escape can only lead to degradation.

Thus the relief provided by aesthetic beauty would prove inadequate. The hero turns then to sexual beauty which is no more effective. The rest of 'Spleen et Idéal' consists of moments of relief that alternate with an ever-growing sense of despair. It is of the essence of this experience that alleviation is short-lived and followed by monumental bouts of *post coitum triste*. The book establishes a pattern of experience: anticipation followed by frenzied realisation ending in stale disappointment, a pattern which underlies a whole paradigm of escapes into intensity, including those of the libertine and of the addict. In each case, relief is pathetically short-lived and succeeded by an increasing need which can only be met by an increasing dose which increases the need ...

Baudelaire has anticipated what William Burroughs was to describe as 'absolute need': a need which may be alleviated but which never can be satisfied. Each alleviation renders the next relief harder to achieve. Baudelaire's hero turns to experiences of an increasing intensity in order to react at all. He loses any concern in the authenticity of his experience, as once he elected to ignore the ambiguity of beauty. He is quite prepared to settle for the chimera of the *paradis artificiel*, the painted imitation of a world of value and harmony. His loss of contact with reality is such that he will accept any illusion that stimulates him in a way that parodies the real thing:

Laissez, laissez mon coeur s'enivrer d'un mensonge.[15]

Unfortunately, as is the case with drugs, alcohol and libertinage, relief becomes harder to achieve as the very capacity to feel is steadily eroded.

Intoxication becomes the very formula of the experience which Baudelaire describes, intoxication by intensity. This is reflected in casual expressions such as the *s'enivrer* quote above and emerges more fully in the prose poem 'Enivrez-vous':

Il faut être toujours ivre. Tout est là; c'est l'unique question. Pour ne pas sentir l'horrible fardeau du temps qui brise vos épaules et vous penche vers la Terre, il faut vous enivrer sans trêve.

Mais de quoi? De vin, de poésie ou de vertu, à votre guise. Mais enivrez-vous ...

'Il est l'heure de s'enivrer!' Pour ne pas être les esclaves martyrisés du Temps, enivrez-vous; enivrez-vous sans cesse![16]

Intoxication is seen as an escape from time – the supreme Romantic ambition. From Rousseau to Proust escape into timelessness through creativity remains the most serious aspiration of the artist, but it is an escape which Baudelaire never achieves; he can only enjoy the illusion of escape, never escape itself. 'La Chambre Double' describes the beatific experience of laudanum which culminates in the following lines:

> Non! il n'est plus de minutes, il n'est plus de secondes! Le temps a disparu; c'est L'Éternité qui règne, une éternité de délices![17]

But inevitably the experience is interrupted and the poet comes down to earth as time reappears:

> Oh! Oui! le Temps a reparu; le Temps règne en souverain maintenant; et avec le hideux vieillard est revenu tout son démoniaque cortège de Souvenirs, de Regrets, de Peurs, d'Angoisses, de Cauchemars, de Colères et de Névroses.
>
> Je vous assure que les secondes maintenant sont fortement et solenellement accentuées, et chacune, en jaillissant de la pendule, dit: – 'Je suis la Vie, l'insupportable, l'implacable Vie!'[18]

So bemused do the heroes of both Baudelaire and Dostoevsky become in their attempt to escape through intensity that the nature of the stimulus becomes unimportant. It only matters that it be strong enough to distract. Thus intensity can put a premium on self-destruction itself. Baudelaire's character excites himself by contemplating the likelihood of his own imminent damnation, having reached the stage when any stimulus will serve; just as the heroin addict comes to love the needle which is the cause of his own destruction. The hero gradually grows so bemused that he quite loses the ability to evaluate the experiences he undergoes. He simply moves on an axis between feeling and non-feeling.

Baudelaire goes to some lengths to make the point that true satisfaction cannot be reached through the cultivation of intensity. His character seeks to satisfy an essentially spiritual craving through sensation, and is hence doomed to failure. To focus the theme of a perpetual quest for metaphysical satisfaction through the physical, Baudelaire introduces the image of the lesbian lovers, whose quest has taken them beyond the pale of convention and spiritual good order. They seek for infinity through physical experience which can only leave them dissatisfied. Their desire can be aggravated but never assuaged. There is no more perfect image for the Baudelarian attempt at escape than these desperate *chercheuses d'infini*, with the *âpre stérilité de votre jouissance*.

But beyond the self-destructive plunge of Delphine and Hippolyte looms a self-destruction of an even more acute kind. From this point on the pursuit of intensity contents itself with mere sensation, plunging into unreflective sensuality. Feeling of any kind becomes welcome, whatever the quality. It is this that accounts for Baudelarian sado-masochism.

Pain for Baudelaire is a major source of intensity. One of the prose poems, 'Le Mauvais Vitrier', describes the savage treatment that the poet accorded a glazier. He summons him to his attic, then sends him away in a rage, on learning that he sells no coloured glass which might permit him to see 'la vie en beau'. When he re-appears on the street the poet drops a flower pot on his wares:

> Et, ivre de ma folie, je lui criai furieusement: 'La vie en beau! La vie en beau!'
> Ces plaisanteries nerveuses ne sont pas sans péril, et on peut les payer cher. Mais qu'importe l'éternité de la damnation à qui a trouvé dans une seconde l'infini de la jouissance.[19]

The momentary exultation of a Stavrogin-like act of savagery is its own reward. The intensity of the experience overrides all considerations of its cost. For a moment, the world of commonsense ceases to exist, and nothing matters beyond the pure quality of the experience itself.

As will be confirmed by Stavrogin, this is essentially the psychological climate of the sex-crime. 'A celle qui est trop gaie' describes intensity achieved through sexual sadism. The psychic health of his mistress drives the hero to an orgy of destruction which culminates as he dreams of penetrating her through her wounds, the poem concluding in a positive vertigo of intensity.

The strongest of all Baudelaire's expressions of intensity achieved through destruction is 'Une Martyre'. It is a delirious 'still-life'. The poem describes a boudoir in which a headless corpse, legs spread wide, lies bleeding on a bed. The head, jewels in its hair, is on a nearby table. The scene ends in the tentative suggestion of necrophilia:

> L'homme vindicatif que tu n'as pu vivante
> Malgré tant d'amour assouvir,
> Combla-t-il sur ta chair inerte et complaisante
> L'immensité de son désir.[20]

Once again the emphasis is on inassuageable appetite. It is only proper that the quest for intensity should lead us to the sex-crime. The infliction of pain offers opportunities for intensity that greatly exceed the resources offered by the procurement of pleasure. Pleasure is seldom so intense that it provokes loss of consciousness; moreover, it lacks that extra register of feeling offered by the infliction of pain – the possibility of deriving intensity from pity and remorse.

Although the sex-crime may be the ultimate in social degradation, the degradation of the spiritual is taken further still. The hero finally reaches the point at which he derives intensity from the pain which he inflicts upon himself. Destruction of the self becomes a means of escaping from the self. This is the attitude of poems such as 'Héautonti-morouménos' ('Mine own executioner').

Masochism is specifically described by Baudelaire as a perverse form of pleasure-seeking. He terms it a kind of narcotic—witness the preface to 'Les Paradis Artificiels':

> Car, tout aussi bien que d'une drogue redoutable, l'être humain jouit de ce privilège de pouvoir tirer des jouissances nouvelles et subtiles même de la douleur, de la catastrophe et de la fatalité.[21]

The notion of masochism as a *paradis artificiel* – artificial in the sense that it is often self-induced and always distortive – is important to an understanding of Baudelaire, crucial to an understanding of Dostoevsky. In the latter's work it regularly takes the form of a moral masochism; intensity achieved through exultant self-humiliation. Sexual humiliation, in particular, plays such a rôle in both the life and the work of Baudelaire. An essential aspect of his attraction to his mulatto mistress Jeanne Duval was her sexual indifference towards him, as expressed, for example, in the following lines:

> Je t'adore, à l'égal de la voûte nocturne,
> O vase de tristesse, ô grande taciturne,
> Et t'aime d'autant plus, belle, que tu me fuis,
> Et quand tu me parais, ornement de mes nuits,
> Plus ironiquement accumuler les lieues
> Qui séparent mes bras des immensités bleues,
>
> Je m'avance à l'attaque, et je grimpe aux assauts,
> Comme après un cadavre un choeur de vermisseaux,
> Et je chéris, ô bête implacable et cruelle!
> Jusqu'à cette froideur par où tu m'es plus belle![22]

The ultimate stage of his masochism goes well beyond humiliation and self-inflicted wounds. To achieve the definitive *frisson* his protagonist ensures the damnation of his immortal soul. He consciously adores the principle of evil which he recognises as responsible for his very urge to destroy himself. This is the sense of the penultimate section of *Les Fleurs du Mal*, 'Révolte'. With its deliberate and virtually unhysterical adoration of Satan it exceeds even Dostoevsky in the sheer degree of its plunge into intensity.

The last poem of the book, 'Le Voyage' looks back on a life devoted to attempts at escaping the limitations of reality. The human condition is seen as a state of perpetual dissatisfaction, while it is recognised that escape from that condition is not possible. 'Tout homme qui n'accepte pas les conditions de la vie vend son âme', and yet the world in which action is not sister to the dream is, almost by definition, unacceptable.

'Le Voyage' makes it clear that it is set in a world which can never satisfy:

> Amer savoir, celui qu'on tire du voyage!
> Le monde, monotone et petit, aujourd'hui,
> Hier, demain, toujours, nous fait voir son image;
> Une oasis d'amour dans un désert d'ennui![23]

The *amer savoir* is the supreme lesson to be learnt in the nineteenth century; the bitter lesson of romantic disillusion. It is learnt by Julien Sorel in prison, by Frédéric Moreau in his last meeting with Mme Arnoux, by Pierre Bezukhov amid the joys of married life. It is the same lesson that is both learnt and transcended by Proust's hero. In a world in which action was not sister to the dream, escape was not possible and to believe otherwise could only lead to self-destruction. The realisation expressed itself in Flaubert as serene despair. Baudelaire's reaction was more ambiguous.

'Le Voyage' may reject the pursuit of intensity in this world, but it ends with the protagonist looking forward to death itself as a relief from his *tedium vitae*. Baudelaire's definitive attitude is perhaps better expressed in one of the prose poems. It begins by listing a series of alternative means of escape. The title is 'Any where out of the world'. It opens:

> Cette vie est un hôpital où chaque malade est possédé du désir de changer de lit.

It concludes with a sentence which is the ultimate expression of the Baudelarian attitude:

> Enfin mon âme fait explosion, et sagement elle me crie: 'N'importe où! N'importe où! Pourvu que ce soit hors de ce monde!'[24]

Baudelaire's work is a comment on Romanticism. Including both the Romantic rejection of the world and its longing for escape, it handles these familiar themes in a new way. Instead of making them the basis for an immediate expression of feeling – the shaping and projection of fantasies of *Sehnsucht* – the poet describes their impact upon the psyche and gives a critical account of the psychological damage that they do. Thus he is not content simply to make use of the hysterical rhetoric of Gothic; he traces the degradation of his hero to the point at which only the Gothic experience can provoke a response. The poet looks beyond the purely aesthetic value of the Gothic *frisson* to consider its rôle as a psychological phenomenon.

This critical quality which infuses all his work converts what might have been Romantic confession into a case-history. The quasi-impersonal style, the analytic approach, explores aspects of perverse psychologies including his own, which Baudelaire felt to be characteristic of his age. It is this analytic attitude, focused upon contemporary distortions of the psyche, which links Baudelaire to Dostoevsky.

Crudely, our reading of Baudelaire is based upon the following analysis: factors such as the rise of the pecuniary ethic, the industrial revolution, positivism, the decline of religion, had shaped a world without whole meanings, a world which could no longer satisfy the full spectrum of human needs. Man was faced with two alternatives: to live in a state of perpetual discontent, or to distort and destroy his consciousness, the seat of that discontent, by means of intoxicants, illusions and the cultivation of an existential vertigo which did not come cheaply. Intensity of experience becomes the supreme good, because it denies reality. This is the view that forms the basis of the poet's moral indictment of his age.

If ever a writer were concerned with intensity of experience, it is Dostoevsky. Seen through the focus of Baudelaire's schemata, his obsession with every kind of intensity, from stylistics to theology, becomes something more than the ravings of an epileptic Slav. Whatever the reasons for his personal involvement in intensity, its central rôle in his works renders these perhaps the greatest and the most comprehensive articulations of the stress-patterns of his age.

Looking at Dostoevsky through Baudelaire does more than point up the importance of the intensity drive. Baudelaire's explicit associations between what otherwise might appear unrelated areas of experience, *ennui* and the city, intensity and the ambiguity of beauty, are not nearly so clearly made by Dostoevsky, although the individual elements are all present in his work. However, they seem to exist independently of one another. Baudelaire's tighter analysis, which makes certain associations more specifically, provides us with a framework which structures the loose and baggy monsters of Dostoevsky, showing that they have a much greater degree of inner coherence, stemming from a unified creative vision, than has hitherto been suspected.

On the surface it would be hard to imagine two artists with less in common than Baudelaire and Dostoevsky. Baudelaire was the most delicate of writers, one of the greatest stylists of his language. His poetic output is slight, but every word is the product of immensely careful calculation. Dostoevsky, on the other hand, was the prolific master of a kind of literary overkill. Technically, he wields a steam-hammer that cracks everything from nuts to mountains. However, his work perpetually transcends its forms. He relies on instinct and intuition more than on calculation, and as an artist who believes the ends to justify the means, he is sublimely indifferent to the technical details of execution.

Baudelaire analyses his world in a way that both defines and explains its craving for intensity. Dostoevsky grasps the importance of the intensity drive instinctively, and is instinctively aware of its causes. Baudelaire's analysis clarifies Dostoevsky's statements, in the sense that it teaches us how to look at them. But the authors are much too different for anything to be gained from a conventional 'comparative' approach. Although we have derived our frame of reference from Romanticism and from Baudelaire, the account of Dostoevsky's world must be carried out in its own terms. It is with a critical analysis of that world, and not with coincidental resemblances to Baudelaire, that the rest of this work will be concerned.

PART TWO

Un monde où l'action n'est pas
la soeur du rêve

CHAPTER FOUR

The City

Viewed in the light of the Baudelairian framework, Dostoevsky's writing falls into three parts: an account of cultural disintegration, and the resulting pressures upon the individual; the escape into intensity; proposals for a solution. It should at once be made clear that the first two parts greatly outweigh the third, both in volume and significance. Indeed, it will emerge that even Dostoevsky's solutions are contaminated by the intensity drive.

Lest this tripartite treatment implies over-systematisation, it should be pointed out that Dostoevsky is the least systematic of writers. It is not suggested that this pattern informs the design of his novels; it relates to the system of values and beliefs which articulates them. This account is intended to clarify the issues posed by the novels, and does not claim to explain the works. It is an analysis of their context and circumstances.

Dostoevsky's account of the disaster areas of his age is both subtler and more elusive than more conventional treatments of the theme. He did not consider himself a descriptive realist, had no sense of the novel as documentary. He went beyond realism, aiming at the creation of a picture more profound, more accurate than that of any realist. He is concerned with deep as opposed to surface structure. Indeed he condemns the realists for their limitations, hinting at his own intent – to use fiction to probe areas of contemporary experience, areas of psychic shock, that were beyond the reach of the documentary novelist. In other words, he sought to reach beyond reality to seize the myths upon which that reality was founded:

> My dear fellow! My views on reality and realism are quite unlike those of our realists and critics. My idealism is more real than they are. My God! If someone were to describe the spiritual upheavals in our inner life which we Russians have been through in the last 10 years; would not the realist protest that this was fantasy; whereas it's all true, genuine realism! It's realism all right, but it goes deeper, they remain on the surface . . . Their realism cannot explain the hundredth part of what has actually happened. But my idealism actually anticipated the fact.[1]

This describes Dostoevsky's level of analysis. He will attempt to write the psychological chronicle of his age, and, like Baudelaire, is more

51

concerned with inscape than with landscape. Consequently, the part played in his work by the equivalent of 'Tableaux Parisiens' is essentially secondary. By the time of *The Brothers Karamazov* we find ourselves in a town which remains nameless for three-quarters of the book. We know nothing about it except that it has a network of back alleys.

Nevertheless, his earlier work pays due attention to externals. Indeed, Dostoevsky is, if only incidentally, one of the greatest chroniclers of the nineteenth-century city.

It is appropriate to begin our examination of his account of the state of culture with his treatment of the city, not only because it provides another link with Baudelaire, but because city life for Dostoevsky was the supreme emblem of that new civilisation from which man felt it necessary to escape at all costs. The city will provide a tangible setting for Dostoevsky's more abstract indictments.

It was London that first seems to have focused the image of the city for Dostoevsky. The traumatic impression it made upon him forms the centre-piece of his travel notes *Winter Notes Upon Summer Impressions* (1863). His first contact with the capital of the industrial revolution taught him what city life really meant. In London he witnessed human misery on a hitherto undreamt of scale and came into contact with the aimless bustling and isolation of the crowd.

He saw London as the incarnation of the new culture because it was so blatant. Where Paris worshipped the pecuniary ethic furtively, making a pretence at being *la ville lumière*, London's devotion to the spirit of capitalism was unashamed:

> When day follows night, that same proud, sombre spirit reigns once more over the gigantic city. It is not concerned by the events of the night, nor by what it sees by day. Baal reigns and does not even require obedience, because he is certain to get it. His self-confidence is boundless; scornfully and calmly, he distributes alms on an organised basis, for good order's sake . . . Baal does not conceal savage, shocking facts, as they do in, say, Paris. The poverty, the suffering, the protest, the brutalisation of the masses are of no concern to him. Scornfully he permits all the suspect and evil practices to exist openly at his side. He does not, like the Parisian, make a nervous effort to persuade himself that things are all as they should be. He does not, as they do in Paris, hide the poor away, in case they alarm him or keep him awake. The Parisian, like the ostrich, likes to bury his head in the sand to avoid seeing the approaching hunters.[2]

With its emphasis on the unique imperative of the pecuniary ethic, regardless of its cost in human misery, Dostoevsky's vision might have come straight from the devastating portrait of London painted by

Friedrich Engels. Indeed Dostoevsky shares the premises of Marx and Engels, it was their conclusions and the manner of their thought which he was unable to accept. The following description of London life warrants quoting in full, for it is the most complete picture we have of the externals of nineteenth-century civilisation as Dostoevsky saw them:

. . . here too we find the same stubborn, brutish and outmoded struggle, the struggle to the death between Occidental man's sense of individual origins and the necessity of living together in some kind of harmony, to form some kind of communal ant-heap; an ant-heap perhaps, but at least it is a community, the alternative being cannibalism. In this respect, moreover, as in Paris, we witness the same desperate wish to preserve the *status quo*, to stamp out all desire and hope in oneself, curse the future, in which perhaps not even the champions of progress believe, and bow down to Baal. But please do not be misled by the high-flown style: only those who are aware and in touch are conscious of all this, it is reflected, on an instinctive and unconscious level in the behaviour of the masses. But the bourgeois of Paris, for example, is consciously happy and confident that all is as it should be, and he will lay into you, if you doubt whether all is as it should be, lay into you because, for all his self-confidence, there is something that continues to frighten him.

Things are the same in London, but what huge overpowering sights it offers! It is quite different from Paris, even to look at. The city which never rests by day or night and which is as broad as an ocean, the howl of the machines, the railways laid above the houses (and soon under them), the entrepreneurial spirit, the apparent chaos which, in essence, is the apogee of bourgeois order, the polluted Thames, the sooty air; the delightful squares and parks, the strange parts of town like Whitechapel, with its half-naked, savage, staring inhabitants. The City with its millions, its world trade, the Crystal Palace, the Great Exhibition. The Exhibition is extraordinary. You sense the terrifying power which has brought these countless people from all corners of the earth together into a single herd; you acknowledge the titanic concept; you understand that here something has been achieved, that here is a victory, a triumph. You begin to feel afraid. Might this not be the dream come true you think; isn't this the end of the road, the 'herd united'. Won't you have to accept it as the whole truth, and hold your peace henceforth? It is all so triumphant, victorious, proud, that it oppresses you. You observe these hundreds of thousands, these millions of people, who have assembled, obediently, from the four corners of the globe, with a single thought, quickly, obstinately, silently crowding into this colossal palace, and you feel that something irrevocable has just taken place. It is a scene from the *Bible*, something Babylonian, a prophecy from the *Apocalypse* that is happening before your eyes. You feel that you need a vast amount of enduring will-power and spiritual self-discipline not to bow down before the facts and worship Baal . . .

Certainly I admit that the spectacle carried me away. But had you seen the pride of that mighty spirit which created that colossal scene, how proudly confident it was of victory, you would have shuddered at its pride, its obstinacy, its blindness, shuddered for those it governs. Faced with the colossal size, the towering pride of the ruling spirit, with the triumphant execution of its projects, the spirit of the hungry grows docile, seeks salvation in gin and vice, and begins to believe that all is as it should be. Beneath the crushing burden of the facts the masses lose their spirit . . . In London you can see the masses on a scale and setting that are unique. For example, I am told that half a million workers with their women and children, flood into the city on Saturday nights, crowding into certain parts of town, and celebrating the Sabbath, till five in the morning, swinishly gorging and getting drunk enough to last the week. They spend the week's savings which they have earned in a bitter labour of the damned. In the butchers' shops and eating houses the gas-lights burn bright, and light up the street. It is as if there were a ball for these white niggers. The crowds throng the open taverns and the streets, eating and drinking . . . Everyone is drunk, but joylessly, sombrely, heavily and silently drunk. Only occasional curses and bloody brawls interrupt the suspect lugubrious silence. They all try to drink themselves unconscious as quickly as possible. The wives stay with their husbands and get drunk with them; the children run and crawl among them. On such a night, between one and two in the morning, I once strayed and wandered for ages along the streets among the countless throngs of this sombre city, finding my way by sign language, as I spoke not a word of English. I found my way, but my impression of what I saw upset me for the next three days. Crowds and crowds of people with everything on such a colossal scale, so blatant that you could feel as something tangible, something that hitherto you had only imagined. It is not even a crowd that you see here, but the systematic, obedient, officially encouraged obliteration of consciousness. And looking at these social pariahs, you feel that it will be a long time before their prophecy fulfils itself, a long time before they receive palm fronds and white raiment, and for a long time yet, they will continue to cry up to the throne of the Almighty: 'How long O Lord?' They know it too, and for the time being they take their revenge on society by joining the Mormons, the Quakers,

... We are amazed at the stupidity that makes people join the Quakers, and we do not understand that this represents a departure from our social formula, a stubborn, unconscious departure, an instinctive departure, at all costs, for the sake of one's own salvation, a horrified, frightened flight from *us*. These millions, abandoned, driven away from life's banquet, shove and trample each other in subterranean darkness, into which they have been cast by their elder brothers, groping their way to knock at some gate or another, searching for a way out to escape death in the black hole. It is their final desperate effort at a last stand, an escape from everything – from the human image itself, just to be themselves and apart from us.[3]

This is the author's encounter with Megalopolis. No mere account of a visit to London, it is a nightmare myth of the city itself, London town being no more than a catalyst to the imagination. The passage renders a view of the nineteenth-century city that is to inform his whole work, shaping the stereotypes which he will employ to describe his own capital. He responds to his vision as to a glimpse of the future. This London becomes the definitive city, the supreme manifestation of the spirit of the age, a prophetic emblem that pointed the way the rest of Europe was going.

Dostoevsky's London is the incarnation of the nineteenth-century ideals of free-trade, progress, utilitarianism; the commonsense world of the pecuniary ethic, the secular society. Henceforth Dostoevsky would devote his creative powers to the exposure of those values. In that sense, this vision of London is responsible not just for Dostoevsky's treatment of the theme of the city as such, but for the overall direction of his entire work. It is the supreme account of a world in which reality is forever at odds with the dream.

The passage opens with the suggestion that the human spirit is so crushed by a society which cannot see beyond the profit principle, that man will resort to any narcotic which promises to relieve him of the burden of his consciousness. Although Dostoevsky's analysis concerns working-class culture, its nature is identical to that proposed more generally by Baudelaire; man turns to sensation to compensate for a lack of whole meanings.

The immediate consequence of this materialist culture for Dostoevsky was an agglomeration he referred to as the human ant-heap: an agglomeration which has no objectives beyond sheer animal survival and the meeting of physical needs. This was the 'ideal' of the age, a reductionism that sought to eliminate all differences, cultural and individual, to turn the human race into a 'united herd', made of appetite, needs, and nothing else.

55

Dostoevsky finds the limitations of this view intolerable. It was those very limitations, the attempt to define man as the sum of his material needs, which had created the sullen drunkenness, the religious hysteria of Dostoevsky's vision of Cockney life. More important, it was also to create his own freaks' gallery of sex-criminals and murderers. Dostoevsky's characters are all, in the final analysis, driven to destructive extremes of action by their desperate need to break out.

The passage also establishes the tone in which Dostoevsky will write of the city. The language is highly emotive, designed to move as well as to inform. Indeed, Dostoevsky's urban passages are excellent examples of his own use of the rhetoric of intensity. This aspect of his style has been characterised by the expression 'urban Gothic'[4] and the term is a happy one.

The Gothic code aimed, simply, at intensity of aesthetic sensation, and to this end everything else was sacrificed. Dostoevsky considers the pursuit of intensity at all costs as symptomatic of a cultural collapse which he was partly describing, partly attempting to resist. The key to the quality of his insights, to his talents as a chronicler of that collapse and the paradox that lies at the centre of his work, is his own complicity in the intensity drive.

This complicity reveals itself in many ways, not the least of which is his extensive use of the rhetoric of the *feuilleton;* hence the propriety of the term urban Gothic to describe his treatment of the city. Although his execution may lack the meticulous descriptive care we find in the Gothic passages of Baudelaire's urban poetry, Dostoevsky shares Baudelaire's aesthetic code. He too sees the city as an unreal monstrosity, as the

> Fourmillante cité, cité pleine de rêves,
> Où le spectre en plein jour raccroche le passant.[5]

Of course Dostoevsky also applies the Gothic code to the description of his own capital. At the time when he started to write there was nothing very original in adopting a negative view of St Petersburg. Both Pushkin and Gogol had treated the theme extensively enough. Pushkin's St Petersburg was the seat of culture as opposed to nature. It encouraged artificiality, hypocrisy and conspicuous consumption. It made for loneliness, compounded human misery and sent statues galloping in pursuit of little men who dared to voice their dislike of it. For Gogol, the city was an alien world in which a superficial glitter obscured the fact that it was the home of lunatics, whores, zombies and disembodied noses. It was an 'enchanted spot', the most unreal place in the world, and the most dangerous.

As well as being the embodiment of alienation, loss of identity and the destruction of the individual, St Petersburg was also a monument to planning. It was designed, it did not just grow. It is the total anti-thesis to the organic quality of life, an antithesis that creates Tolstoy's Moscow/St Petersburg contrast. The huge scale of its architectural masses and spaces, the extraordinary width of the Neva, the sprawling low profiles of its buildings, the sheer lunacy of a design that transposes the forms of intimate Palladian architecture onto a Brobdignagian scale, all conspire to make its inhabitants, and its visitors, feel crushed and dwarfed. Even the paving stones feel unusually hard underfoot. The abstract, mathematical quality of its design, and the impression this makes upon the imagination, emerge in this vision of the capital by Andrey Bely:

> The wet, slippery avenue was intersected by a wet slippery avenue at an angle of 90 degrees. A policeman stood at the cross-roads.
> There were exactly the same houses, the same grey streams of people, the same greenish yellow fog.
> But parallel to the avenue was another avenue, with the same rows of little boxes, the same house numbers, the same clouds.
> There is an infinity of lines of intersecting shadow. The whole of St Petersburg is an infinity of lines of avenues raised to the nth degree.
> Beyond St Petersburg there is nothing.[6]

It is this rational quality that shapes literary visions of the capital from Pushkin to Bely. It is both a projection of the will and a monument to unfeeling, rational planning. Both inhuman and extraordinarily beautiful, with no topographical *raison d'être*, it is an eighteenth-century Brazilia of the North. The recognition of its abstract and recti-linear foundation creates Dostoevsky's underground man. He suffers from an excess of consciousness, a condition which he finds amplified by living in St Petersburg, 'the most abstract city in the world'.

These are the terms in which Russian literature creates its stereotype of the capital. It is a monument to the planned city, as opposed to city planning.

This quality must have recommended it to Dostoevsky as a suitable setting for his indictment of contemporary culture. He was all too aware that his was an age of uncompromising faith in reason, logic and planning. He felt the planned environment to be an anti-human obscenity which he refers to as the ant-heap, or, echoing his visit to London, 'the Crystal Palace'.

There were other respects in which St Petersburg was well qualified to represent the ravages of the new urban civilisation. It may have lacked an industrial proletariat on a gigantic scale – it was the sheer size of the slums that impressed Dostoevsky in London – however, it had other advantages.

According to the census of 1881, less than a third of the population were native to the city; an aspect of the capital that Dostoevsky captures by describing it as a place of isolation, the negation of the organic unity of family life. In the latter half of the century its death-rate increased steadily, and was comfortably in excess of the birth-rate. The *Encyclopaedia Britannica* (9th edition) gives the following account of the city in the last quarter of the nineteenth century:

> The mortality at St Petersburg being very high (34.2 in 1883 from 29.7 in 1868–82) and the number of births being 31.1 per thousand, the deaths are in excess of the births by 2,500 to 3,000 in an average year; in 1883 there were 26,320 births (1,151 still-born) and 30,150 deaths . . . The chief mortality is due to chest diseases, which prove fatal on the average to 9,000 persons annually; diseases of the digestive organs also prevail largely; European and perhaps also Asiatic cholera is almost endemic, an average of 3,700 deaths annually being due to this cause. Infectious diseases such as typhus (from 4,280 to 5,100 deaths during the last few years), diphtheria, and scarlet fever (3,500 deaths) are common. Owing to a notable increase of these three infectious diseases the mortality figures for the last few years are above average. Of 28,212 deaths nearly 2/5 (12,369) were among children under five. The number of marriages in 1883 was 6,183, (only 7.1 per 1,000 inhabitants); out of a total of 26,320 births, 7,977 (30%) were illegitimate; and no fewer than 31% of all children, both legitimate and illegitimate, born in St Petersburg, are nursed in the foundlings' homes . . . More than 100,000 persons enter public hospitals annually . . .[7]

These figures take on additional significance when compared with those given for other capitals. In Paris these were, in 1881, 25.8 deaths per thousand and 27 births. The corresponding figures for London were 21.5 deaths and 35 births.

Its appalling climate, with its consequent toll of human life and misery, earned Dostoevsky's capital special title to act as the mirror of urban civilisation, to capture the decline in the quality of life. Novels such as *Crime and Punishment*, *The Idiot*, *The Adolescent* are utterly steeped in the atmosphere of the capital, and the atmosphere of city life as such. Although by Dostoevsky's time it was no longer possible to write directly of the unreal city, as had Gogol and Pushkin, he was able to handle this vital St Petersburg theme obliquely. In the following passage he employs it as a projection of his character's sense of spleen and disgust:

> Early morning anywhere – including St Petersburg, has a sobering effect. Last night's inspired ideas seem to evaporate in the cold

morning light, and there have been mornings when I have recalled certain fantasies of the night before, and actions too, with shame and remorse. But let me say that I think mornings in St Petersburg – seemingly the most prosaic mornings in the world – are perhaps the most fantastical of all. That is a personal opinion or observation, rather, but I'll stand by it. On one of those rotten, raw, foggy mornings, St Petersburg lends substance to the wild fantasies of Pushkin's Herman from *The Queen of Spades* (a colossus, a unique, total Petersburg type, a type from the Petersburg period). A hundred times I have had a strange, persistent fantasy in that fog. 'But what if this fog were to lift and clear, would not the whole of this rotten, slimy city go with it, vanishing like smoke, leaving behind the Finnish bog it used to be, with a bronze horseman on a . . . hard-ridden horse remaining behind as a decoration!' In short I can't put my impression across because it's just a fantasy – poetry and therefore nonsense; but still, I was, and am, haunted by the same senseless question: 'Everyone is busy and in a hurry, but who can tell, perhaps it's all part of somebody else's dream, and not one person here is genuine, not one action real? One day the dreamer will awake and it will all vanish'.[8]

Such passages bring Dostoevsky close to Baudelaire, with his emphasis upon a descriptive intensity bordering upon hallucination, without going into naked fantasy. This is the technique Baudelaire employs in poems such as 'Les Sept Vieillards'. He sees seven identical old men following each other towards him in the fog; we can just accept the possibility of ageing septuplets as being within the bounds of reality; but what if there are eight? As we follow Raskolnikov, wandering through the city muttering to himself, we can never be quite sure whether or not we are in the midst of one of his nightmares. It is significant that the detective, Porfiry, describes such behaviour as characteristic of the capital:

> . . . I am convinced that in St Petersburg, lots of people talk to themselves as they go along. It's a town of psychotics [lit. half-madmen]. If we had any [persons of] science, doctors, jurists, and philosophers would all be able to do most valuable research in St Petersburg, each in their own field. You don't often come across as many dark, violent and weird pressures upon the personality as you do in St Petersburg. Just take the climate! Then, it's the administrative centre of all Russia, and its characteristics must put their stamp upon everything.[9]

It is through the focus of these violent and weird pressures that Dostoevsky presents his vision of the capital. He writes of it in a code

59

of mental instability and physical discomfort. For example *Crime and Punishment* creates what is tantamount to a new descriptive genre: the 'feverscape'.

The novel is set in high summer in a poverty-stricken milieu. There can be no question of escape to a *dacha*. The descriptions blend the realistic depiction of a town in a heat wave with Raskolnikov's state of delirium, one condition complementing the other:

> Outside it was terribly hot; stifling hot, with jostling crowds, lime, scaffolding, bricks, dust and that particular summer stink, that every inhabitant of St Petersburg knows so well, if he cannot afford to rent a *dacha* – it all increased the nervous tension of the young man, who was quite tense enough already. The unbearable stench from the beer-parlours which were so numerous in that part of the town, the countless drunks, although it was a week-day, completed the disgusting, melancholy picture . . .[10]

The city in summer is not just a source of depression, it is an irritant. It grates upon the nerves, exasperates, as if a perpetual metaphysical sirocco, a 'murderer's wind', were always blowing.

Such is the masochism of Dostoevsky's characters that we find them actually cultivating this aspect of the city, as Baudelaire's character would cultivate his spleen. Raskolnikov chooses the most depressing route across town:

> He often used to take this crooked little alley that led from the square to Sadovaya Street. Recently he had felt impelled to wander through all these places, whenever he felt sick – to make himself even sicker![11]

In the same way both Velchaninov, the hero of *The Eternal Husband*, and Dostoevsky's most fantastic and phantasmagoric creation, Svidrigailov, the definitive 'Burnt-out Case', elect to remain in St Petersburg in high summer:

> He couldn't bring himself to go out to a *dacha*. The dust, the stifling heat, the white nights of St Petersburg that exasperated the nerves – that was what he liked about St Petersburg.[12]

The same view of the city informs *The Insulted and the Injured*, Dostoevsky's version of 'A St Petersburg Story'. He describes the city through a mood of death and decline, so that it embodies those qualities, becoming an amalgam of cause and effect:

> 'So B is dead? I'm not surprised. What a life, and what a place to live. Just look!'
> With a quick reflex gesture he pointed down the foggy street, lit with lanterns flickering weakly in the raw twilight, to the dirty

houses, the paving-stones glistening with moisture, the passersby, gloomy, bad-tempered and soaked through, to the whole picture which was encompassed by the dark inky dome of the St Petersburg sky. We went out into the square, a monument stood before us, lit from below by gas and further on loomed the huge dark mass of St Isaac's scarcely distinguishable against the dark-toned sky.[13]

The passage brings out another of the characteristics of the capital: the overpowering presence of the sky. No doubt because the land upon which it is built is so flat, and the height of its buildings relatively low, the city gives the impression of a sky which seems larger, wider, than usual, and, at the same time, particularly when overcast, there is a very real feeling that the sky weighs down upon one. Dostoevsky has used this and other physical characteristics to create a mood of sombre intensity. The same mood informs the conclusion of *The Insulted and the Injured*:

It was a sombre story, one of those sombre, painful stories that often pass unnoticed, in secret almost, beneath the oppressive St Petersburg sky, in the dark corners of a huge town, in the mighty seething turmoil of life, blind egoism, conflicting interests, gloomy vice, and secret crime, in the midst of this Stygian hell of pointless and abnormal existence.[14]

Dostoevsky uses melodramatic tones to establish the quality of urban experience. He shares this treatment of the city with other writers, such as Balzac, Dickens, Sue, Hugo and Baudelaire. This may be seen as the cross-fertilisation of literary conventions, but it is a movement engendered by the reality which those conventions depict. It was because those writers saw the new reality of the nineteenth-century industrial city in a certain way, that they used a very specific convention with which to express their vision. Dostoevsky describes the city as a world of materialism and appetite gone mad. There are certain aspects of his treatment of his capital which call for special mention. The *Encyclopaedia Britannica* pointed out that less than a third of its inhabitants were St Petersburg born. This makes the city a suitable medium to render the alienation and rootlessness which Dostoevsky felt to be so characteristic of his age. He saw the traditional values of grass-roots Russian culture, organic community and family life, being destroyed by the centrifugal, disintegrative pressures of modern society. City life was the incarnation of those divisive forces. For example, it encourages the disintegration of the family. The city is the place in which people live alone, apart from the rest of their family; the only relationship into which they enter with their neighbours is a non-relationship founded upon a lack of interest and anonymity.

Thus Raskolnikov lives in virtual isolation. The effect of his crime is to increase that isolation, cutting him off from his family and rendering him incapable of communicating with them. The city is equally responsible for the disintegration of the Marmeladov ménage. The daughter becomes a whore in order to support the rest of the family. Consequently she must leave home. Her mother eventually dies of TB – a St Petersburg disease doubtless precipitated by undernourishment – as she and the remnants of what was once a family take to the streets.

The city is the place to which people come leaving their family behind them. The very existence of the capital constitutes a disruption of family life. Witness the following conversation between two workmen in *Crime and Punishment*:

> 'You've got everything in this St Petersburg,' cried the younger one enthusiastically, 'except for your mother and father it's all there'.
> 'Except for that you can get anything,' agreed the elder with authority.[15]

The author's account of London singles out the same theme. He writes of working-class children who, finding the violence and drunkenness of their home unbearable, simply left, vanishing into the crowd.

The crowd, the vast anonymous mass that swallows children and others whole, echoes other visions of the city. In *Les Misérables* Hugo describes the total dissolution of the Thénardier family. Gavroche, the eldest son, assists his father to escape from prison, quite unaware that it is his father. On the same night he gives his younger brothers shelter without recognising them, and the next morning they leave to vanish into the crowd.

Its rôle as the administrative centre of Russia provides another way in which the capital generates isolation and poverty. One of Dostoevsky's stock sources of urban pathos is the figure of the provincial of slender means who has come to the capital to solicit a favour or obtain administrative justice. He has been deprived, unjustly, of a government post, and has come, often with his family, to seek reinstatement. He hopes that the remains of his savings will keep him until justice has been done, but they are running low, and he still has not managed to obtain an audience with the man who can put everything right . . . Dostoevsky is by no means the first writer to touch upon this theme. Gogol has already used such a figure in his Captain Kopeykin. But where Gogol's narrative treats the theme in a manner that is grotesquely facetious, Dostoevsky plays it for pathos.

In *The Idiot* Ippolit describes a meeting with such a character. He

immediately recognises him for what he is, suggesting that this was a
familiar figure, another St Petersburg type.

> 'It's obvious, you must have lost your job, and have come here to
> explain and find another?'
> 'How can you tell?' he asked, in astonishment.
> 'It's obvious at first sight,' I replied, laughing despite myself.
> 'Lot's of people come here from the provinces, with expectations.
> They do the rounds living as best they can.'[16]

Inevitably, in Dostoevsky's world, they seldom get justice. They come,
almost invariably, to the end of their tether before justice is done. This
is because they have come to seek justice in the city of lost illusions, the
place in which, almost by definition, justice can not be found. In
The Insulted and the Injured, Ikhmenev has brought his family with
him to the capital, in order to defend a lawsuit. It has been brought
against him by his employer, an evil prince for whom he had worked
as a land-agent. During his stay in St Petersburg, the prince's son
seduces and abducts his daughter, and her father disowns her, splitting
the family apart. Inevitably his funds are running low, and of course
the law-suit goes against him.

The two principal characters of *The Eternal Husband*, Velchaninov
and Trussotsky, have come to the capital for similar reasons: they are
both brought there by litigation. We find another such situation in
The Adolescent. A would-be governess commits suicide, overwhelmed
by poverty and despair. Her background is not elaborated. The theme
of the needy and distressed provincial is reduced to the bare bones of
an abstract pattern. The implication would be that the situation was
so familiar to Dostoevsky's readers that the following lines told them
all they would need to know:

> Vasin said about the neighbours that they had been there about
> three weeks and were from somewhere in the provinces; that their
> room was extraordinarily small, and it was perfectly obvious that
> they were very poor; that they were stuck there waiting for some-
> thing.[17]

Enough said. The phenomenon of the waiting provincial was clearly
all too familiar. The poorer quarters of the city were full of despairing
victims, living for indeterminate periods in furnished rooms, upon
hope and their dwindling savings, making their particular contribution
to the quality of life in the capital.

Dostoevsky's emphasis on isolation, the lack of community, the
casual, haphazard nature of city life, and the sheer lack of feeling
which its inhabitants display for one another, create a picture which
has great authority. This is because he is not building upon stereotypes

of big city life, he is creating them. No one, not even Balzac or Zola, has shown himself so sensitive to the big anonymous city in which the penniless individual can sink like a stone. Perhaps circumstances favoured the Russian writer. In France, Paris was everything, and provincial life was buried in moral torpor, existed in a state of suspended animation. Accordingly French authors lacked the possibility of a meaningful alternative to life in the capital, which might bring out that capital's deficiencies. In Russia, there was a sharp and viable contrast between traditional patterns of country-life and the European modes of the city. This in itself offered the Russian author a conceptual framework which his French equivalents lacked. A second advantage was of course the fact that St Petersburg was, in many ways, a particularly wretched place. It's climate, it's sheer inhumanity, it's scale, must all have helped to make it a suitable vehicle for the analysis and expression of the traumatic quality of life in the nineteenth-century city.

Dostoevsky's St Petersburg is a world of materialism and appetite, a harsh unfeeling place, in which, should you have the misfortune to go under, you will vanish for ever. It is the place in which the Marmeladovs of this world are allowed to become so much human rubbish. It is the degraded quality of life in these surroundings, the fact that such a place can never offer any hope of finding genuine satisfaction, that makes its inhabitants turn, for escape or for distraction, to the cultivation of intensity. In a world in which neither idealism nor meaning can be possible mere sensation is made to take their place. The Dostoevskian city-dweller feels the need to obliterate the consciousness through sensation, at all costs.

Dostoevsky couches his account of the city in the code of urban Gothic. It is a characteristic of this rhetoric that squalor and poverty are dramatised. In his appeals to the reader's sentimental 'Will to Pity' Dostoevsky knows no restraint, he is a maximalist. He shares with predecessors, such as Eugène Sue, an affection for a rhetoric of intensity. It is as if Dostoevsky manages himself to escape the full horror of his subject matter by turning it into a source of aesthetic sensationalism. This is the author's own escape into intensity, his own self-defence.

It is this deference to the intensity aesthetic which accounts for the peculiar note of exultation with which he describes the wretched poverty-stricken St Petersburg sub-culture. In a sense he is almost enjoying these accounts of human misery and degradation. He wallows in the plight of a Marmeladov. There is a kind of savage force, a determination to spare us nothing, in his account of Katerina Ivanovna Marmeladova and her children taking to the streets. Such pathetic passages almost become self-justifying aesthetic experiences. There exists a profound complicity between Dostoevsky and his subject-matter.

In a sense, this spectacle of squalor is enjoyable; Dostoevsky shares with some of his most unnerving creations, such as Svidrigailov, a profoundly developed *nostalgie de la boue*. Squalor moves his sentimental heart-strings, and also appeals to something else, something better left unexplored.

CHAPTER FIVE

The New Ideologies

As a 'mythographer' Dostoevsky is not really concerned with externals. Although the city plays an important part in his work it remains a mere setting, and one which his most important novel, *The Brothers Karamazov*, does without. He is more interested in mental states than in physical reality. Action itself is only relevant as a manifestation of inner events. It is their expressive nature, their rhetorical eloquence, that draws him to acts of violence. For all the indisputable importance of murder, suicide and rape in his creative world, it is finally the mental attitudes that generate such actions that are his real concern.

This is even reflected in his account of the city. His vision of London was turned, immediately, into a moral emblem. It becomes the embodiment of the spirit of capitalism, it is because it is able to *represent*, to serve as a patchwork of signs, that it is of interest to Dostoevsky.

His description of the climate of his times concentrates upon values, attitudes, world-pictures, rather than upon reality as such. Thus the railway, which for artists such as de Vigny and Ruskin was the manifest embodiment of philistinism and 'progress', is treated symbolically by Dostoevsky in a passage of comic mysticism. Lebedev in *The Idiot* is not only a clown and a professional go-between, he is also an interpreter of the Apocalypse. He advances the thesis that railways symbolise the spirit of materialism. It is typical that Dostoevsky should have chosen an 'unworthy mouth-piece' to present his own views. Both Shatov and Myshkin also speak for the author, and neither of them command much respect as spokesmen. Lebedev is convinced that:

> . . . the star Wormwood, in the Apocalypse, that falls to earth upon the source of the waters, is the network of railways . . .[1]

'So it follows,' said Ganya vehemently, from the other corner, 'That you believe the railways to be cursed, that they will destroy mankind, that they are pestilence descended upon earth to sully the springs of life? . . .'

'No, not the railways,' Lebedev retorted, both losing his temper and enjoying himself hugely. 'It's not the railways that will sully the springs of life; it's the whole lot that's cursed, the whole mood of recent times, the whole lot, the intellectual and the practical, that may really be cursed . . . Cursed, cursed for certain.' Lebedev made the point emphatically.[2]

Railways and all other manifestations of the new culture were merely symptoms; the root of the trouble lay elsewhere. Once again Dostoevsky is in accord with Baudelaire, who also saw beyond the paraphernalia of progress:

Théorie de la vraie civilisation
Elle n'est pas dans le gaz, ni dans la vapeur, ni dans les tables tournantes, elle est dans la diminution des traces du péché originel.[3]

Both authors see a decline in spirituality as the true cause of the Wasteland of their age. Dostoevsky regarded such a decline as a monument to crass human stupidity. Man had grown stupid enough to believe that all problems of every kind might be answered by the assiduous application of sound commonsense and empirical reasoning; anything else was anti-scientific and hence the work of prejudice, ignorance and superstition. But, by entrusting himself to empirical solutions alone, man thereby rejected his heritage of whole meanings: a set of values which might ensure that empiricism would remain, in the last instance, subject to the control of an overriding sense of nobler meaning and purpose. Without such a control the empirical method could only bring about an aggregate of piecemeal technical solutions without any form of binding unity to them.

Empiricism had formed the intellectual backbone of middle-class philosophy for nearly two centuries. It was initiated by the scepticism of Bacon and Montaigne. It is they who instigate the movement away from a concern with the whole meanings which integrate man into a greater pattern of cosmic harmony. They fragment that harmonious world-view and in its place propose working solutions, *modi vivendi*, *morales provisoires*. Their attitude is subsequently applied to metaphysics and epistemology by Locke. It is later taken by Voltaire and the *Philosophes*, and turned into a middle-class *Lebensmoral* for eighteenth-century progressives. It became a tool with which to destroy long-standing political and social institutions that, serving no obvious purpose, failed to stand the acid test of Poujadist commonsense. The tradition is directly responsible for that practical and utilitarian positivism which turns the nineteenth century into the shop-keeper's golden age. For the unbridled application of the principle of common-sense, enlightened self-interest and nothing else created a civilisation of shop-keepers and prepared for the desert of twentieth-century big business and commercial technology. Being what they are, applied commonsense and self-interest can never check the encroachment of profitable pollution upon human happiness. This is because happiness cannot be *quantified*, and therefore must needs fall outside the frame of reference employed by commonsense.

The metaphysical essentials of Dostoevsky's case against the values of his culture emerge in the following letter, in which he is discussing his Grand Inquisitor:

'You are the Son of God, so you are all powerful. Here be stones, see how many there are. You need only command and the stones will turn into bread.

Command that the earth may bring forth produce, without work, teach the people skills that will permit them to live henceforth without work. Do you not realise that man's greatest vices and misfortunes were caused by hunger, cold, poverty and the unbearable struggle for life?'

That is the first question the spirit of evil sets Christ. Admit that it's a tricky one. Modern *socialism*, here and in Europe, puts aside Christ and is primarily concerned with *bread*, it calls science to witness that the sole cause of all human misery is – poverty, the struggle for life, 'it was the fault of the environment'.

To this Christ replied: 'Man does not live by bread alone,' i.e. he stated an axiom about man's spirituality. The devil's idea could only create human cattle, but Christ knew that man cannot be brought alive by bread alone. If there is not also a spiritual life, an ideal of Beauty, man will grow miserable, die, go mad, kill himself or indulge in heathen fantasies. Since Christ bore the Ideal of Beauty in himself – His Word, he decided it was better to instill the Ideal of Beauty in men's hearts; this would create a sense of brotherhood and then men would work for each other's benefit, and would grow rich. Whereas, were they given bread they would become enemies out of boredom.

But what if Bread and Beauty both were granted? This would deprive man of work, personality, self-sacrifice, the benefit of others, – in short it would remove the whole ideal of life. Hence it was better simply to celebrate the spiritual idea alone.

The proof that this short passage of the Gospel was indeed concerned with this idea and not simply with the fact that Christ was hungry and the devil encouraged him to turn a stone into bread, is to be seen in Christ's reply, which revealed a secret of nature: man does not live by bread alone (that is to say unlike animals).

If it were a simple matter of Christ appeasing his hunger, why raise the question of the spiritual nature of man in general? . . . Incidentally; remember Darwin's recent theories about man's descent from the apes? Without going into any theories, Christ simply states that in man, besides an animal world there is also a spiritual one. Let man be descended from what you please (The *Bible* does not explain how God moulded him out of clay) but God breathed into him the breath of life. But sickeningly enough, his sins can turn him back into an animal.[4]

This assertion of man's essential spirituality is the point of departure of Dostoevsky's work. Any social system that ignores it must needs be deficient. By concentrating on physical needs alone, materialism, capitalist or socialist, can only degrade man, turn him back into an animal and create a wilderness of boredom. Because such systems lack whole meanings, and ignore a whole dimension of human experience, they build a world which is essentially incomplete, in which there can be no satisfaction. Man responds to this lack of wholeness with an aggravated, dissatisfied kicking against the pricks, a kind of ontological restlessness and endless unrealisable aspiration.

In *The Devils* Shatov develops this view of the limitations o contemporary culture:

Not one nation has yet established itself on science and reason; there has never been such a case, not even for a moment, out of stupidity. Socialism must by definition be atheism, since it announces, from the very start, that it is an atheistic institution, and proposes for itself a uniquely scientific and rational basis. Reason and science have always, since the beginnings of time, played a secondary, subservient rôle in the life of nations; so it will continue for ever.[5]

Dostoevsky contends that that which is most important in man lies beyond the scope of commonsense. Commonsense had created a society which had lost all harmony, unity and meaning: a world in which everyone was over-aware of his own individuality and of what he owed to himself. To look after number one was the new categorical imperative, which claimed to have rendered the Christian ethic obsolete.

In his rejection of an age which had come to regard the applied skills as the highest form of wisdom, Dostoevsky does not discriminate between socialist and capitalist. He rejects Western culture wholesale, the difference between its principal manifestations being less important than their similarities. Revolutionary progressives and men of commerce shared the same flaw. This kind of indiscriminate indictment is very characteristic of the Orthodox tradition. For example, the Eastern Church never permitted itself to be drawn into the struggle between Catholicism and the Reform. It considered that the Western Church had long since turned away from the true path and that was that. Dostoevsky's lack of discrimination between capitalism and socialism partakes of a similar attitude. All modern Western thought was corrupt, in that it sought to reduce man to less than the sum of his parts.

The horrors of the new ideology emerge in the following conversation from *The Idiot*:

'. . . I challenge all you atheists; how do you save the world and find the right path to tread, – you persons of science, industry, association, salaries and all that. How? By credit? What's credit? Where does credit lead you? . . .'

'It leads you to universal solidarity, an equilibrium of interests,' observed Ptitsyn.

'And that's all! Taking no moral base but the satisfaction of personal egoism and material needs?' . . .

'But surely the universal necessity to live, eat and drink, the full scientific conviction that you will not satisfy this necessity without universal association and solidarity of interests, is, it seems to me, a powerful enough notion to act as a fulcrum, a "source of life" for future generations,' said Ganya hotly. 'The necessity to eat and drink, . . . that is to say simply the sense of self-preservation?'

'But is a sense of self-preservation not enough for you? It's a natural law, human nature.'[6]

Ganya and Ptitsyn seek to reduce the complexities of human action and motive to the simple patterns of appetite, patterns which will, incidentally, justify their own actions provided these fulfil their profit-oriented criteria.

Luzhin, in *Crime and Punishment*, is another advocate of the new morality. He is generous enough to consider the lot of others; he finances the journey of his bride-to-be and future mother-in-law to the capital – but makes them travel third class. He describes himself as 'a positive man, but sharing in many respects . . . the views of our younger generation'.[7] He is guilty of the same moral views that convinced Raskolnikov to murder for money. He sacrifices compassion to self-interest, and believes in the rule of technical justice:

'If I've been told, till now to love, and have done so, what has come of it?' continued Petr Petrovich, a trifle hastily perhaps. 'I've torn my coat in two, shared it with my neighbour, and we've both ended up half-naked; as the Russian proverb goes: "Chase several hares at once, and you won't catch a single one." Science says: "Love yourself most of all, since everything is founded upon self-interest. Love yourself alone and conduct your affairs properly, and your coat will remain in one piece." Economic truth adds that the more private enterprises, the more coats, society has in one piece, the firmer its foundations the better to build the common good.

Thus, by amassing wealth for myself alone, I am, so to speak, amassing on behalf of everybody and contributing to my neighbour getting a good deal more than half a coat – and not out of private, individual generosity, but as the consequence of a general prosperity. The idea is a simple one, but I fear that it took a long time to dawn, as it was obscured by enthusiasm and fruitless dreaming, when you would think that with a bit of commonsense . . .'[8]

Of course, Luzhin is a distinctly evil character who abuses utilitarian notions to justify his own pursuit of profit. However, it is his readiness to reduce human behaviour to the crudest of models that makes him a 'new man'. Dostoevsky objects to what might be described, in a loose sense, as the behaviourist world-view. Behaviourist science is rooted in the empirical method and nineteenth-century positivism. In its pursuit of methodological rigour, it elects to ignore those aspects of human behaviour such as faith and love, which it cannot measure. It tends to dismiss such qualities as 'unscientific'. Indeed behaviourism has come a long way towards the fulfilment of the Dostoevskian night-mare of the 'ant-heap', the 'herd united'.

The philosophical consequence of behaviourism is the negation of free will and of ethics: man is reduced to the product of stimulus and response. *The Brothers Karamazov* furnishes Dostoevsky's last words on the subject. Dmitri learns of the new ideology from the unspeakable Rakitin, who introduces him to the thought of one of the high priests of positivism, Doctor Claude Bernard.

Bernard's *Introduction à la physiologie expérimentale* was one of the sacred texts of positivism. Zola used it, almost word for word, as the basis of his naturalist handbook, *Introduction au roman expérimental*. Bernard is alleged to have introduced the scientific method into medicine, and is said, virtually single-handed, to have turned it from an art into a science. From Bernard's work Zola, for one, derives a theory of human behaviour according to which it may be accounted for, entirely, by a combination of hereditary and environmental factors. Bernard, and Zola after him, express themselves in the arrogant language of scientific reductionism, and display a scientist's impatience with notions such as the soul, or even the mind, together with an exclusive faith in the world of sensory experience.

Dostoevsky, and even more so, Dmitri Karamazov, are unable to accept this denial of man's human qualities. During his trial it is suggested by the defence that Dmitri could not have helped killing his father, could not have helped spending at once all the money entrusted to him – as opposed to keeping half of it in a bag hanging from his neck like a dead albatross. It is such observations that Dmitri interrupts with disgusted cries of 'Claude Bernard'. The same disgust

71

emerges more lucidly in the following passage. He has just learnt who Bernard was:

'. . . I'm sorry for God . . .'

'What do you mean?'

'Imagine, it's all in the nerves, in the head, I mean these nerves in the brain (damn them) . . . these, these kind of little tails, the nerves have got these tails, and, well, they start to tremble – I mean I look at something with my eyes, like that, and an image appears but not at once, in a moment, and a second later a moment turns up, not a moment dammit, an image, an object or an event, damn it that's how I perceive, and then think, all because of the tails, and not at all because I have a soul and am made in an image – that's all rot. Mikhail explained it all to me yesterday, and it shattered me.

Science is terrific Alyosha. I can see that a new kind of man will arise. But still, I feel sorry for God.'[9]

Dostoevsky saw in the kind of denial of human freedom which the views of Bernard implied, not just an intolerable restriction upon humanity, but a source of grave social instability. In this respect he agrees with another great critic and chronicler of the state of nineteenth-century culture, Alexis de Tocqueville. De Tocqueville perceives, in this kind of denial of personal responsibility, a threat to social order:

We no longer have faith in anything, especially in ourselves. A work which tries to prove that in this world man obeys his *constitution* and can scarcely affect his destiny by his own free will, is like giving opium to a sick man whose heart is already slowing down.[10]

It is the steady encroachment of the behaviourist world-view and its denial of human freedom in the interests of 'social engineering' that creates the character of Dostoevsky's underground man, with his sense of metaphysical spite and his addiction to intensity. He is unable to accept the socialist Utopia of an antiseptic, behaviourist Welfare State. It places too low a price upon his humanity:

You believe in an eternal and indestructible crystal building, in which you won't be able to stick out your tongue in secret, or even make a rude sign in your pocket. But perhaps I fear that building precisely because it's indestructible and made of crystal, and you won't be able to stick out your tongue, even in secret.

You see: if, instead of a palace there were a hen-house, and it were raining, I might well go into that hen-house to avoid getting wet, but I would not mistake it for a palace simply because it kept off the rain. You may laugh, you may even say that in that particular instance there's no difference between a hen-house and a stately home. Agreed, if the sole purpose of life is to keep dry.

But what am I to do if I believe that there are other things in life, and that if you are going to live, you might as well do it in a mansion? That's what I want. You will only stop me from wanting it by altering me . . . In the meantime I will not mistake the hen-house for a palace . . . I refuse to say that I've had enough when I'm still hungry; I know that I won't settle for a compromise, for a perpetually recurring zero; just because it exists in *reality*, and according to the laws of nature. I will not accept as my ultimate desire, a solid building, with flats for poor tenants on a thousand year lease, with Vagenheim the dentist, just in case.[11]

Positivism, planning and commonsense conspire to deny man his right to be impractical, to indulge in irrational behaviour. The intolerable restriction upon freedom which they bring about engenders the need to escape by plunging into sensation, a plunge which usually takes the form of anti-social action. Dostoevsky's account of the potentially violent response to excessive social engineering and planning is not without a certain relevance today.

In his Underground Man Dostoevsky created a character with responses a hundred years ahead of his time. He anticipated the despairing reaction to the planned obscenities of twentieth-century technology and its ant-heaps of applied commonsense. It was as if Dostoevsky glimpsed, through the relatively harmless sub-Palladian Baltic architecture of 'the most deliberately thought-out city in the world', the terrible vision of what was to come. In comparison with twentieth-century high-density development, from the Stalinallee to Tower Hamlets, Dostoevsky's St Petersburg was a haphazard and organic paradise.

Dostoevsky feels that the modern world is committed to the pursuit of reasonable and egalitarian happiness. It is against this pattern that he proposes the image of the monastic life, in *The Brothers Karamazov*. The Russian Monk was to be a defender of the faith, asserting spiritual values in a world in which all other things were falling apart. The monk was to attempt to restore those whole meanings which the modern world had lost. Father Zosima expresses this conception, which he sets against a secular world of an ever increasing degradation:

As yet they preserve undistorted the image of Christ, in solitude and devotion, in the purity of God's truth, they have received it from the elders of the church, from apostles and martyrs, and when the time comes, they will reveal it unto the world, when the world's truth shall have collapsed. This is a solemn notion. A star will shine forth from the East.
That is what I believe the monk to be . . . Look at the secular

world, has it not distorted God's image and God's truth? They have science, but science only deals with the world of the senses. The world of the spirit, the nobler half of man's being, is utterly derided, driven out with a certain exultation, even with hate. The world has announced the reign of freedom . . . and what do we see in their freedom; nothing but slavery and self-destruction! The world says: 'You have needs, so satisfy them, for you have the same rights as the rich and the famous. Do not be afraid to satisfy them, in fact you should multiply them.' That is what the secular world teaches today. That is their idea of freedom. And what results from this right, from this multiplication of needs? For the rich – isolation and spiritual suicide, for the poor, envy and murder; for they have been accorded rights, but not shown how to satisfy them. They inform us that the world is steadily becoming as one, is creating a brotherly community, by reducing distances, transmitting thoughts through the air. Alas, put not your trust in that kind of unity. Those who understand freedom as the multiplication and immediate satisfaction of needs, distort their own nature, for they create in themselves a multitude of pointless and stupid desires, habits and illusions. They live for envy of one another, for sensual satisfaction and rivalry. To have banquets, carriages, calls, positions and obsequious attendants is held to be a necessity, and to that end they sacrifice their very lives, their honour, their love of their fellow men, and even kill themselves if they fail. We find the same in those who are not wealthy, while for the time being the poor drown their envy and their inability to satisfy their needs in drink. But soon they will drink not alcohol, but blood.[12]

This is the author's most complete account of the state of nineteenth-century culture: a world in which what you have is perpetually out of phase with what you want. Dostoevsky's picture is less abstract, less interiorised than that of Baudelaire, but the analysis is the same. Both writers describe a world of illusions and appetites, a world in which everybody expects his due: he has his rights. This notional egalitarianism creates a world in which there can be no satisfaction. 'Needs' have come to take the place of whole meanings, and needs can never be satisfied definitively. Society lives in a climate of divisive envy and running discontent. The poor envy the rich and the rich have lost any sense of the responsibility conferred upon them by wealth.

Father Zosima's analysis has a socio-political dimension. It is to the rise of egalitarianism that he ascribes the degeneration of his society into mindless and unrestrained appetite. The gradual disappearance of privilege and the corresponding rise of more or less democratic institutions had already been singled out by de Tocqueville as the most important trend of nineteenth-century culture. The Frenchman regards it as a mixed blessing. For all its short-comings a hierarchically organised society, based upon privilege, had two vital advantages. It had made for a sense of stability and security: those qualities which we had suggested were ultimately responsible for the *douceur de vivre* of the *ancien régime*. In the second place, the existence of privileged groups constituted a check against the potential tyranny of the executive. De Tocqueville describes the dangers inherent in the trend towards democracy in the following lines of *L'Ancien Régime*:

> . . . au milieu des ténèbres de l'avenir, on peut déjà découvrir trois vérités très claires. La première est que tous les hommes de nos jours sont entraînés par une force inconnue qu'on peut espérer régler et ralentir, mais non vaincre, qui tantôt les pousse doucement et tantôt les précipite vers la destruction de l'aristocratie; la seconde, que parmi toutes les sociétés du monde, celles qui auront toujours le plus de peine à échapper pendant longtemps au gouvernement absolu seront précisément ces sociétés où l'aristocratie n'est plus et ne peut plus être; la troisième enfin, que nulle part le despotisme ne doit produire des effets plus pernicieux que dans ces sociétés-là, car plus qu'aucune autre sorte de gouvernement il y favorise le développement de tous les vices auxquels ces sociétés sont spécialement sujettes, et les pousse ainsi du côté même où, suivant une inclination naturelle, elles penchaient déjà.[13]

It is the author's insistence upon the steady rise of egalitarianism which is our chief concern in this passage, however the contention that from democracy to tyranny *il n'y avait qu'un pas* has its own relevance to the history of Russia.

De Tocqueville clarifies Zosima's suggestion that egalitarianism and the erosion of privilege are a sign of the times; his association of egalitarianism with the development of appetite, envy and discontent is echoed by another French writer, de Lamennais:

> L'égalité absolue ou la destruction de toute hierarchie sociale, ne laissant subsister d'autres distinctions que celles de la fortune, produit une cupidité extraordinaire, une soif insatiable de l'or; or, quoi qu'on fasse, les hommes voudront s'élever, c'est-à-dire se classer; et comme la richesse participe elle-même de la mobilité du gouvernement et de la société toute entière, elle devient corruptrice au plus haut degré. Les désirs sans bornes et sans règles se précipitent vers tout ce qui promet cet or, seule noblesse désormais, seul honneur, seule considération et dans ce mouvement rapide, le temps manquant à tous pour apprendre à posséder, tous se jettent dans les jouissances avec une sorte de fureur . . . Dans le désordre universel, chacun

cherche avec anxiété la place due à son mérite, à ses services, à ses besoins, ou à ses convoitises. De là des prétensions innombrables, des murmures, des plaintes, des haines passionnées, un fond général d'aigreur et de mécontentement qui croît sans cesse.[14]

De Lamennais' analysis is Dostoevsky's. If we conflate the picture of nineteenth-century culture created by Dostoevsky, de Tocqueville, de Lamennais, and Baudelaire, we see a world that had gone dreadfully wrong. The quantitative approach to the analysis of human action, and the denial of humanity which that involves, coupled with that doctrinaire belief in absolute social equality, had created a culture-pattern in which appetites had replaced values, and the supreme categorical imperative was 'I want it now'; a culture-pattern that was restless, unstable and potentially explosive.

That this analysis has its relevance to our own time suggests that what Dostoevsky has to say about the spirit of his age is of more than academic interest. In essence, he has sketched out the psychological climate of the permissive and consuming society. It is a world in which everybody knows that they have the right to defer to their every appetite, their every consumer's caprice, a world that runs on envy, discontent and keeping up with the Jones's; a place in which no satisfaction survives the point of sale, no pay-award satisfies a working class which is by definition permanently envious and discontented. With Zosima's account of transmitting ideas through the air and speeding up travelling times, Dostoevsky has even anticipated the 'global village'. But it is a village without village life, in which nobody knows their neighbours.

CHAPTER SIX

From the Banker to the Psychopath

Yes, I'm very skilled at the interpretation of the Apocalypse . . .
You will agree with me that we are now in the age of the third horse,
the black one, the horseman holds a balance in his hand, since ours
is an age of measures and contracts, and everyone is simply interested
in their rights . . . And they still want to preserve freedom of the
spirit, a clear conscience and a healthy body, and all God's gifts.
But they won't preserve them through their rights alone, and this
age shall be followed by the pale horse, and he whose name is Death,
and thereafter comes Hell.[1]

Lebedev chooses the third horse as the emblem appropriate to an age
in which the only aristocracy was the aristocracy of money. The ever-
increasing influence of the financier had already been an important
aspect of Balzac's critique of French society in the 1830s, the society of
Guizot's famous injunction: *Enrichissez-vous*. The increasing importance
of money over other forms of distinction can be seen in the changing
ambitions of Dostoevsky's own characters. Raskolnikov (1866) simply
wants power. He is a traditional character from nineteenth-century
fiction, inheriting his values from Stendhal's Julien Sorel, and Balzac's
own mephistophelian Vautrin. He is included in Pushkin's assertion
that everyone aspires to become a Napoleon. Not so *The Adolescent*
(1875). He is virtually a parody of disinheritance; the bastard son of
a gentleman out of a serf, he bears the princely name Dolgoruky.
A classless, rootless individual, with no stabilising influences, not even
the support of a regular family, he has to create himself from scratch.
In this respect the novel is the definitive *Bildungsroman*, demonstrating
the dependence of that form upon cultural instability. Such books are
not generated by stable cultures, since there the individual inherits
rules and patterns of behaviour which provide him with guidance
enough. The novel of education, in which isolated heroes learn the
hard way, from their own experience, is the product of periods of rapid
cultural change, in which the experience of one generation has no
relevance to its successor. In this respect *The Adolescent* is a reflection
of the chaos of Russian society in the age that followed the reforms.
The hero's model is no longer Napoleon however, it is Rothschild:

My idea is – to become Rothschild. I beg the reader to relax and
take me seriously. I repeat that my idea is to become Rothschild, to

77

grow rich as Rothschild; not just to be rich, but rich as Rothschild.[2]

Dolgoruky looks to Rothschild rather than Napoleon because he has no heroic illusions. He knows that he is a mediocrity in a mediocre world and he has chosen a path along which mediocrity is no handicap:

> The whole strength of my idea is that money is the only way that brings even mediocrity to the top. I may not even be a mediocrity, but I can tell, from the looking-glass, that my appearance is against me because I have an ordinary face. But were I as rich as Rothschild – who could rival my appearance, – would I not have thousands of beautiful women at my beck and call; indeed I am convinced that they would actually, in all sincerity, end up by finding me handsome. I may be intelligent, but however intelligent I might be, there will always be someone more intelligent still – and I'm done for. But were I a Rothschild – would the man who was more intelligent be of any importance in comparison? He would not even be allowed to speak in my presence! I may be witty; but put me next to Talleyrand or Piron, and I'm eclipsed, but once I'm a Rothschild, where's Piron?[3]

Stendhal was correct in his belief that the age of heroism, of the soldier, was over. But the implication of the title, *Le Rouge et le Noir*, that the future lay with the priesthood, was mistaken. As he came to see when writing about the July Monarchy, the black of *Le Noir* was not to be clerical cloth, but the sober, confidence-inspiring livery of the banker. The banker Leuwen, who brings the government down for utterly frivolous reasons, is allowed, despite his calling, to retain the style of a dandy. But, by making Rothschild his ideal, something of a contradiction in terms, Dolgoruky vowed himself to a lifetime's po-faced seriousness and devotion to the pecuniary ethic.

For, in the world described at the end of the preceding chapter, the pecuniary ethic has become the sole driving-force. All other considerations are eclipsed by material gain. Dostoevsky sees his age as a time when the spirit of calculation and profitability reigns supreme. This supremacy is heralded by another manifestation of the steady encroachment of egalitarianism: the moral abdication of the aristocracy. Dolgoruky is not the first Dostoevskian character to suggest Rothschild to be the true aristocrat of the age. The evil prince, the villain of *The Insulted and the Injured* (1861), has already made the point to his son. The prince represents a betrayal of the sense of obligation and honour which should be the distinctive feature of the aristocrat and gentleman. He abuses power and responsibility to satisfy his intense but shallow appetites. In the following scene he makes a sneering *profession de foi* to a poor but honest listener, whose revulsion the prince enjoys:

> . . . what am I to do when I know for sure that the basis of all

human virtue is the profoundest egoism? The more virtuous the action the greater the egoism. Love yourself – that's the only rule I recognise. Life is a business deal; don't throw your money away, but pay for your pleasures and you will fulfil your obligation to your neighbour – that's my morality, if you really must know, although frankly, it seems to me that it's better to get out of paying your neighbour, and make him work for nothing. I neither have nor wish for ideals; I have never yearned for them. You can get through life gaily and pleasantly enough without ideas and, *en somme*, I'm very glad I can get by without prussic acid. For if I were more virtuous I might not manage without it . . . No! there is so much that is good in life. I like status, rank, a mansion; huge stakes at cards . . . But above all women, women of all kinds; I even like hidden, dark orgies, a little on the odd, the peculiar side, even a bit sordid sometimes.[4]

The prince has abdicated all forms of social responsibility to become something of a Baudelairian libertine, with a *nostalgie de la boue* which he will share with Svidrigailov. But his attachment to the darker corners of human experience is less important than the betrayal of his position and responsibilities.

Abdication of responsibility by a gentleman plays an important part in the short story 'The Gentle One' ('Krotkaya', 1876). The hero is a practical man quite lacking in a sense of honour. Once he was an officer and a gentleman, but was obliged to resign his commission and his place in society when he declined to fight a duel for a trivial provocation to the honour of his regiment. From that moment he sinks through society like a stone, experiencing the lowest depths of urban depravity in 'Vyazemsky's house' – the centre of small-time debauchery that had also been visited by Svidrigailov. Eventually the ex-gentleman becomes a pawnbroker.

The erosion of a sense of honour is essentially a consequence of the cult of self-interest, which destroys any sense of one's obligation to others. Dostoevsky looks to a sense of honour and obligation as a means, perhaps the only means, of achieving a kind of stability in an otherwise disintegrating world. Hence the importance of the aristocrat who betrays his rôle. The point is made by a schoolmaster who attaches his comments to Dolgoruky's chronicle:

Were I a Russian novelist with talent, I would certainly take my characters from the hereditary Russian gentry, because only in that kind of cultured Russian can one find the semblance of good order, and a good impression, that are essential to a novel if one is to produce a noble impression upon the reader. I am speaking seriously, although as you know, I am not of the gentry myself. Pushkin even noted as the subject of a future novel, 'The traditions of a Russian family' and, believe me, here is to be found everything that has been beautiful to date. At any rate, here is everything that we perfect. I am not saying this because I am definitely convinced of the order and the justice of this beauty; but there were here, for example, complete forms of honour and obligation, which, beyond the gentry, have not even begun in Russia . . .

Whether this honour was good, the obligations fulfilled, is another story; more important for me was the perfection of the forms, and the existence of some kind of order . . . For heaven's sake, the most important thing of all for us is some kind of order of our own! That was our hope . . . something constructive, and not this eternal smashing, these splinters flying in all directions, this litter and dirt in which we've been stuck . . .[5]

The schoolmaster is no snob. He is remarkably detached about the gentry, simply regarding them as the sole possible means of achieving an indigenous stability which might halt the collapse into chaos.

In most other societies, at most times, man is motivated by something beyond immediate self-interest, but for Dostoevsky the nineteenth century was an age in which the pecuniary ethic had become the sole imperative. Witness this description of Paris:

The Parisian loves to bargain, but even when he cheats you blind, he cheats, not for profit alone, as he used to, but out of virtue, a kind of sacred necessity. To accumulate a fortune and own as many things as possible has become the Parisian's supreme moral code. Where once this was a mere truth, it now has an odour of sanctity about it. There used to be a few other things besides money, so that someone with no money who had other qualities could count on a little respect; no longer. Now you must have money and accumulate as many things as possible, and only then can you expect some sort of respect. Otherwise, not only may you not count upon the respect of others, you may not even count upon your respect of yourself.[6]

Dostoevsky asserts the need for a sense of honour to oppose this degeneration. Significantly a sense of honour plays an important part in the novels of another writer concerned by the encroachment of baseness and the pecuniary ethic. Stendhal, Nietzsche's favourite novelist until he read Dostoevsky, portrays idealistic young heroes who try to cope with a world in which there are no ideals left. It is their inability to play the game and reconcile themselves to base reality and its compromise, that leads to their practical undoing and their spiritual apotheosis. Julien Sorel has to learn to rise above the world of petty vanity, ambition and self-interest, before he can find peace with

himself and his lover. Fabrice del Dongo is an uncompromising
idealist, in contrast with the practical statesman Mosca, who, for all
his nobility of feeling, is finally spiritually corrupt. In order to please
his father, Lucien Leuwen must quite literally be smeared with mud,
as he goes about the honourable government business of the July
Monarchy – election rigging. These characters all recoil from the
world in which they find themselves. In one respect they are strangely
close to some of Dostoevsky's own creations. They model themselves
upon Napoleon, and aspire to an apotheosis of the will. They believe
that their might is their right, and happily step over the frontiers of
conventional morality in their cult of self-glorification. (But where
Stendhal applauds their transgression of a morality which he sees as
the creation of a corrupt and hypocritical society, Dostoevsky does
nothing of the sort.) Stendhal's characters are prevented from developing into selfish maniacs, as do Raskolnikov, Kirillov, Stavrogin,
by their unique sense of personal honour. Living in a world in which
honour no longer exists as a public code, they set their own solipsistic
standards: standards which they must never fail.

Although the Stendhalian sense of honour differs from that of
Dostoevsky in respect of its solipsistic basis, both authors describe their
societies in terms of the opposition of some kind of honour to the
pecuniary ethic, the new morality. Stendhal, especially in *La Chartreuse
de Parme*, essentially a pastoral novel, allows himself the luxury of
treating his characters' honour in the idealistic language of Quixotic
wish-fulfilment. Dostoevsky tends to be more down to earth and
therefore less serene. However his characters are capable of a lack
of self-interest that can be positively Stendhalian: witness their capacity
for conspicuous consumption. The supreme example is Dmitri Karamazov's last night of freedom at Mokroe. It ends with the entire
village dancing, as Dmitri, beaming drunken approval, hands cigars
out to peasants and tops up their glasses with champagne.

The most intense and concise moment of conspicuous consumption
however comes when Nastasya Filipovna throws Rogozhin's hundred
thousand roubles on the fire. She tells Ganya he can have the money
if he retrieves it – only to have him collapse in a dead faint, so great
has been his effort at self-control. Rogozhin adores her for burning the
money:

> 'There's a queen,' he kept saying, turning first to one and then to
> another, at random.
> 'She's my sort all right.' He cried, quite beyond himself.
> 'Which one of you sneak-thieves would do a thing like that?'[7]

Even Raskolnikov is essentially disinterested. From the moment he
is mistaken for a beggar and given money which he throws into the

river, he keeps giving money away – to the Marmeladovs, to the drunken girl he meets on the street. His genuine distaste for money is also reflected in his utter lack of interest in the booty for which he ostensibly committed a double murder.

Alyosha Karamazov has the same attitude towards money:

> Alyosha was clearly one of those young people who were like God's fools, if he were suddenly to come into a capital sum, he would readily give it all to the first person to ask him – for good works, or even to a crafty swindler . . . In general he seemed not to know the value of money, metaphorically speaking that is . . . Petr Alexandro-vich Myussov, a man who was distinctly punctilious about money and the middle-class virtues, once . . . said of Alyosha 'Here is possibly the only person in the world whom you could abandon, alone and penniless, in a strange square in a town of a million inhabitants, and he will run no risk of dying of hunger or cold, because he'll get fed and lodged at once, or else he will lodge himself, and it would cost him no effort or humiliation, cost the benefactor no trouble and he might even enjoy it.'[8]

Such persons of generous feeling and honour are contrasted with the 'new man', a cautious egotistical calculator who believes only in his own advantage. He has a humourless capacity for self-interest, a spiritual pettiness and a sense of vanity in place of a sense of honour. He is content to stand to reason. Now this account of the Dostoevskian villain could equally well apply to some of Stendhal's creations, such as M. de Rênal, M. de Valenod of *Le Rouge et le Noir*, and countless other characters consumed by envy, vanity and self-interest of truly gallic proportions. Moreover, in Stendhal's world, as in Dostoevsky's, men of honour go to the wall.

Dmitri Karamazov, the definitive man of honour, is constitutionally incapable of smallness. The scale of his spirit transcends his violence. As he puts it to Alyosha, Karamazovs may plunge, but at least they plunge straight.[9] It is his sense of personal integrity that is his saving grace. It emerges in his encounter with the new men who judge him by their own standards. His interrogation and subsequent trial represent the clash of two ethical systems, one founded on honour, the other on prudence. The confrontation is strikingly reminiscent of the trial of Julien Sorel. Sorel informs the jury about to find him guilty of attempted murder that they would condemn him not for what he did, but for what he was – a threat and an insult to the middle classes. The details of Dmitri's condemnation are very different, but once again the verdict is motivated by the jury's view of the accused as someone who rocked their boat. This emerges in the title of the chapter in which the verdict is announced: 'The peasants stood up for themselves.'

The clash between honour and prudence emerges in Dmitri's explanation of how he financed the orgy at Mokroe. It will be recalled that he had retained half the money entrusted to him by Katerina Ivanovna, in order to have funds should Grushenka agree to go off with him. He is appalled at his own capacity for calculation:

> I didn't understand her then. I thought she wanted money and would not forgive my poverty. So I spitefully count off half the three thousand, and cold-bloodedly sew it into a bag, sew with calculation, sew before getting drunk, and then, when I've finished, go off to drink the second half! No, it was despicable. Now do you see?

But they do not. To his interrogators Dmitri's behaviour looks like plain commonsense:

> The prosecutor burst out laughing, as did the investigator. 'I'd say you showed good sense and common decency, restraining yourself, and not blowing it all at once,' giggled Nikolai Parfenovich. 'What's wrong with that?'
> 'But I stole it, that's what! For God's sake, your failure to understand appalls me.'[10]

It should. Dmitri realises that the people into whose hands he has fallen, and whom he has to convince of his innocence, might just as well be Martians. If they cannot understand his sense of shame at the awareness, let alone the admission, of his despicable premeditation – his banker's approach to an orgy – then what chance does he have of convincing them of his innocence?

It is calculation that Dmitri detests in himself. He accepts his spontaneous actions, although he is always ready to face their consequences. It is calculation and cunning that he is ashamed of:

> 'By the way, why did you in fact take steps to divide the money? Why, for what purpose, can you explain?'
> 'Gentlemen, the purpose is the whole point!' cried Mitya. 'To divide it was despicable, that is to say that it was a calculation and calculation, in this case, is despicable . . .'[11]

The new men cannot understand that had Dmitri killed his father, he was constitutionally incapable of concealing the fact in the hope of evading justice. His natural sense of honour would require him to bear the consequences of his action as a matter of course. He tries to make the point to his interrogators, as he gradually realises whom he has to deal with:

> Damn it, gentlemen, you make me feel dirty [lit. you have sullied my soul]. Do you really suppose that I'd try to hide it from you if

I had killed my father, fence, lie, cover up? No, Dmitri Karamazov is not like that.[12]

The trial itself is an indictment of a kind of justice which is unable to accept Dmitri's word of honour as evidence:

He explained nothing, added not a single explanatory fact to his earlier fantastic confession; that's all unimportant he said, believe my word of honour! Oh we'd like to believe, we're longing to believe, even his word of honour. Are we jackals thirsting for human blood? Give us just one fact in the accused's favour and we shall rejoice.[13]

The prosecutor's speech resumes the clash between the two attitudes by opposing honour to – facts. Dostoevsky writes of the world of the Third Horseman, a world governed by the rule of fact. Positivism and the egalitarian dynamic had combined to create a society in which the aristocracy had given up, and rootless young men set Rothschild up as an ideal. Like Stendhal, Dostoevsky is revolted by this decay in values. Like Stendhal he opposes the new men of his age with heroes who were extreme in their disregard for their own material advantage. The eccentricity of their purity, the pathetic inadequacy of the gestures they make, ensure that they go to the wall. Dostoevsky describes a world in which honour was doomed, in which Dmitri Karamazov was handcuffed on arrest and forbidden to speak to his erstwhile friends, who had ordered handcuffs, not because they suspected him of parricide, but because they were thereby able to avenge themselves upon someone whose spirit was more generous than their own – and, besides, familiarity from a suspected murderer was embarrassing.

Enlightened self-interest not only erodes the sense of honour, it also destroys any sense of moral responsibility. When a diminished sense of responsibility is added to a reaction to the ant-heap, which tends to take the form of a craving for excitement at all costs, the result is those acts of violence which Dostoevsky chose as the centre-pieces of his novels. Dostoevsky was writing the mythology of a generation in which a diminished sense of responsibility had combined with an aggravated craving for sensation to give it a licence to kill.

Here again Dostoevsky and Baudelaire come close together. *Les Fleurs du Mal* build up to a crescendo of violence, as the poet-hero turns to sensations of an ever increasing intensity, that culminate in the savage and erotic fantasies of the sex-crime.

Baudelaire, who it will be recalled described the disappearance of a sense of original sin as the supreme sign of the new civilisation, agrees with Dostoevsky's contention that modern man has been relieved of his sense of responsibility by the new philosophy. Like Dostoevsky,

Baudelaire derived his own sense of intensity from masochism, and set too much store by the joys of remorse to deny himself the pleasure to be derived from *la conscience dans le mal*: that *conscience* which prevented mankind from turning into human cattle, into the Gadarene swine of *The Devils*.

The new philosophy eroded that consciousness, that capacity to feel guilty, by denying man his freedom. When his every action is to be accounted for in terms of stimulus and response, the criminal becomes the unfortunate victim of his circumstances. It is a view of criminality given short shrift by Dostoevsky – for example, through the mouth of Razumikhin, the law student of *Crime and Punishment*:

> 'We began with the socialist view. You know: crime is simply a protest against abnormal social structures, that's all – no other reasons are allowed . . .'
>
> 'Nothing else!' Razumikhin said heatedly, 'It's quite true. I'll show you their books; they say it happens because "The environment drove them to it" and that's it. Their favourite expression! From which it follows that in an ideal society all crime would disappear, as there would be no need to protest so that everyone would grow honest overnight.'[14]

In the meantime, as an entire generation felt absolved from guilt, the immediate result was a sharp increase in the crime rate.

The rate of increase was stepped up by contemporary man's restless thirst for intensity. Dostoevsky saw his age as the time of the psychotic. Like Baudelaire, for whom his age was one in which man's spirit was irritated by the abuse of stimulants of every description from hashish to satanism, Dostoevsky understood that his generation lived on jangling nerves. Both writers describe as characteristic of their age a certain pattern of experience, long periods of sloth are punctuated by short bursts of feverish activity, both violent and perverse. After months of brooding in the isolation of his tiny oppressive room Raskolnikov tucks an axe under his overcoat, goes out, and sinks it into the skulls of two old women. This is the kind of action the author had in mind when, in his *Diary of a Writer*, he describes his age as a time of dark frustrated desires and feverish despair:

> The author sees his time as a powerful, self-confident age, which is also sick; full of the most nebulous ideals, the most impermissible longings.[15]

The thwarted idealism, the gap between dream and reality, the sense of personal frustration and disillusion that form the bedrock of nineteenth-century fiction, accounting for the sour ironic serenity which is found in works as far apart as Goncharov's *Ordinary Story* and Flaubert's

Education sentimentale, creates in Dostoevsky's world and in Baudelaire's an irritated sensibility that stretches the nerves too tight. The detective of *Crime and Punishment* brings out the psychotic quality of his contemporaries when he characterises the double murder of the pawnbroker and her sister:

> This is a fantastic, sombre, contemporary affair, an affair of our time, when men's hearts have grown troubled; when people say that 'blood refreshes'; when the sole aim in life is material comfort. It's an affair of bookish day-dreams; of feelings irritated by theoretical speculation; resolution was apparent in the early stages, but a peculiar kind of resolution, the resolution of the plunge . . . Let's admit that he was ill at the time, but look he's a killer, and believes himself a man of honour, looks down on others and goes about like a pallid angel . . .[16]

Indeed, Raskolnikov is the archetypal new criminal. He has the aggravated sensibilities of his age. He is never at one with his world, but always set against it. His nerves are permanently stretched to breaking point. His moral and physical isolation have made him pathologically introspective. It is significant that Dostoevsky has made him a university drop-out. His creator makes it clear that, as an ex-law student, he had been exposed to the half-baked ideas of the new morality. In him two currents of nineteenth-century thought combine. We find the 'power morality' inspired by the example of Napoleon. A tradition reaching from Stendhal, Balzac and Nietzsche to the wilder extravagances of German and Italian fascism, suggests that for 'truly exceptional persons' the restrictions of conventional morality are meaningless, since the scale of their actions is its own justification. In Raskolnikov this ethical megalomania is reinforced by a second strain, the utilitarian morality which suggests that conspicuously philanthropic ends justify the most unlovely means. In Raskolnikov the will to power combines with the ethical justification of terrorism with disastrous consequences. In a letter, his creator presents him, precisely, as the pathetic victim of certain fashionable ideas:

> A young man . . . who, thanks to sloppy thinking and a shaky grasp of things, falls victim to certain strange, half-baked ideas that are in the air, and decides to get himself out of his appalling predicament at a blow. He decides to kill a certain old woman who lends money against interest. She is stupid, heartless, sick, greedy and charges a Jew's rate . . . She's good for nothing, 'Why does she live', 'What use is she', and so on. These questions confuse the young man. He decides to kill and rob her in order to make his mother . . . and his sister . . . happy, take his degree, go abroad and be honest for the

rest of his life, steadfast and unswerving in the execution of his humane duty to mankind, thereby expiating his crime, if such an action can be so termed.[17]

Not only is Raskolnikov a neurotic, prone to brainstorms and cerebral fever, he is sufficiently under the influence of 'modern' ideas to believe that this plan need only stand the test of reason.

The rational killing, the killing that 'makes sense', is the supreme characteristic of Dostoevsky's mythology of the new culture. It justifies Raskolnikov's action on philanthropic grounds. In the same way, the sordid and pathetic murder of Shatov is justified by a lunatic *raison d'état*. Dostoevsky's myths of murder make the tragic absurdity of such actions clear, but not, it would seem, clear enough. European culture acknowledges the half-baked ideas of Raskolnikov: the acknowledgment is reflected in its language and the clear-cut and hair-raising distinction which language makes between 'murder' and 'assassination'.

Dostoevsky saw Raskolnikov as symptomatic of a general moral distintegration. The author is very conscious that European man could no longer take comfort in the thought that violent crime was an essentially working-class phenomenon. The educated classes were now becoming capable of casual violence. Zametov makes the point, in *Crime and Punishment*:

> . . . I'm interested in something else, a whole subject. Besides the fact that the working-class crime-rate has risen over the last five years; besides the ceaseless widespread robberies and arson, the thing that really astounds me is the fact that crime in the upper classes has been increasing at the same rate. For example, an ex-student robbed the post on the high road; progressives utter forged securities – as a result of their social predicament; in Moscow they caught a gang who had forged lottery tickets, one of the ringleaders was a university lecturer in world-history, abroad one of our secretaries was killed for obscure financial reasons. And if this old woman, the money-lender, has been killed by a member of the upper rather than the lower classes . . . how are we to explain this moral disintegration of our civilised society?[18]

Clearly Zametov does not regard Raskolnikov's crime as an isolated instance. It is part of a whole paradigm of violence. The answer to Zametov's rhetorical question, both for Dostoevsky and for Baudelaire was that society, having lost its grasp upon whole meanings and values, was quite simply falling apart. It had lost all sense of moral integrity, and was no longer able to satisfy the metaphysical and material demands of its citizens.

This sense of collective dissatisfaction expressed itself through the single-minded cultivation of self-interest, enlightened and otherwise, a cultivation which found its definitive expression in cold and savage acts of violence. In this respect there was a classic historical precedent to Raskolnikov in the shape of the notorious murderer and poet Pierre-François Lacenaire. His trial and execution were a *cause célèbre* in the Paris of the 1830s. The son of a relatively prosperous Lyons merchant, he received a good education, although his home life was far from perfect. On leaving school, he made desultory attempts to go into commerce; joined the army, deserted, and eventually ended up in Paris, down and out. He resorted to crime without compunction, devising a scheme to murder and rob debt-collectors.

Lacenaire was not a very successful killer. It is his literary talent that distinguishes him. He was a prolific poet, and wrote his memoirs whilst awaiting execution. He wrote in a stilted, old-fashioned rhetoric of sensibility, which would have rendered his work perfectly comprehensible to a contemporary of Rousseau. Lacenaire uses this utterly inappropriate code to provide the most matter-of-fact account of his crimes. He writes with an unnerving lucidity, without a hint of fear, remorse or even bravado. The memoirs read like the work of someone whom surgery has deprived of a moral sense.

The impact of Lacenaire upon his age was the equivalent of that of Leopold and Loeb, or, more recently, of Charles Manson and his gang. In each case it is the cold-blooded savagery of the educated man that disturbs. Dostoevsky was quite obsessed by the image of the educated criminal. It proved to him that civilisation had refined, but not reduced the blood-lust. Thus, it was the total lack of any moral sense, of any awareness of guilt, that terrified him in the young radicals; their mediocre vulgarity of thought and feeling were only matched by their callow ruthlessness. The qualities are embodied in the band of protesters grouped around Ippolit, in *The Idiot*:

'. . . be careful of these home-grown Lacenaires of ours! I'll say it again, crime is all too often the way out for this talentless, impatient and greedy trash.'

'Is that really what Lacenaire was?'

'The essence is the same, although the doses may vary. But just you see if this young man is not capable of cutting throats "for laughs" – as he said he would in the confession which he made to us. Those words are going to keep me awake at night.'[19]

It was the emergence of this new type of unrepentant criminal who 'couldn't help it' which made Dostoevsky anticipate the coming of a blood-bath. Prince Myshkin speaks for the author in the following characterisation of the new-style criminal:

Yes, I know that there used always to be lots of equally terrible crimes; I recently visited some prisons and managed to get to know a few criminals and people remanded – stronger men even than this fellow, men who killed ten people without compunction. But I noticed that even the most hardened and unrepentant killer at least understood that he was a *criminal*, that is to say that his conscience told him that he had done wrong, even though he was unrepentant. They were all like that, but the people Evgeny Pavlovich was talking about do not even want to think of themselves as criminals, they believe, in their heart of hearts, that they had a right . . . were justified even, in doing what they did. That, I believe, is the terrible difference. And look at them, they're all young, a defenceless age when it is all too easy to be corrupted by ideas.[20]

Finally, it is the new ideas, the suggestion that might is right and no one is to blame which are responsible for that cold-blooded violence which he proposes as the signature of his age. With the decline in a sense of honour, the rise of egalitarian ideas, the growing irresponsibility of the privileged classes, and the emergence of Rothschild and Claude Bernard as culture-heroes, Dostoevsky saw a new culture, self-confident, self-seeking and violent; the age of the terrorist and the psychopath, a culture that had begun with Lacenaire, and would extend to Lee Harvey Oswald, and beyond.

CHAPTER SEVEN

The Dawn of Chaos

The loss of a sense of whole meanings, of a collective purpose, the increasing importance of a pecuniary ethic which was no ethic at all, had both produced and combined with a craving for intensity, to create a society which Dostoevsky's mythology has characterised in the figures of psychopaths and terrorists. Raskolnikov, Rogozhin and Verkhovensky are proposed as typical. They are the products of their 'civilisation':

> Just look around you: blood flows in rivers, and cheerfully into the bargain, like champagne. There's your 19th century for you . . . There's your Napoleon, Napoleon the Great and the present one. There's North America – the Eternal Union. There's comic-opera Schleswig-Holstein. And what is it that civilisation softens in us? Civilisation just develops the range of man's responses and . . . that's all. And through the development of that range man will doubtless reach the point where he will derive pleasure from blood. Haven't you noticed that the subtlest murderers have almost all been civilised? . . . Civilisation may not actually have made man more bloodthirsty, but he's grown bloodthirsty in a worse, a more despicable way.[1]

The Underground Man goes on to point to a close relationship between bloodshed and tedium, suggesting that in the Utopia of the planned environment, man would resort to any kind of savagery in the effort to relieve his boredom. Dostoevsky thereby establishes an all-important sociological formula – the greater the degree of planning, the greater the need for intensity as an escape from that planning.

In the meantime the characteristics which were responsible for a soaring crime-rate were also bringing about a general diminution in social stability as such, a diminution which allowed Dostoevsky to anticipate an eventual apocalyptic blood-bath, which the progress of civilisation would do nothing to avert. This glimpse of what was to come is an important element in Dostoevsky's account of the world '*où l'action n'est pas la soeur du rêve*'.

He saw the old order disappearing as an age of materialism, planning and chaos took its place. The examination of widespread cultural collapse forms the background to his account of the behaviour of individuals. It takes the shape of the erosion of values such as the respect for authority, political, social and religious, respect for one's parents, and all the other values and psychological attitudes that contribute towards a society's endorsement of its *status quo*.

Members of any society are perpetually faced by a series of social choices: between actions contributing to the maintenance of order and actions contributing to disorder and to social chaos. When a sufficient number of persons at any one time opt for 'chaos solutions', the fabric of their society simply falls apart. One instance of such collapse is the disintegration of the *ancien régime* in 1789. It was a revolution that occurred without revolutionaries. What began as the refusal of the Estates General to disperse at the royal command turned into a rising tide of mob violence which became a revolution. The old order simply collapsed when its fabric came under strain. De Tocqueville's superb analysis of the *ancien régime* is in many ways an examination of the extraordinarily broad base of the tendency to choose chaos solutions in the years immediately preceding the revolution. It is this anarchic attitude of mind, an attitude that was not widely sustained for very long, and not any particular 'cause', which brought that revolution about.

Something comparable happened in Russia in 1917. G. Katkov's authoritative history of the February Revolution is at pains to point out that there can be no question of ascribing the events that began with a few disturbances in the streets of Petrograd, to end with the overthrow of the autocracy, to a hard core of purposive and plotting Bolsheviks. The revolutionaries were utterly unprepared for their revolution. Above all one is struck, in Mr Katkov's account of the years immediately preceding the events, by the remarkably widespread tendency to choose chaos solutions. This was not confined to any particular class or group. Virtually the whole of Russia, educated and proletarian, had, as its political premise, the profound conviction that the absolute authority of the monarchy must end. Only mediocrities or sheer madmen such as Protopopov, the improbable last Imperial Minister of the Interior, professed any support for the *status quo*. Everybody else from the most conservative member of the State Duma onwards, seemed to act against the régime.

Dostoevsky anticipated future events by pointing to an increasing preference for chaos. It was the formation of that collective anarchic attitude of mind which is the prerequisite of a revolutionary situation, that he describes in his account of cultural collapse.

The terrorist Petr Stepanovich Verkhovensky analyses the forces which contribute to that collapse, in a passage that reads like a lunatic rewriting of de Tocqueville. Like de Tocqueville he enumerates the kinds of damage that may be done to a collective sense of social stability by the widespread erosion of respect for its institutions:

Of course I'm a criminal, not a socialist, ha! ha! Listen, I've counted them all; the teacher who laughs with his pupils about their God and their cradle, is one of us. The lawyer who defends an educated murderer with the suggestion that he is more sophisticated than his victims and that he was obliged to kill because he needed the money, is one of us. The schoolchildren who kill a peasant to see what it feels like, are with us. Jurors who find criminals not guilty, without more ado, are with us. The prosecutor who is terrified of not being liberal enough in court, is most certainly one of us. Civil servants, writers . . . so many are with us without knowing it!

In the meantime schoolboys and idiots obey us as never before; schoolmasters are bilious with rage; there is colossal vanity everywhere, and incredible animal appetite . . . Do you know how many we'll convert by means of instant ideas alone? When I left, Littré was advancing the thesis that crime is a form of madness; by the time I got back crime was no longer even a madness, just plain commonsense, a duty almost, at the least a legitimate protest. 'How could an educated man help killing, if he needed the money.' But this is nothing. Before the days of cheap liquor the Russian God used to save them. Now the masses are drunk, mothers drunk, children drunk and the churches stand empty . . . Give this generation a chance to grow up! . . . It's a pity that there is no proletariat, but there will be, there will be![2]

Verkhovensky properly considers chaos, the erosion of traditional values, the decline in moral consciousness, the rejection of authority, and the celebration of the criminal as signs that the culture is at risk. The passage provides a vitally important link between the acts of individual violence which we reviewed in the preceding chapter, and that more general dissolution which forms the subject of the present one.

It is in the context of such a dissolution that *Crime and Punishment* is set. Svidrigailov, who has a real nose for degeneracy, returning to the capital after an absence of some years which included the time of the reforms, notices an atmosphere of chaos and dissipation:

The populace are on the booze, educated young people have nothing to do, and consume themselves in impossible day-dreams, cripple themselves with theories; Jews have congregated out of nowhere, hoarding money and debauching everyone else. That was the familiar smell I sniffed out the moment I arrived in this town.[3]

The Devils is Dostoevsky's myth of chaos as such. He makes his revolutionaries both dangerous and ludicrous. They are not exactly responsible for the chaos he describes. They are a focal point rather than a cause. Here again history seems to have justified Dostoevsky's allegory, in the shape of the Bolsheviks' rôle or non-rôle in the February Revolution. Of course this is not to suggest that Dostoevsky's band of maniacs offers a serious analogy of the intensely dedicated and disinterested conspirators grouped around Lenin and Krupskaya, who devoted a lifetime to plotting the overthrow of Tsarist Russia. Dostoevsky's novel functions on a level of myth, not fact, and it is on that level that it must be understood.

The Devils describes a provincial capital turned upside-down by a collective madness which brings about murder, arson, riot and a lynching – the total disappearance of any form of authority or leadership being precipitated by a blend of bad luck, destructive malice and sheer stupidity. It would be positively perverse to see, in the unfortunate influence of the Governor's wife upon the course of events, a terrible if confused vision of the influence of the last Tsarina upon the luckless Nicholas II, despite the fact that both von Lembkes are clearly of German extraction; and yet there is no denying that Dostoevsky's portrait of the stubborn yet henpecked Governor and his dominating, misguided consort has a strange propriety.

The author does not see any one factor as the direct cause of the disintegration, rather it is a question of a general collapse into anarchy, a collapse heralded by the appearance of certain 'storm signals';

> I already said that all sorts of rabble had turned up. In times of trouble, unrest and change, rabble always turns up. I don't mean the so-called 'progressives' that are always trying to head the trend, . . . with aims that are, admittedly, idiotic, but which are nevertheless more or less clearly defined. No, I mean the scum. Scum floats to the surface in any period of transition, and it is to be found in every society. Not only is it without any purpose, it lacks even the ghost of an idea, and can only express . . . unrest and impatience. In the meantime, without realising it, scum almost always falls under the control of the hard core of 'progressives' that have a real sense of purpose; they control it as they please, unless the hard core is itself composed of complete idiots – which, incidentally, has been known to happen.[4]

The surfacing of the scum signifies a steep increase in the 'chaos count', the beginning of mob rule.

As both the cause and the effect of this rising tide of chaos, Dostoevsky points to a *trahison des clercs*. In *The Devils* in particular, he describes along with the collapse of political authority and the rule of law, the disappearance of any form of moral authority. The theme is an aggravated version of the aristocrat who betrays his obligations. Another such betrayer was the public prosecutor described by Verkhovensky as being afraid of appearing illiberal. Better to be in the wrong than to be unpopular. The attitude is a direct reflection of moral bankruptcy, in that those persons who should give a lead have lost all confidence in the values which they represent:

> In the meantime the most frightful people had gained the advantage, and began loudly criticising anything sacred, whereas in the past they had never dared to open their mouths. The leaders, who had managed to stay on top until then, suddenly began to take them seriously, and fell silent themselves; some even lapsed into shameful giggling.[5]

We find the same abdication of responsibility in *The Adolescent*. Versilov suggests that they live in a time when the best have lost conviction and the worst have Yeats' passionate intensity:

> 'They are neither stupider nor more intelligent; they're mad, like everyone else.'
> 'Can everybody be mad?' I turned to him with involuntary curiosity.
> 'All more or less decent people are mad. Only the mediocre and the incompetent are enjoying themselves . . . There are no ethical ideas any more; suddenly they've all vanished, and, what's more, it's as if they had never existed . . . This is a time of *juste milieu* and callousness, a passion for boorishness, idleness, incompetence, and the need for instant results.'[6]

This decline in moral authority is accompanied by the development of the 'fashionable conscience'. In stable cultures it is fashionable to align oneself with stereotypes of order and tradition. But, as the chaos count increases, fashion swings towards the admiration of disorder, it becomes fashionable to feel intense dissatisfaction with the *status quo*, expressions such as *consensus* become dirty words, and one's revolutionary aspirations frequently express themselves by certain alterations in one's dress:

> All it took some of our young ladies was to cut their hair, put on dark glasses and call themselves nihilists, for them to persuade themselves that, with the glasses, they had acquired their own 'convictions'. Others just needed to feel a drop of some kind of universal humanitarian emotion, and they acquired the certainty that they were, in that respect, unique, at the very forefront of the trend towards enlightenment.[7]

The most perfect incarnation of the fashionable conscience is Andrey Semenovich Lebezyatnikov in *Crime and Punishment*. He is a martyr to political fashion:

> Despite all these qualities Andrei Semenovich was truly stupid. He

94

had attached himself, with passion, to progress and 'our young generation'. He was one of those countless and various legions of vulgarians, the sickly still born and half-educated mules, that attach themselves, in a flash, to the most fashionable ideas in the air, vulgarising them immediately, and parodying every cause to which they may devote themselves, often in all sincerity.[8]

Dostoevsky pulls out the comic stops when describing him in action. He is discussing the life-style of fashionable radicalism:

'It's a question of taking someone's hospitality and then spitting on it, is that it?'

'Not spitting, protesting. I serve a useful purpose. I can contribute, incidentally, to progress and propaganda. We must all do what we can for progress and propaganda, and perhaps the ruder we are the better. I can plant an idea, a seed . . . From that seed will grow a fact. In what way do I give offence? At first they'll take offence, and then they'll see for theselves that I am making a positive contribution. Look, they condemned Terebyeva (she's in a commune now) for leaving her family, and . . . sleeping with someone, she wrote to her parents saying that she did not wish to exist surrounded by prejudice, and was going to live with someone; people felt that she was too rude and hard on her parents, that she could have been kinder, written a gentler letter. Nonsense, there was no point in being kind, on the contrary, here was a chance to protest. Take Warens, who spent seven years with her husband, abandoned two children and left him once and for all, with a letter: "I have realised that I cannot be happy with you. I shall never forgive you for concealing from me the existence of an alternative society in the form of the commune. I have just learnt about it from a noble spirited man to whom I gave myself, and we are starting a commune of our own . . . Don't hope to get me back, you're too late. I want to be happy." That's what I call a letter.'

'Terebyeva, is that the one you said was starting her third civil marriage?'

'It's only the second really! But were it the fourth, the fifteenth, what does it matter! If I were ever sorry that my parents were dead it's now. I often dream how, if they were alive to-day, I would set them alight with my protests . . . I'd show them. I'd amaze them. Really, it's a shame I'm all alone.[9]

For all the references to communes, free love, radicalisation and the generation gap this was really written about a hundred years ago. Dostoevsky has caught the idiot tones of passionate conviction to perfection.

The lunatic fringe is summed up once and for all by the spiritual father of *The Devils*, the old-style liberal revolutionary Stefan Trofimovich Verkhovensky, whose generation was unwittingly responsible for the sins of its children:

> Gentlemen, I have discovered their secret. The secret of their success is their stupidity. . . . Yes, gentlemen, were this a deliberate, calculated, assumed stupidity – it would be a stroke of genius! But we must be fair, there has been no deceit. It is the most naked, the most simple, the most basic stupidity . . . Were it to express itself a little more intelligently, we would all see the poverty of this short-winded stupidity at once. But as it is, we're all confused; no one can believe that it is as basically stupid as it appears. "There must be more to it" – they all say to themselves, looking for the secret, trying to read between the lines – and that does the trick! Stupidity has never received such a fantastic reward, regardless of how often it may have earned it . . .[10]

These various factors combine to create a rot which, for Dostoevsky, set in with the Paris Commune. The point is made by Versilov. Although he is a person of manifold contradictions, as prone to sudden surges of a craving for intensity as any Dostoevskyian character, he feels, on his good days, that as a Russian gentleman he has an obligation to try to maintain the finest qualities of his culture. He is a kind of repository of social honour and social stability – a one-man version of Montesquieu's view of the rôle of an aristocracy as a *dépôt de lois*, the upholder of traditions. Versilov understood that Western Europe was in a state of cultural decline, it had become a graveyard, a monument to expired values which had lost all vitality. He had witnessed the beginning of the end on the first day of the Commune:

> . . . my dream of the sun setting on the first day of European man became, as soon as I awoke, the sun setting upon European man's last day! It was a moment when the sound of a kind of death knell rung out over Europe with a particular clarity. I don't just mean the war and the Tuileries . . .[11]

Unfortunately, that so-called European corruption which was symbolised by the burning down of the Tuileries, was beginning to affect Russia. Father Zosima sees it happening. He associates it with the rising aspiration of the merchant class and the ravages of industrialisation:

> . . . sin is in the people too. The flame of decay spreads before our eyes, blazing up higher with every hour. The people too are beginning to cut themselves off; we're starting to see *kulaks* and fast-breakers;

merchants want more and more status and try to flaunt their education, when they haven't a scrap, and to this aim they turn away from their ancient customs, and are even ashamed of their fathers' faith. They pay calls on princes, and are nothing but perverted peasants. The people have grown rotten with drunkenness, and cannot stop drinking. How hard is this drunkenness on the family, on wives and on children even! I have seen ten-year-old children in factories – sickly, wretched, stooping and already corrupt. A stifling shed, clattering machines, work all through the day, foul language and drink, is that what the soul of a young child should have? It needs sun, children's games, a constant shining example, and at least a little love.[12]

Zosima focuses on particular aspects of the process of dissolution. He is concerned with the threats posed by new appetites and ambitions to those traditional values which had, in the past, served as a guarantee of cultural stability. Here the merchant classes, with their firmly established traditions of custom and discipline, are shown to be turning their back on their culture. Zosima also amplifies Verkhovensky's contention that drink is ruining the working classes. Dostoevsky associates this with the reforms, suggesting that the liberation of the serfs set the entire Russian peasantry on a drinking spree that lasted for more than ten years. Since the state grew to rely on the resulting revenue, it could not afford to stop the peasants from drinking. Vodka balanced the national budget.

Dostoevsky also ascribes other aspects of the general decline to the reforms. It was the introduction of trial by jury which had led to special pleading and miscarriages of justice; hence the public prosecutor courting popularity, the eloquent advocate who persuaded jurors to find murderers not guilty since it 'wasn't their fault'. Moreover, the legislative and administrative chaos which the reforms had brought about had not only brought the idea of law into disrespect, they had also encouraged the proliferation of shysters such as Luzhin, who grew rich on litigation. The full impact of this particular transformation of Russian society is expressed, eloquently, by the maniac who finally disrupts the charity function in *The Devils*:

Twenty years have passed since then. Universities have opened and expanded. Drill has become a distant memory: the army is thousands of officers short. The railways have consumed all our funds, and have formed a spider's web across Russia, so that in about fifteen years we shall be able to go somewhere. Bridges only burn down occasionally, and towns burn to rule, in rotation, in the fire-season. Judgments of Solomon are to be heard in the courts, and jurors only take bribes because of the struggle for life, when the alternative is starving to death. The serfs are free and flog each other in place of the landowner. Seas, oceans of vodka are drunk, to the benefit of the budget, and in Novgorod, opposite the ancient and useless cathedral of St Sophia, they have proudly erected a huge bronze globe in commemoration of a thousand years of chaos and disorder . . . Fifteen years of reform. And never, in the most absurd periods of hopelessness, has Russia attained . . .[13]

CHAPTER EIGHT

The Terror to Come

Dostoevsky saw that the immediate prospect for his culture was a period of chaos and disorder. He also realised that the consequence of the degeneration of values which we have described was a search for new whole meanings, new gods, new certainties. Thus he accounts for the appeal of socialism as a reaction against the meaningless and haphazard world created by *laissez-faire* empiricism and commonsense. It is a pathetic, dangerous, misguided, but initially well-meaning quest for whole values, a quest doomed to failure because its materialistic premise renders it incapable of the kind of wholeness to which it aspires. Dostoevsky refers to socialism specifically as the action of an uprooted generation, searching for some kind of cultural stability. Paradoxically it is the rootless Prince Myshkin who makes the point in the speech which culminates in his smashing of the vase. He suggests that people are attracted by the absurd and inhuman doctrines of socialism because they provide a centre:

> 'What's the reason for this sudden frenzy? Don't you know? It's because he's found a homeland . . . he reached dry land and fell on his knees to kiss it! It is not vanity . . . alone that creates Russian atheists and Jesuits, but spiritual pain and longing; longing for a cause, for a country – in which they no longer believe because they have never known it. It is so easy for a Russian to become an atheist, easier than for anyone else. Our people do not just become atheists, they *believe* in atheism as in a new faith, failing to perceive that they have professed a belief in zero.[1]

It is the longing for certainty, for wholeness of meaning that accounts for radical attitudes. In the final analysis therefore, Dostoevsky holds the way in which his culture is developing responsible for the forces that would eventually destroy it. Belief in atheism is preferred to no belief at all, even though it is a belief in nothing.

Dostoevsky describes the left as the side that turns its back on its own traditions of whole meaning, on its own culture and civilisation. This is not to deny the sincerity of its supporters; moreover, the man who spent ten years of his life a political prisoner would be unlikely to endorse the *status quo* blindly. His distrust of the left is inspired by their appallingly narrow view of human needs, their reductionism, the *a prioristic* assertion of untested theories. He lacks confidence in their capacity to improve the human lot, as we see from this entry from *Diary of a Writer*:

> It may well be that . . . the aims of all our European progressives are noble and humanitarian. But there is absolutely no doubt that were all these noble teachers of ours accorded the chance to destroy the old society and build a new one – there would emerge such darkness, such chaos, something so crude, blind and inhuman, that the whole edifice would collapse beneath the curses of mankind, before it was ever completed. Once it has rejected Christ, human intelligence can arrive at astounding conclusions . . . Europe . . . rejects Christ, and we, of course, are bound to follow Europe.[2]

It is possible to argue once again that Dostoevsky has been vindicated by subsequent events – although the curses of mankind have not yet brought about the collapse of the Soviet Union.

Dostoevsky's essential objections to socialism are succinctly expressed in the following description:

> the summit of egoism, the summit of inhumanity, the summit of economic absurdity, the supreme annihilation of human freedom.[3]

Thus socialism has many of the shortcomings of the society that it seeks to reform: the same blindness, the same selfish bias, the same idiot confidence in materialism and commonsense. Above all, Dostoevsky condemns socialism for offering equality in the place of freedom. It is this that lies at the very heart of his case against them. Socialists aspire to the erection of the 'ant-heap', in which everyone will unite into the 'single herd'. Dostoevsky's extrapolation of egalitarianism into the totalitarian state, in which everybody is equal because no one has any rights, once again echoes de Tocqueville. It will be recalled that the Frenchman saw tyranny as the probable outcome of egalitarian trends. His account of the end of the *ancien régime* makes the point that *liberté* was a short-lived aim of the Revolution; it was *égalité* that remained its enduring preoccupation. He also points out that no set of political institutions can guarantee freedom, unless the citizens actually want to be free. On the whole, he feels that they do not. Freedom will always be sacrificed in return for comfort. Balzac comes to the same conclusion after the failure of the July Revolution to bring about a republic. An open letter of his on the events of July contains the expression:

> Prenez ma liberté, je ne vous la vends pas, je vous la donne, à condition de me rendre heureux et tranquille.[4]

This is precisely the attitude which Dostoevsky fears will be exploited by socialism. His Grand Inquisitor realises that the people will accept an enslaving régime in return for the satisfaction of their material needs. It is this readiness that enables him to remove their freedom and turn them into human cattle:

> Never, never would they feed themselves without us. No science will give them bread as long as they remain free, but eventually they will lay down their freedom at our feet, and say to us 'Make us slaves, but feed us.' They will eventually understand of their own accord, that freedom and sufficient bread are incompatible, never, never, would they be able to share it equally. They will realise that they can never be free, because they are weak, vice-ridden, insignificant and rebellious.[5]

The authoritarian régime, be it Catholic or socialist, would exercise control through the trinity of Power, Secrecy and Authority. This analysis of oppression reaches to the core of the totalitarian state in which a clerisy of *apparatchiks* shoulders all responsibility, relieving its subjects of the burden of their freedom, and guaranteeing their material welfare. It reigns, finally, through terror and authority, imposing prescribed behaviour patterns upon a nation with the mentality of slaves.

The Grand Inquisitor tells Christ how the Church deliberately betrayed His teachings, His belief in freedom, while exploiting the authority of His name. People found such freedom intolerable, and longed like Balzac's Parisians for reassurance, authority and material comfort. He reminds Christ that He is still a trouble-maker, and were He to remain it would prove necessary to re-crucify Him in order to ensure the enduring authority of His church.

Once again we find a prophetic strain in Dostoevsky. If one were to substitute Marx for Christ, Marxism for Christianity, we would have an instant twentieth-century parable, describing Soviet Russia's distortions of Marxism. What was proposed as a doctrine of total liberation was turned into a mandate for terrorism and oppression. Once again, the Grand Inquisitor would found his case on the fact that freedom was intolerable, and that, were Marx to return to mid-twentieth-century Russia, it would prove necessary to intern him as a revisionist. The interchangeability of Catholicism and socialism is justified for Dostoevsky by the part played, in both, by authority and the rejection of spiritual in favour of secular power:

> Socialism is the continuation of Catholicism and the Catholic essence! It too, like its brother atheism, was the product of despair . . . in order to take over the lost moral force of religion, to quench mankind's spiritual thirst . . . It too is freedom through force, unification through blood and the sword. Do not dare to believe in

God, do not dare to own property, do not dare to have individuality, '*fraternité ou la mort*, and two million heads roll.' By their works shall ye know them![6]

Ultimately, the Grand Inquisitor is as much a political as a religious myth. It investigates the mythology of authoritarianism, whereby there is a reciprocal relationship between the oppressor and the oppressed. The arrangement suits them both and is essentially sado-masochistic. Dostoevsky has reached into the overpowering political sexuality of Authority, a force to which everything is sacrificed in return for a sense of stability and the eradication of doubt. Slavery is preferred to uncertainty.

Dostoevsky realised that the disappearance of whole meanings, the erosion of all values and certainties might make the Grand Inquisitor welcome. Men would turn to his régime since any authority would be preferable to the vacuum; for the Grand Inquisitor offers a parody of whole meanings. Where whole meanings had made for a stable balanced world, locked into an organic unity by a sense of all-pervading collective purpose, the world of the Grand Inquisitor would also offer unity, a unity based not on whole meanings and a collective sense of high seriousness, but upon terror.

The deeply seated psychological need for terror which his myth brings out is itself a reflection of the intensity drive, its second cousin. Like intensity it derives from a dissatisfaction with a particular state of culture. As a mythographer Dostoevsky embroiders de Tocqueville's admittedly prophetic suggestion that egalitarianism can slip all too easily into absolute autocracy. He makes us *feel* how it may come about that people will come to love the hand that crushes them. De Tocqueville supplies the facts, Dostoevsky the feeling tone.

His insight into the anatomy of totalitarianism and repression, his anticipation of the police state, emerges fully in another political myth: the lunatic Utopia of Shigalev in *The Devils*. Camus recognised the importance of Shigalev in *L'Homme Révolté*, his own study of totalitarianism, and in his creative work. *Caligula* is a study in Shigalevian terror and oppression, Caligula being the only free man in a universe of slaves.

Shigalev's system is strangely reminiscent of the totalitarian implications of Rousseau. As did Rousseau in *Du contrat social*, Shigalev begins by seeking to create a maximum degree of freedom compatible with a state of culture, only to arrive at a conclusion that advocates a maximum degree of oppression. Like Rousseau he bases his system upon the terrible formula *compelle intrare* – 'We shall force them to be free'. Shigalev's conclusions are not invalidated by the fact that he was quite obviously mad; it will be recalled that Versilov characterised his age as a time when everyone was mad. Shigalev introduces his work as follows:

> I get my facts muddled, and my conclusion is in direct contradiction of my premise, my point of departure. Starting from unlimited freedom, I conclude with unlimited despotism. I would add, however, that there can be no other solution of the social problem.[7]

Shigalev's view of his conclusion is a frightening parody of all doctrinaire political theory. The theorist will trust his conclusions regardless; such is his blind faith in the infallibility of his methods. Given the facts and a rigorous intellect no other conclusion is possible. It is appropriately Petr Verkhovensky, the spirit of chaos, who explains the system. It is based upon egalitarianism and spying:

> Shigalev is a genius. Like Fourier; only bolder, more powerful; I'll take him up. He invented equality . . . His note-books are excellent . . . He's got spying. Every member of his society spies on everyone else and is obliged to make denunciations. Each belongs to all, and all to each. All are slaves and equal in slavery. In extreme cases there is denunciation and murder, but the thing is equality. First of all, educational standards will be lowered, as will science and talent. Higher education is only accessible to the talented, and we'll get rid of those. The talented always seized power and were despots. They cannot help being despots, and always did more harm than good; they'll be exiled or executed. We will cut out Cicero's tongue, put out Copernicus' eyes. Shakespeare will be stoned – that's Shigalev's system! Slaves must be slaves; without despotism there was neither freedom nor equality, but there must be equality in the herd . . .
>
> I'm for Shigalev. We don't need education or science. There's enough to last a thousand years without science, but we must establish obedience . . . The longing for education is an élitist longing. As soon as you get a family or love, you find the wish for property. We shall stifle desire; we'll instigate drunkenness, gossip, denunciation; we'll instigate unbelievable debauchery; we'll kill all geniuses in childhood. All will be reduced to a common factor, total equality . . . Only the necessary is necessary – that will be the world's motto from now on. But it also needs terror; we, the rulers, will take care of that. Slaves must have masters. Utter obedience, utter conformity, but once every thirty years Shigalev lets terror loose, and they all fall on one another, dog eat dog, up to a point, simply as a release from boredom. Boredom is an aristocratic feeling; under Shigalev there will be no desires. Desires and suffering are for us, the slaves will have Shigalev.[8]

Shigalev offers certainty. He removes all possibility of ontological unease and insecurity. Massed together into a single herd, there can be no danger of identity crisis or excessive individualism. His society renders discontent impossible. The society even contains its safeguards against tedium. Controlled outbreaks of aggression cater for that, within, rather than against, the social fabric. Shigalev provides a balanced diet of bread and Roman circuses. By emphasising equality above all else Shigalev recognised the essential aspiration of his age – witness de Tocqueville. He shares with the Grand Inquisitor the knowledge that freedom is a burden. It generates too many anomalies, is socially untidy. Man aspires to equality before the law, the absolute merging of all identity into a single herd of slaves.

Dostoevsky proffers his myths of oppression as comments upon the psyche of his own age; their prophetic value is incidental. That those myths were to become a reality within half a century merely confirms the accuracy of the original analysis. This is ultimately based upon the recognition of the dispersed quality of nineteenth-century culture, of the consequences of the disappearance of a stable and coherent pattern of values and the corresponding emergence of piece-meal solutions and the commercial opportunism of Luzhin. The result was a cultural and spiritual vacuum. The workers Dostoevsky described in London, dulling their senses with gin on Saturday nights, were metaphorically speaking the raw material of Shigalev's society. Dostoevsky's account of the climate of his age ends in these extrapolations into political terrorism as its logical culmination. Even this parody of stability was preferable to the state of unstructured chaos in which nineteenth-century man found himself. That Shigalev's 'Utopia' was to be based on violence, oppression and mindless egalitarianism should come as no surprise, for these were the qualities that already informed the dream life of the world Dostoevsky knew.

Although Dostoevsky proposes his myths as characteristic of European society, there are reasons why they are particularly appropriate to Russia. It will be recalled that Dostoevsky described as specifically Russian the propensity to embrace radical atheism as a new faith. The Russian character, being temperamentally drawn to a rigid orthodoxy of attitude, is peculiarly sensitive to a state of unstructured chaos, to the disappearance of fixed points of reference. The relative freedom of personal action and opinion developed in the West since the Renaissance, and brought to a peak in the Enlightenment, is quite foreign to it. Thus, in Russia, even atheism becomes a kind of orthodoxy. The condition of religious and cultural agnosticism, the unformulated 'Butskellite' vagueness which most Westerners find tolerable, is quite unacceptable to the Russian temperament. This demands clearly defined parameters, extreme situations and rigid discipline. It is this that explains the passionate conviction, the sincere revolutionary idealism of the generations of 1905 and 1917. It also makes clear why democratic institutions that depend upon a politically apathetic electorate, such as prevail in the West, are unlikely ever to take root in Russia, why the Soviet government was unable to permit the liberalisation of Czechoslovakia. The rôle played by the principle of authority makes it infinitely easier for Russia to feel close to Stalin and to Shigalev than to understand the unstructured *laissez-faire* of the West.

Historically, Russian culture has never understood the concept of civil, religious or personal freedom. It has always advocated the principle of orthodoxy. Since Russia has always been an autocracy, always lived by this principle of unswerving conformity, it is not conditioned to freedom; freedom, as the Grand Inquisitor properly says, is indistinguishable from anarchy.

The apparently more monstrous aspects of the Russian national character, such as the purges, can only be understood when it is realised that freedom, as it is understood in the West, is as foreign to Russia as is the code of the *samurai* to our own way of life. Russia's need for stringent conformity can be seen at virtually any moment in its history. For example, in the sixteenth-century handbook on domestic manners, *Domostroi*, every precept is founded upon the principle of a firm imposition of rôle and authority; wives who fail in their duty must be beaten 'lovingly' and 'scientifically' to bring them to their senses. The same period witnessed the emergence of an ecclesiastical attitude that outlawed personal opinion – *mnenie proklyato*, opinion was accursed. Similarly, the great schism of the seventeenth century was the outcome of an uncompromising literalist orthodoxy. The new and philologically corrected versions of the Holy Texts were widely held to be unacceptable, *simply because they had been changed*. The Old Believers suffered torture, the stake and mass self-immolation, rather than accept innovation.

The inability to handle freedom is reflected more clearly still in the short period succeeding the 1905 Revolution, when Russia enjoyed freedom of the press for the only moment in her history. The results were too violent, the satire and the vicious graphic designs too extreme to be tolerated. The impact of a liberated press, upon a nation which had lived beneath censorship from its origins, was much too strong, and censorship was rapidly reintroduced.

Our understanding of Dostoevsky's account of his age is assisted by the realisation that the Russian temperament is peculiarly unsuited to loose, indeterminate structures. Indeed it is this temperamental sensitivity to anarchy that must, in the final analysis, explain the depth and accuracy of Dostoevsky's own account of the response to the loss of whole meanings. He ascribes the rootless quality of his own times to the European cultural heritage, and, in the sense that it derives from Renaissance empiricism, he is correct to do so. He makes the point in *The Adolescent*, which is specifically about the new rootlessness that is shown to be experienced as trauma:

> ... until about a generation ago, one did not need to pity these interesting young men so much, for in those days they almost always ended up by becoming part of our own cultured classes, and became one with them. And if, at the outset, they were aware of all their disorder, their accidental quality, the lack of family stability even, the lack of family traditions and fine stable forms, this was all to the good, since they subsequently sought these qualities out and learned to appreciate them. Things are a little different now, – because there is nothing to grasp hold of.[9]

Thus the young generation lived in a cultural vacuum, which it abhorred; hence its radicalism, its advocacy of revolutionary violence, its pursuit of intensity, and, ultimately, its endorsement of Shigalev.

This abhorrence of the vacuum is reflected in Dostoevsky's characters by a longing for order. This is not just the longing for spiritual good order, *hygiène morale,* which we find in Baudelaire, although it includes it. Dostoevsky's characters long for a more general stability. They look beyond self-discipline to the image of an ideally ordered society, and they detest disorder.

The Russian word for disorder – *besporyadok*—covers a wider semantic field than its English counterpart, and this itself is an indication of the importance of notions of order and conformity in Russian culture. *Besporyadok* includes notions such as bad-housekeeping, untidiness, slap-dash *laissez-faire*, and moral turpitude. It occurs much more frequently than the English equivalent and is part of the active vocabulary of the spoken language: a term of condemnation covering every kind of negligence and man-made chaos from the trivial to the spiritual.

Personal disorder is a crucial constituent of the Karamazov family. Dmitri is all too aware that disorder, chaos and unbridled excess lie at the root of his being. He expresses his loathing for his own lack of self-discipline as he prepares for the orgy at Mokroe:

> 'Do you know my friend,' he suddenly said, with feeling, 'I have never liked all this disorder . . . I lack order, higher order. But . . . it's all finished now, no use crying about it. It's too late and to hell with it! My whole life was disorder, order is what's needed.'[10]

We find him in his element at Mokroe, in a welter of chaos and disorder:

In short something disorderly and ridiculous began, but Mitya was in his element, the more absurd things got, the more animated he grew.[11]

The notion of order is absolutely crucial to Ivan Karamazov, the ostensible author of the Grand Inquisitor myth. His parable of oppression derives originally from a craving which he detects in himself:

if I did not believe in life . . . in the order of things, were I ever convinced that it's all a disorderly accursed and perhaps even diabolical chaos . . .[12]

He advances, *as the worst thing he can think of*, the possibility that he might discover the world to be disordered and chaotic; in other words, that he might discover what the twentieth century would describe as *the absurd*, an apprehension of the world as a haphazard and meaningless chaos without any network of necessary causal relationships. Ivan's dread of disorder is of the greatest importance in the understanding of Dostoevsky's world-view. He fears that metaphysical disorder which is *the consequence of a loss of faith in whole meanings*. The twentieth-century notion of the absurd can itself be seen to be the eventual derivative of that loss of faith which is first mirrored by Baudelaire and Dostoevsky. From Baudelaire's poet who smashed the glazier's wares for an infinite surge of pleasure, and from the cold-blooded murder of Raskolnikov, to the equally cold-blooded murders of Gide's Lafcadio and Camus' Meursault, *il n'y avait qu'un pas*. It is as someone haunted by the dreadful possibility that the world might be the place of absurdity and disorder that Ivan advances his advocacy of spiritual and political authoritarianism. No one abhors the vacuum more than Ivan Karamazov. The Grand Inquisitor guarantees order, in a world in which order is threatened by the very notion of freedom. It will be recalled that Lafcadio committed his murder to demonstrate to himself that he was free to do so. Consequently, Ivan's Grand Inquisitor condemns freedom itself because it is a potential source of disorder:

You desired the free love of man, that he might follow you freely . . . In place of the rigid ancient law, man must henceforth make up his own mind with a free heart about good and evil, with nothing but Your example to guide him. But could You really not understand, that he would reject and dispute even Your image and Your truth, if he were to become oppressed with such a strange burden as freedom of choice? They would eventually cry out that the truth was not in You, since it was impossible to leave them in a greater state of confusion than You did . . .[13]

By the same token it will be recalled that Ivan, in conversation with

Alyosha, did not deny God, but he denied His creation. In particular he found it impossible to accept a world which admitted the suffering of children. In other words, Ivan rejects God's creation because he is unable to reconcile himself with certain aspects of it which he finds anomalous; he rejects that world as *insufficiently ordered*. The need for order, and the haunting fear of metaphysical chaos and absurdity, lie at the heart of Ivan Karamazov. He feels, like no other character in fiction, the full traumatic impact of the disappearance of whole meanings.

Dostoevsky's understanding of Ivan, and the unnerving insight he displays into the anatomy of authoritarian terrorism, shows us how deeply his own spirit was penetrated by a need for orthodoxy and order. The imaginative leap that would otherwise have been required in order to enter into the mentality of a slave would have been too great. After ten years of penal servitude and exile, Dostoevsky was all too well placed to understand that freedom was foreign to his national character. For all his burning assertions of individual freedom of the spirit, and his rejection of the ant-heap of totalitarianism, he remains, on another level, the advocate of an unswerving orthodoxy which rejected all foreigners and all heretics out of hand. The jingoistic pan-Slavism of his later years shows that however much he might have rejected the *Shigalevshina*, he enjoyed a certain complicity with its principles.

Dostoevsky's complicity with the anatomy of terrorism and authoritarian oppression is a characteristic ambiguity. Just as he provides an indictment of the intensity cult through a literary code based upon an aesthetic of intensity, so his assertions of freedom are accompanied by a stern sense of orthodoxy. Moreover, he writes about the objects of his criticism, about Raskolnikov, Stavrogin and Shigalev, from the inside. His intimacy of understanding is, frankly, suspect. Similarly, his insight into sadism and the sex-crime goes too deep, his feel for the almost sexual force of political oppression is too strong. Both as a Russian, and as an ex-convict, he knew the fascination of total oppression, its soothing obliteration of the individual consciousness. The paranoid intensity that echoes through the political figures of *The Devils*, the monstrous spiritual evil of the Grand Inquisitor, are the work of an insider. For all his truly magnificent sense of human freedom and dignity, freedom itself was only to be reached through rigid orthodoxy and a degree of jingoistic conformism which was tantamount to being tied to the soil. Dostoevsky chose freedom rather than oppression, yet his temperament craved for a rigidly structured order. His view of freedom is a characteristically Russian one: man may be as free as he pleases as long as he keeps in step.

It is this paradoxical complicity with his subject matter, the strain of passionate intensity which runs through his myths of oppression, that explains why Dostoevsky's treatment of these themes, more than any nineteenth-century history, can help us understand and enter into the world of terrorism and totalitarian madness – the world of Hitler, Stalin and Ubu Roi.

CHAPTER NINE

The Individual: Pressures and Responses

We suggested that Romanticism was the first wave in the recognition that society no longer provided harmony, stability or the satisfaction of certain essential needs. It was fundamentally a literature of escape. Dostoevsky paints a more informed and detailed picture of that world which put the Romantics to flight. He describes an age of urban development, cast-iron and spiritual impoverishment. Nineteenth-century culture had created a world which could only satisfy the appetites; it could not meet spiritual demands. Hence it was an age of universal dissatisfaction. All harmony, brotherhood, community disappear, and human experience is rendered through a language of violence, chaos and division. Dostoevsky describes a climate of alienation, discontent; an age of appetite and bloodshed, an age without peace in which man is condemned to the pursuit of unattainable goals.

Although his response echoes that of the Romantics in its feeling tone, it is essentially better informed, more aware. Romantic rhetoric, its individualistic culture-heroes such as Werther or René, its celebration of local colour and Gothic revivalism, its assertion of the unique value of individual feeling, all tended to obscure the essence of Romanticism, the fact that it was finally a gesture of rejection and escape. The significance of that gesture can only be understood by examining its motivation, by seeing, for example, that the Romantic celebration of nature was the creation of the industrial revolution.

Baudelaire is already more specific than his predecessors. He isolates both the causes and the effects: witness the prominence his work accords to the theme of the city. However, his literary codes remain essentially abstract. The poet expresses himself in the allusive language of allegorical tropes. He writes of 'un monde où l'action n'est pas la soeur du rêve', where Dostoevsky writes of tenements, sex-crimes, political terrorism and the ethics of self-interest, thereby translating the profoundly felt but vague dissatisfactions of the Romantics into hard facts.

The difference between Dostoevsky and earlier generations is reflected in the choice of media. Up to and including Baudelaire the Romantics had found lyric verse the most appropriate medium of expression. This is because their responses remained on the level of individual and instinctive feelings. The lyric response rests upon an instant and all-embracing intuitive apprehension. It is an impulse that

110

remains all of a piece. Dostoevsky clarified that impulse, analysing it by situating it in a concrete context which made its motivation clear; hence his need for the narrative and descriptive resources of prose fiction.

This is why the dissatisfaction which is captured by Baudelaire's essentially lyric response emerges with a different clarity in Dostoevsky's studies of the individual under pressure. The new world places the individual in a state of stress, as he becomes exposed to divisive and destructive forces that were unknown to his ancestors. These forces are of course reflected in the centrifugal tendencies of modern society. Dostoevsky's work abounds in expressions alluding to 'the chemical disintegration of our society'.[1] One of the most obvious forms which the disruptive pressures took was the disintegration of the family. This is why he regards its disruption as a particularly significant sign of the times:

> never has the Russian family been more disrupted, more divided, more ill-matched, more ill-constituted . . .[2]

Besides creating social chaos, such disruption destroys cultural continuity. It places at a risk that steady process of transmission of values from one generation to the next, which forms the backbone of any stable culture. The older generation has lost its sense of purpose, and no longer believes in the values which it should transmit:

> . . . the loss, in the fathers of to-day, of any sort of common idea, with reference to their families, common to all fathers, binding them to one another, in which they might believe, and which they might teach their children, thereby transmitting their own faith in life.[3]

Consequently the younger generation is left without moral guidance, obliged to find its own way. Collapse of the family means that 'our younger generation is condemned to seek out its ideals for itself'.[4] Hence of course the enduring relevance of the *Bildungsroman*.

Of course, Dostoevsky is by no means alone in grasping the seriousness of the family's disruption. It is one of the central themes of nineteenth-century fiction. Tolstoy brings it to the centre of his work. It features in other writers such as Eugène Sue and the Victor Hugo of *Les Misérables* where its rôle is equally central. It also features as a crucial theme in the poetry of Lautréamont – the supreme poet of disintegration, chaos and cultural entropy. Equally, Karl Marx mounts an assault upon the notion of the family in *German Ideology*, as the basic social unit of the capitalist world.

The disrupted family, while playing an important part in a great number of Dostoevsky's works, is crucial to his penultimate novel, *The Adolescent*. Dolgoruky is the embodiment of the new rootlessness, the new disinherited. Described as 'a bastard with a lackey's soul',[5] he thereby anticipates the definitive image of the disinherited son, the parricide Smerdyakov, the bastard lackey. Dolgoruky is described as a member of an 'accidental family':

> tell me, Arkady Makarovich, that this family is a chance phenom- enon, and I shall rejoice. But is it not more true to conclude that already large numbers of Russian families are becoming *accidental families*, contributing to the general disorder and chaos? . . . Yes, Arkady Makarovich, you belong to an *accidental family*.[6]

The theme of family disruption is, of course, brought to a climax in the ironically entitled *Brothers Karamazov*. Here the theme is used to express the very essence of chaos and cultural disintegration. The Karamazovs are the supreme accidental family. The father played no part in the upbringing of his children. One of them is employed by him as a cook, another, his sexual rival, he cheats of his birthright. The family comes together for the first time when the children are grown up. It communicates on an axis of hate and sexual jealousy – sexual rivalry between father and son being almost as intense an image of disruption as incest – that final negation of kinship. The book is packed with images of disintegration. Its central incident is a parricide, and Ivan reminds us that we all long for our father's death.

Much has been made of the novel's closeness to Greek tragedy, since that too deals with the infringement of essential taboos such as incest and parricide. It is proper that such parallels should acknowledge the novel's elemental force. Yet there is a difference. Anthropologists have suggested that the myths upon which the tragedies were founded reflect the traumatic experience of man's initial submission to the rule of law: the imposition of culture upon nature. Such myths were essentially constitutive, describing the formation of civilised society. Dostoevsky's myths are disruptive, describing its final splitting asunder. Small wonder that they should treat the same themes; but they treat them in reverse. There is a fascinating if somewhat glib parallel to be drawn with the processes of language acquisition and language loss. It has been shown that the order in which a child builds up his series of phoneme sets is the reverse of the order in which an adult, whose speech faculty has been impaired by brain damage, loses his. He ends with the basic oppositions with which the child began. Similarly, Greek myth begins the foundation of civilised society with the very themes with which Dostoevsky would announce its end.

In *Crime and Punishment* break up of the family is associated with its extension – a process which Dostoevsky terms *obosoblenie*: isolation, or insulation, i.e. of the self.

Much is made of the total isolation of Raskolnikov, his withdrawal from all communal life, from all contact with his family and friends.

112

It is this that accounts for his melodramatically savage treatment of his long-suffering mother and sister. His relationship with them expresses itself almost entirely through a series of leave-takings. So great is his sense of withdrawal that he is unable to accept family ties and love:

> Why do they love me so much if I don't deserve it! If only I were alone and no one loved me, and I loved no one. *None of this would happen!*[7]

Raskolnikov positively revels in his state of total withdrawal:

> It would be harder to let oneself go any further, but in his present state of mind Raskolnikov actually enjoyed it. He had definitely withdrawn from everyone, like a tortoise into its shell, and even the face of the maid who looked after him, and who visited him occasionally, brought him to a frenzy of irritation. It's what happens to some monomaniacs who depend too much upon themselves.[8]

In his confession to Sonya he suggests that it was this sense of isolation that made him a murderer:

> Then I withdrew into my corner like a spider. You've been to my den, you've seen . . . But do you know, Sonya, that low ceilings and cramped rooms suffocate the mind and the spirit! . . . But I didn't want to go out. I deliberately did not want to. I stayed in for days, didn't go to work, wasn't hungry even, I just lay there . . . If Nastasya brought food, I'd eat, if not I'd go without all day, I didn't ask for any out of spite! There was no light at night, I'd lie in the dark, and didn't want to earn the price of a candle. I had to study, and I'd sold my books . . . I preferred to lie and think . . . and I kept having strange dreams, all kinds of dreams.[9]

This overpowering sense of isolation is proposed as a special instance of that general withdrawal into the self which we first witnessed in the Romantics. It is this that Dostoevsky alludes to in writing of:

> our lamentable isolation, our ignorance of the masses, our break with national values . . . for isolation is disintegration.[10]

He is more explicit still in the following passage:

> Each for himself and himself alone, any contact with his fellows is for selfish ends – that is most people's moral principle these days. N.B. it is the basic idea of the bourgeoisie, which replaced the former order at the end of the last century, and has become the main idea of the age throughout the European world.[11]

Dostoevsky sees the movement, which began as Romantic egotism, become the enlightened self-interest of the new morality, underwriting a general dissolution of any sense of communal values in favour of individualism. Although he describes this as a European phenomenon, there were reasons why it should have been experienced in Russia more keenly than elsewhere. There it could be seen to be the product of that peculiarly Western European culture-pattern which had, after all, been grafted onto Russian institutions relatively recently. The educated Russian was able to contrast European culture with an autochthonous alternative. This native culture was quite unlike that of the Western lower classes; it was not a sub-culture but a 'counter-culture'. A merchant could be as wealthy as any prince, and still live according to traditional values, folkways and whole meanings. It may well have been the possibility, peculiar to Russia, of witnessing a living alternative to the state of nineteenth-century European culture, that rendered Dostoevsky's dissatisfaction with that state so lucid and acute. Equally that same awareness of an alternative accounts for peculiarly Russian movements such as populism and Tolstoyism.

This extra dimension of awareness permits Dostoevsky to furnish an indictment of that sense of isolation, egotism and alienation, in which writers such as Chateaubriand, Stendhal and indeed Lermontov had positively exulted. He provides an essentially critical treatment of that theme, which is both an acknowledgment and an indictment of that quintessential Romantic phenomenon – solipsism. Dostoevsky shows how it can come about that Stendhalian egotism or the heroic mono-mania of the Balzacian obsessive can lose their heroic dimension all too easily, and collapse into the petty *arrivisme* of the characters of Flaubert and Maupassant; the step from Romantic solipsism to bourgeois self-interest is easily made: Raskolnikov had magnificent dreams which led him to a squalid murder.

Dostoevsky sees isolation turning all too easily into alienation. Solitude ceases to be enjoyed, and comes to be experienced as intense personal anguish. This is one of the characteristics of the idiot prince. Myshkin is an alienated character whose very existence is a contradiction in terms. A Russian prince who knows nothing of Russia and speaks his native tongue like a foreigner, he is cut off from his fellows both by cultural circumstance and by physical handicaps. His sense of not belonging, of being out of things echoes a mood of Baudelaire's poet-hero who found himself:

> Un faux accord
> Dans la divine symphonie.[12]

It is precisely this sense of discord which Myshkin experienced in his madness:

Before him was a radiant sky, beneath him a lake, around him a clear unending horizon. For a long time he looked on in agony. Now he remembered how he had stretched his arms out to this clear, unending blue sky, and wept . . . What sort of banquet was this, what sort of eternal endless feast-day, to which he had long felt drawn, from his very childhood, and which he could not attain. Every morning such a clear sun would rise; every morning there was a rainbow on the water-fall, every morning the sunny peak of the highest mountain, there, on the edge of the sky, would burn with a purple flame; 'every little fly that buzzed beside him in the warm sunshine was part of that choir; it knew its place, loved it and was happy!' Every blade of grass grew and was happy! Everything had its way and everything knew its way, coming and going with a song; he alone knew nothing, understood nothing, neither sounds nor people, a stranger and an outcast.[13]

Myshkin's feeble-minded condition rendered the theme of not belonging as acutely as possible. But his alienation is merely an intensified version of that loneliness and isolation which the author more usually proposes as being culture-bound, embodied in such creations as Raskolnikov and the Underground Man. This sense of anguished isolation, the traumatic realisation that you are alone, without the support of any kind of family or community, was the price the individual, from Romanticism on, had to pay for his state of culture.

The pressures which that culture exerted upon the individual cut him off, drove him, finally, into a corner. Dostoevsky's treatment updated these Romantic themes of alienation, by handling them in a realistic code which included a sociological and historical dimension. He transplants alienation from the storm-tossed Gothic nights of Romanticism to the here and now of the nineteenth-century city. He does as much for that supreme manifestation of Romantic insecurity and identity crisis – the divided self.

Dualism virtually created the Romantic view of personality, from Goethe on, and this, of course, was a reflection of Romanticism's fundamental sense of instability and disintegration. Dostoevsky first treats the theme in a traditional manner that echoes Gogol and E. T. A. Hoffmann. *The Double* is the story of an unremarkable civil servant dogged by an *alter ego* who gradually usurps his place and finally secures his incarceration in an asylum. The hero is perpetually asserting that he is autonomous, a complete individual, but of course he is nothing of the sort. His double, a despicable fawning and hypocritical careerist, gives him the lie.

Dostoevsky soon abandoned the crude and fantastic aspects of the theme, as he became more absorbed by the psychology of dualism. The divided self becomes central to his account of the individual's response to pressure, and the tensions which he experiences. Dualism is proposed as the supreme characteristic of modern man, reflecting the divisive world in which he has his being. The loss of a coherent system of whole meanings which might hold that world together, and the impact of the technological and piecemeal solutions which had brought that loss about, made for a personality that was dispersed, uncentred. As a result, Dostoevsky understood that modern man was capable of a much broader range of sensations and attitudes than were his ancestors. Because he lacked a unifying framework of values, he cultivated various aspects of his self, regardless of whether or not they contributed to the formation of a whole being:

> . . . people in those days (I promise you, this always struck me) were quite different from people to-day, they were a different breed . . . it's as if they were a different race . . . people seemed more single-minded then, now they are more nervous, more sophisticated, more sensitive, and seemed to have two or three ideas at a time . . . today's man is broader, and I promise you, that prevents him from being the unified man of ages past.[14]

In singling out division and nervous tension as the particular marks of modern man Dostoevsky is again in agreement with Baudelaire. The latter defined modern man by his extraordinary capacity for sustaining mutually contradictory attitudes. Dualism is at the very root of his being. He derives this dualism from his two 'simultaneous postulations' towards God and Satan. 'Man is born double,' wrote Baudelaire, 'the man of genius aspires to unity.'

Like Baudelaire, Dostoevsky singles out as a vitally important characteristic man's capacity to keep his two postulations going at once; to live in a condition of sustained contradiction. The young Dolgoruky makes the point:

> I had an intense longing for spiritual good-order of course, but I'm at a loss to say how it could accompany God knows what other longings . . . I have often wondered at man's capacity (and particularly Russian man's) to nourish in his soul the noblest ideal beside the most abject baseness, in all sincerity.[15]

Dmitri Karamazov makes a similar point in his crucial 'confession' to Alyosha. He is horrified by his examination of his own character, finding in it a love for the good and the beautiful which is only matched by the strength of his equally sincere love of their opposites:

> What I cannot bear is that a man with the noblest of feelings and great intelligence begins with the ideal of the Madonna, to end with the ideal of Sodom. More frightening still is the type who has

the ideal of Sodom in his heart without rejecting the ideal of the Madonna; his heart yearns for it in all sincerity, in all truth, as it did when he was young and innocent. No, man is broad, too broad, I'd have him narrower.[16]

This account of metaphysical dualism and the transition from 'the Madonna' to 'Sodom' might serve equally well as an introduction to *Les Fleurs du Mal*. Both Baudelaire and Dostoevsky see the ability to sustain mutually contradictory attitudes of this kind as central to the psychological experience of their age. The all-important capacity for dualism and contradiction is reflected on every level of Dostoevsky's work. For example, Raskolnikov's name (*raskol* meaning schism) echoes the great division of the Orthodox church in the seventeenth century, which continued to divide Russian society until the Revolution. Another reflection of fundamental dualism lies at the very heart of the author's conception of *The Idiot*. His working papers suggest that he initially conceived of a single hero, who eventually divided into the double figure of Myshkin and Rogozhin. This becomes particularly significant when taken in conjunction with his professed intent to portray a 'positively beautiful hero' in this work. It is as if he were only able to do so by isolating a particular aspect of his initial conception, freeing it of certain characteristics, and acknowledging the partial quality of his creation by making him an idiot.

The notorious difficulty which faces the *novelist* who seeks to portray a positive character is a critical commonplace, but one should beware of extending it to all art forms. The epic, for example, encounters no such difficulty. In fact the difficulty is, if not an exclusive, then at least a particular characteristic of the novel, and of the world which the novel, 'the form of absolute sinfulness', represents. The inability of the novel to handle positive characters, to make Tolstoy's Levin come alive, or Oblomov's unspeakable friend Shtolz into anything but a priggish bore, is an important characteristic of a specific form, not a quality of art in general.

Dostoevsky cannot encompass both a whole and a positive character, so he sacrifices wholeness. Myshkin and Rogozhin are day and night. The novel opens with their meeting, and ends, essentially, with their joint vigil over the corpse of Nastasya Filipovna. Their characters pair off into complementary opposites. Rogozhin is, by word, deed and background, the very embodiment of a certain vivid and intense Russianness, the Russianness of sheepskin jackets and tar-stained boots. He has a tremendous vitality which overrides all considerations of good-form, a vitality which Russian describes as *razmakh* (*lit.* a sweep of the arm), for he sweeps all obstacles aside. The prince, on the other hand, is a stranger; brought up abroad he speaks Russian like a foreigner. Although he too may override convention, he is quiet and diffident, if without timidity. The opposite of Rogozhin's physical exuberance, he is a physical and mental invalid. Where Rogozhin is the embodiment of sexual violence, Myshkin seems to be impotent. Where Rogozhin is a merchant, and hence beyond the pale of cultivated European society, Myshkin is a prince. Finally they are linked through their names. Rogozhin is a good name for a merchant (*rogozha* meaning bast, or matting). In it we also hear *rog* meaning horn, which brings out his strength, his sexuality, and perhaps also the fact that he will finally be a sexual loser, the moral cuckold of Myshkin. Myshkin's name, on the other hand, connotes opposite qualities, for *mysh* means mouse. However, the characters are also linked to each other by the fact that each bears a Christian name which would be more appropriate to the other. Myshkin is Lev, the lion, while Rogozhin is Parfen, the virgin.

The action of the book, its culmination in Rogozhin's murder and the madness of Myshkin, derives from the tension between the two central characters, and the pressures which they exert upon Aglaya, and Nastasya Filipovna. It is because each man is incomplete without the other that Nastasya Filipovna is torn between them. It is their inability to harmonise with one another, the fact that they clash, rather than blend, that destroys them and those involved in them. Eventually Nastasya Filipovna spends the night with both of them together; but she has had her throat cut and Myshkin has lost his mind. Dostoevsky may have succeeded in portraying a positively beautiful individual, but equally, he has created a profound exploration of that divided self which opposes *eros* to *agape*, a sense of spirituality to the libido.

Versilov is another character built upon contradiction and division. Dostoevsky described him as an agnostic who would go to the stake for a vague belief. Immensely proud of being a Russian gentleman, he is the irresponsible head of two families, and lives most of his life abroad. He is quite unable to reconcile the two halves of his being – the responsibilities of his position and his capacity for a surging, arid lust which overrides all efforts to resist it. The dualism is expressed symbolically in a scene in which his hidden half comes through. He takes a family treasure, an old icon into his hand, and continues:

'I don't know what the matter is . . . I just came in for a few minutes to say something nice to Sonya, and I can't find the words . . . Do you know I have the feeling that I am splitting in two.' He looked around with a terribly serious expression . . . 'Really, my mind is splitting in two, it's terrifying. It's as if a double were standing beside one. You are perfectly rational and sensible, but he wants to do something utterly senseless, and often very funny, and you suddenly realise that you want to do it too, heaven knows why, that's to say that you both do and do not want to, you want to despite yourself . . . Do you know Sonya, I'd like to take this icon . . . and, you know, now, this very moment, I'd like to smash it on the corner of the stove. I'm certain it would split into two halves, no more, no less.[17]

He does so, and of course it breaks into two halves as predicted.

Versilov's anxiety derives from Dostoevsky's early story of *The Double*. Small wonder that he is alarmed by this encounter with the 'Rogozhin within'. Where Baudelaire experienced division and contradiction as spleen, a condition of passive and impotent hopelessness, Dostoevsky feels it as trauma, not a metaphysical or mystic *Angst* but a physiological condition. He thereby makes an advance on earlier treatments of that theme, finding nothing in it that required the fantastical extravagance of Romantic fantasy. The feeling that the mind is coming apart at the seams is now presented as a part of everyday life. Versilov's condition is portrayed as a medical fact:

> Versilov . . . for the whole of that last day and the evening before, could have no definite purpose. He was, I believe, even incapable of thought, and was under the influence of a kind of surge of feeling. I do not believe, however, that he was actually mad at the time, any more than now. – But I certainly believe in 'The Double'. What exactly is a double? A double, at any rate according to a medical book written by an expert which I read subsequently . . . a double is simply the first stage of a certain serious mental disorder which can have the gravest consequences.[18]

The explanation is vague enough, but there can be no doubting the author's intention. He treats dualism and split personality as medically attested phenomena. In the final analysis he derives this view from his view of the structure of the mind. Basically Dostoevsky would maintain that we have two brains: one handles the rational processes and all forms of conscious mental behaviour, the other is the seat of instinct, emotion and intuition. The distinction is drawn, a little vaguely, by Aglaya, who believes that Myshkin, for all his idiocy, has a different kind of intelligence:

> . . . although you may be mentally sick . . . your principle mind is a better one than any of theirs, better than they could ever dream of, because there are two minds; the important and the unimportant one, aren't there?[19]

Strangely enough certain modern psychological theories support Dostoevsky. They speak of the 'old' and the 'new' brain. The new brain handles those elements of rational behaviour that Dostoevsky puts into one category, the old brain handling the rest. The terminology suggests that we have evolved some capacities earlier than others. This view of mental events describes as 'the old brain taking over' the familiar sensation when, having firmly resolved to perform some action, such as striking a golf-ball or casting a fly, in a slow and deliberate manner, we suddenly find ourselves threshing like a maniac, utterly wrecking our performance. The old brain has asserted itself and all control is lost. In his *The Ghost in the Machine* Arthur Koestler suggests that most of the otherwise inexplicable evils of human society, its capacity for self-destruction, may perhaps be accounted for by a physiological imbalance, a failure of co-ordination between the two brains.

At all events the old/new brain terminology lends itself perfectly to the description of Dostoevskian mental events. Thus Aglaya has suggested that although Myshkin is unable to handle intellectual skills, he is more than competent on an instinctive level.

In a sense Dostoevsky agrees with Koestler in seeing in a lack of equilibrium between the two brains a major source of potential disaster. However his explanation is essentially cultural rather than physiological. Post-Renaissance man had over-developed the rational skills at the expense of feelings and intuitions. It is finally the old brain which requires that framework of certitudes and whole meanings which the empirical tradition destroyed. The resulting imbalance had removed the basis of a certain sense of purpose and ontological reassurance. Neglect of the area of experience pertaining to the old brain, the area that lies beyond the scientifically verifiable, had made for a dangerously limited view of man and his needs, threatening to create a society in the image of the human ant-heap. The effect of this narrowing upon the individual was to bring about a condition of lopsided imbalance, in which the old brain acted against the consciousness rather than with it and threatened, under stress, to assert itself with a terrible chtonic violence. It is this that accounts for Dostoevskian man's capacity for moments of unpredictable and savage destruction.

The excessive importance which nineteenth-century culture attached to the experience of the new brain made the Underground Man describe consciousness itself as a kind of disease.[20] Dostoevskian characters who attempt to live through their consciousness alone destroy themselves in the end. Raskolnikov, for example, tries to live exclusively on the level of the new brain. His intention to murder is logical – so he murders. He heeds his deductions, but then the old brain reasserts itself with a terrible power. He passes the weeks following his double slaying in a brainstorm, because his two brains are at odds. He eventually betrays himself and confesses, although at no stage could he have

120

been convicted without that confession, because his mental condition has grown intolerable.

The fainting-fit which Ganya Ivolgin experiences in resisting the temptation to reclaim 100,000 roubles from a burning stove is a miniature version of the brainstorm which Dostoevsky's new-brain characters experience under stress. Where more integrated persons such as Dmitri Karamazov can take all the punishment handed out to them, Ganya, Raskolnikov or Ivan Karamazov risk insanity. Raskolnikov doubts the reality of Svidrigailov; his mental condition has deteriorated to the point where he can no longer tell hallucination from reality. Svidrigailov himself is prone to hallucinations. Twice he has seen his late wife, and has a terrifying nightmare of child sexuality on his last night upon earth. Ivan Karamazov, another ice-cold calculator, undergoes a total breakdown. He has the most disturbing and convincing derangement of all, in his encounter with the devil. Significantly, the news of his incipient madness is announced on the same page as we are informed that his half-brother Smerdyakov, another calculating murderer who could not see his action through, is also losing his mind.

Dostoevsky's handling of the theme of the dividing self begins with the account of modern man's capacity to sustain various attitudes and appetites that are essentially at odds with one another. Modern man is too broad, suggests Dmitri Karamazov. Inevitably, he falls victim to contradictory stresses and tensions. The divided self becomes a reflection of the divisive qualities of the age. Just as society is losing its cohesion, so the individual feels that his own mind is coming apart. The characters whose minds are cast in the image of the new society, the world of the calculator, of Lebedev's Third Horseman, are exceptionally prone to mental disorders: for when they come under stress they are quite unable to cope. Their models of human behaviour take insufficient account of their own instincts, and this neglect tends to result in the derangement of the balance of their minds.

The picture which Dostoevsky paints of his age is a black one. It was a time without unity, with no sense of community or co-operation, in which every man was for his divided self. The physical and social consequences were to be seen in the cities, their slums, beggars and sickly children. It was also reflected in the personality of modern man, his profound sense of unease, his restless searching for a satisfaction which could never be found, because he was searching in a world which, by definition, could not satisfy. Consequently, what began with the Madonna, with the longing for an ideal, tended to degenerate into Sodom, the quest for sensation. Once a materialistic civilisation had satisfied all material needs, where would its citizens go from there?

Dostoevsky could see little ahead but universal collapse. Materialism must lead first to the human ant-heap and then to chaos, for it would create a society without a moral sense. Once man had lost his sense of moral responsibility he would become an animal, more specifically, a Gadarene swine, galloping on to destruction.

Dostoevsky writes the mythology of that destruction. His novels probe the deep structure of a society which was in the process of falling apart. He went further than Baudelaire in his analysis, creating not lyric poetry but psycho-dramas. He creates situations and *dramatis personae* who enact the climate of violence and destruction which was the true climate of his age. It was this level of truth he alluded to with the suggestion that his 'Idealist' novels had a truth that vastly exceeded that of mere realism.

This truth accounts for the violence of his world, a ritual violence of gesture, speech and action. His novels anticipate the coming of a universal terrorism, when throat-slitting would be a legitimate political action. The Grand Inquisitor, with his emphasis upon power, secrecy and authority, took us further into the psychology of oppression than any realistic treatment. Equally, Rogozhin the assassin, in his dark house like a spider in his web, makes one understand the world of paranoid suspicion in which Stalin would have his being. Dostoevsky's study of violence, individual and collective, lends body to the assertion that the end justifies the means, as Petr Verkhovensky convinces his herd of sheepish conspirators that Shatov must die.

Neither murder nor the divided self are, for Dostoevsky, the supreme sign of bankruptcy, collective or individual. He accords pride of place to suicide – the murder of the self. The willingness to take one's own life is a particular instance of Raskolnikov's manic conviction that logical man has the right of life and death. Makar Dolgoruky in *The Adolescent* describes suicide as the greatest sin of all.[21]

Suicide is the final stage of man's spiritual bankruptcy, the culmination of his psychological ill-being. Just as Dostoevsky's modern murderers act in cold blood, out of logical conviction, so his suicides are equally convinced by their own logic. They kill themselves because they have exhausted all their resources and have nothing left. Svidrigailov, Smerdyakov and, above all, Stavrogin expose the sheer hopelessness of their arid position.

Stavrogin's suicide is the supreme declaration of moral bankruptcy. Everything was expected of Stavrogin, everyone looked to him for a lead. A figure of mythic intensity, his name means 'Cross-bearer'. His wife, the half-wit cripple girl, saw him as the legendary prince of Russian folklore. To Petr Verkhovensky he was the sun, the spiritual leader of the Apocalypse, Ivan Tsarevich. But he disappoints them all. His wife sees through him first, sees that his centre is hollow, that he is no prince but a mere pretender. He laughs in Verkhovensky's face when the latter confesses his plans for him in a frenzy of adoration. He lets Liza down as a lover when she abandons herself to him for ever, and, as Dr Peace has pointed out, there are implications that he is morally or physically impotent with her. His failure and the weakness he displays in condoning the murder of his wife and brother-in-law are the cause of Liza's acquiescence to her own lynching. The cross-bearer turns out to be a broken reed. The only action which he completes successfully is the one that takes his own life. Dostoevsky describes the discovery of the corpse in great detail, detail which suggests that Stavrogin had taken a degree of care over the preparations for his death which was pathetically unworthy of the beautiful madman who sunk his teeth into the Governor's ear, or stood stock still at the barrier as Galganov tried to shoot him at point blank range:

> The citizen of the canton of Uri was hanging there behind the door. On the small table was a piece of paper with, in pencil, the words 'no one's to blame, I did it myself'. On the same table there was a hammer, a piece of soap and a large nail, obviously a spare one. The heavy silk noose, clearly chosen and set aside in advance, with which Nikolai Vsevolodich had hanged himself, was greased with soap. Everything suggested premeditation and consciousness to the end.[22]

It is characteristic of Stavrogin, a 'new-brain' character, that not even in his dying moments could he rid himself of the disease of his consciousness.

That suicide was a significant sign of the times is suggested by Zametov in *Crime and Punishment*. He is disturbed by the casual way in which people appear to commit suicide for the most trivial reasons:

> Another thing, there're all these suicides – you've no idea how it's spreading. They all spend their last penny and then kill themselves. Young girls, boys, old men . . .[23]

In the speech which describes Dmitri Karamazov's murder as a sign of general moral collapse the public prosecutor also alludes to the rising suicide-rate, taking this as an indication that modern man is losing his belief in the immortality of his soul.[24]

Suicide is the direct consequence of the poverty of the materialistic world-view. Unless man has a sense of purpose beyond material comfort, Dostoevsky feels he will inevitably grow convinced of the pointlessness of his existence and take his own life. He quotes a correspondent who objects to his spiritual world-view as a 'comic and pathetic anachronism' for:

> 'this is the age of cast-iron concepts, of positive opinions, an age whose

motto is life at all costs' (his very words!). This is no doubt why the suicide rate has risen so sharply among the educated classes.[25]

The article goes on to discuss the suicide of a young girl. It is typical of a welter of suicides which he ascribes to a spiritual malaise, an over-powering sense of hopeless emptiness, that same feeling of all-embracing disgust which Baudelaire describes as spleen. Dostoevsky ascribes the process to the distintegration of the family and the parents' loss of confidence in their own values.

Curiously enough, Walter Benjamin singles out the theme of suicide in Baudelaire as peculiarly representative of that poet's experience of modernity. He sketches out a theory of suicide as the only heroic gesture left to modern man. However, in his analysis of suicide Benjamin may well have been prejudiced. He was to take his own life to avoid capture by the Nazis in circumstances which rendered capture rela-tively improbable. Benjamin writes of suicide as follows:

The resistances that modernity sets against man's habitual creative drive are out of proportion to his strength. It is understandable that he weakens and takes refuge in death. Modernity must stand beneath the sign of suicide . . . This suicide is not an act of resignation but a heroic passion. Nietzsche sees suicide in the same light – Christianity cannot be sufficiently condemned for destroying the value of a clean and mighty nihilism . . . by hindering suicide – the art of nihilism.

This is modernity's conquest in the field of passion, with the result that suicide appears as the *passion particulière de la vie moderne*, the *locus classicus* of the theory of modernity. The voluntary death of the hero of antiquity is quite different. 'Where, apart from Heracles . . . Cato of Utica and Cleopatra . . . do you find suicide represented in antiquity.' Not that Baudelaire discovered it in the moderns. The reference to Rousseau and Balzac which follows the sentence quoted is trivial. But modernity certainly had the raw material of such representations and it awaited its master. This raw material had been deposited in precisely those strata which turned out to be the foundations of modernity. The first sketch of a theory of suicide dates from 1845. At that time the representation of suicide had become familiar among the working classes.

A printer, A.B., published in 1841 a little text 'On the conditions of the workers and their improvement by means of the organisation of labour'. It was a highly restrained exposition, which tried to win over the old corporations of wandering journeymen . . . to the workers' associations. It failed, the author took his life, and in an open letter urged his fellow sufferers to follow his example. Suicide might well have appeared to Baudelaire the only heroic act that remained for the *multitudes maladives* of the cities in an age of reaction.

Perhaps he saw Rethel's *Death*, which he greatly admired, as the . . . draftsman before an easel, laying upon the canvas the suicide's ways of death.[26]

This is the attitude that motivates Dostoevsky's 'heroic' suicides. Kirillov proposes to take his own life in order to liberate man from the taboo which denies him the right over life and death: precisely the rôle of suicide in the works of Nietzsche. The fact that man's so-called liberation might only be achieved in an act of self-destruction was an irony which did not escape Dostoevsky. Kirillov wishes to make his fellows stop over-valuing life. When it is put to him that success might lead to universal suicide he replies:

> That's unimportant. They will kill deception. Whoever wants real freedom must dare to take his own life. He who dares to kill himself has found the secret of deception. There is no further freedom; it's all here, there's nothing else. Whoever dares to kill himself is God.[22]

Kirillov's insane aspirations lead him straight to self-destruction, as did the no less insane aspirations of Raskolnikov. The logical outcome of the new culture's efforts at apotheosis is – logical suicide.

Suicide as an emblem of moral bankruptcy is found in *The Adolescent* in the farcical and pitiful death of the young intellectual Kraft:

> . . . Kraft presented his death as a logical deduction . . . he left behind a note-book of learned conclusions about Russia being a second-rate nation, based on phrenology, craniology and even mathematics, so that there was no point in living, if you were Russian. If you like, what is significant here is that although you can come to any logical conclusions you please, shooting yourself as the result of those conclusions – is unusual.[28]

Logic tails off into black comedy, a logical suicide being something of a sick joke. The joke emerges in the tone the author uses to write of suicide, for instance in the appalling flippancy of a young girl's suicide note. She has tried to earn a living as a governess, and failed, was unwilling to sell her virtue, and being down-and-out in the characteristically Dostoevskian situation at her wit's end, she kills herself leaving behind the following facetious note:

Dear Mummy,
   Forgive me for cutting short my début. I have upset you.
                              Olga.[29]

Horribly enough fact overtakes fiction. In his *Diary of a Writer* for January 1877, Dostoevsky quotes a real suicide note from a young girl:

> I am going on a long journey. If I don't succeed let's gather together

and celebrate my resurrection with Clicquot. *If I do*, please do not bury me unless I'm really dead, since it's most disagreeable to wake up in a coffin underground. It's not chic at all.[30]

The ultimate suicide is that of Svidrigailov. Life for him has become a perpetual vacuum, an eternal state of spleen. His sense of *accidie* is even more developed than Baudelaire's. The latter always succeeded in sustaining a level of consciousness which kept his moral awareness intact: the awareness of his own damnation. Svidrigailov has nothing. He acts out of total indifference. He lacks the proselytising spirit of Kirillov, the convictions of Kraft, the exhibitionism of the girl suicide. He is the ultimate Dostoevskian bankrupt, whose bankruptcy, as we shall see, derives from the exhaustion of all capacity for feeling and sensation, an exhaustion brought about through the abuse of intensity. Svidrigailov takes Dostoevsky's account of the pressures exerting themselves upon modern man beyond all pressure. The very capacity to experience tension and inner conflict has long since died in him. He is a living corpse. His state of indifference is only equalled by that of Dostoevsky's Curious Fellow:

I had arrived at the conclusion that nothing in the world matters. I had suspected for a long time that it was all the same to me whether the world existed or whether there was nothing anywhere. I began to perceive and feel with all my being that there was nothing for me.[31]

This is the ultimate stage in an ontological disease which threatens the creations of the new culture, the culture without whole meanings, which professes a belief in spiritual zero. As we shall see in the following part of this study, the immediate response to that culture was the attempt to find a surrogate for whole meaning in intensity of sensation. But the fates of Svidrigailov, Stavrogin and the Curious Fellow show what becomes of characters who seek to live through intensity alone. Like Baudelaire, Dostoevsky realised that at the heart of this response to the cultural predicament there was a nothing. His civilisation was built on the principle of zero. It is this discovery that eventually drives his characters to casual self-destruction, just as it drove Baudelaire to aim, despairingly, for 'Any where out of the world'.

PART THREE

The Age of Intensity

CHAPTER TEN

The Anatomy of Intensity

Part Two examined Dostoevsky's treatment of the world which had lost its sense of whole meanings, in which *l'action* was not *la soeur du rêve*. In the world of cast-iron and positive mental attitudes, idealism is no longer possible. No longer can man feel himself to be part of a great chain of being, a beautiful and harmonious interlocking whole. Instead, he is essentially at threat, obliged to come to terms with disillusion and insecurity. This new world also provided the setting of *Les Fleurs du Mal*. Baudelaire actually begins his book with the account of his protagonist losing his grasp upon whole meanings. His character is born a poet, and a poet for Baudelaire was precisely someone who was able to look beyond the apparently haphazard surface structure of perceived reality to detect what he terms *correspondances* in the sonnet of the same name – occult relationships that underly and unify perceived reality, and link this in turn to a greater, cosmic harmony, bringing about what the poet terms *une ténébreuse et profonde unité*. But it is significant that this view is presented as a secret doctrine, the unity is only accessible to a privileged few, and not for long at that. The poems that immediately succeed this statement of belief describe the gradual erosion of that belief; show us in microcosm that slackening of a grasp on whole meanings and universals which, we would suggest, is directly responsible for the emergence of the new imperative of intensity as a substitute for meaningful experience. We see how Baudelaire's character becomes obliged to resort to sensation as his sole resource. He attempts to satisfy his idealistic cravings through sensation, and the satisfaction which he derives is both derisory and short-lived. Intensity of experience gradually becomes its own justification. Unfortunately, like all forms of addiction, the addiction to intensity requires doses of an ever-increasing strength to make the addict enjoy that moment of vertigo in which all self-consciousness is lost. The addict comes to accept intensity of any kind, regardless of its moral significance and the degradation of the self or others which it can bring about. Sensation becomes self-justifying, for the addict seeks to live by sensation alone. The results are ultimately disastrous as pain, self-destruction and finally damnation itself are recruited as sources of experience.

Baudelaire has charted the anatomy of addiction, tracing out a pattern of experience followed by the drug addict, the alcoholic, the pervert, as well as by lesser figures such as the compulsive consumer.

The poet sees it as the key pattern of his age, creating the central experience of modern man. What makes his account of exceptional value is its clarity. Baudelaire is essentially situated on the threshold of the modern age. He retains a sufficient memory of a different era to enable him to describe the actual loss of whole meanings and the gradual acquisition of the intensity habit. *Les Fleurs du Mal* consciously describes the process of modern man becoming himself.

Dostoevsky never matches the French poet's analytic awareness. He lacks his capacity for creative tight thinking. Nevertheless the picture he paints of his age is informed by the selfsame pattern of experience. Like Baudelaire he sees his time as an age of appetites rather than values, an age in which people require immediate sensation and instant results, in which they would rather feel anything than feel nothing, and in which, as a consequence, the very capacity to feel is dulled. This attitude is reflected in that increasing moral indifference which, as we have seen, Dostoevsky singles out as particularly characteristic of his times. Dostoevskian man is all too willing to sacrifice moral values in return for a shot in the arm.

Baudelaire encapsulates this attitude, this sacrifice of values to sensation, in the desperate cry:

> Qu'importe l'éternité de la damnation à qui a trouvé dans une seconde l'infini de la jouissance.[1]

Baudelaire's exclamation is matched by Dmitri Karamazov, at the height of his orgy, dismissing the knowledge that he has blood on his hands:

> Let anything happen now, what does it matter – for a single moment I would give the world![2]

In both cases everything is sacrificed in return for the experience of a single privileged moment. Intensity of experience, however short-lived, justifies all conceivable means.

Baudelaire derives the cult of intensity directly from modern man's need to escape the apathy and indifference with which he otherwise views his world. This has become a place which can contain no values, no meaning, a place in which nothing can matter any more. Baudelaire's attitude is identical to that of Dostoevsky's Curious Fellow. The only escape from an enduring state of apathy is the artificial stimulus of drugs, alcohol or anything else which distorts reality enough to make it appear more exciting than it is. The poet smashed the glazier's wares because he was unable to supply 'des vitres qui fassent voir la vie en beau!'[3]

This is precisely what is achieved by intensity. It provides rose-coloured spectacles. Through its mediation the world takes on all the excitement, the super-charged vitality, and, most important of all perhaps, the moral significance which it lacks in reality. In his account of the experience of hashish Baudelaire stresses the heightened metaphysical awareness of the addict. His consciousness is filled with a sense of significance, *correspondances*, platonic universals. It is that same awareness that is alleged to come from the use of twentieth-century hallucinogenic drugs such as LSD. In each case the addict enjoys the illusion that he is experiencing precisely those *whole meanings* which elude him in everyday reality. On a more modest, but no less serious level, the rose-coloured spectacles of intensity play their part in the experience of the alcoholic. To the chronic alcoholic life appears intolerably dull and grey, and it is only with the first little drink that colour starts to flow back into the world.

Like Baudelaire, Dostoevsky has grasped that all important relationship between intensity and apathy. Moreover, he also understands that apathy has a historical dimension. It will be recalled, we suggested that the need for an escape into sensation is first found in Romantic culture. Dostoevsky alludes to the Romantic intensity cult, to the age of Lermontov, in order to contrast it with his own time. He suggests that, in the past, intensity of experience was fairly easily achieved, but such is the apathy of his own age that it requires more desperate measures. When introducing Stavrogin the narrator suggests that he was almost incapable of sensation, and contrasts him with an earlier generation:

> ... they said of the Decembrist L——, that all his life he courted danger, grew drunk on the experience, which became for him a physical necessity; as a young man he would fight duels over nothing; in Siberia he hunted bears with nothing but a knife, and enjoyed encounters with escaped convicts in the forests, and they, incidentally, were more frightening than any bear. There is no doubt that these legendary figures were able to experience fear, great fear perhaps, or else they would have been much more placid, and would not have made danger a physical necessity.[4]

But Stavrogin belongs to a later age, an impassive age which had exhausted all the obvious sources of excitement, and which appeared to have dulled its capacity for sensation beyond repair. Bears are no longer enough for Stavrogin, who, it will be recalled, was guilty among other things of a sex-crime and of murder by proxy. The description of Stavrogin is reminiscent of Baudelaire's portrait in 'Spleen' (*Les Fleurs du Mal* LXXVII) of sensual exhaustion, his *roi d'un pays pluvieux* whom nothing can arouse. The passage of *The Devils* quoted above continues:

> But that was many years ago, and the neurotic, tortured and schizophrenic nature of our own contemporaries does not even

admit craving for such immediate and complete sensations as were sought after by other restless and active gentlemen of the good old days. Stavrogin might well have patronised L——, even have called him a braggart and a coxcomb – although he would not have done so out loud. He would have killed his man in a duel, or hunted bear, if he absolutely had to, and would have fought off a robber in the woods – quite as well and as fearlessly as L—— – but without any sense of enjoyment, simply as a tedious necessity, listlessly, lazily, even looking on it as a bore. Of course it is in spite and in malice that the progress has been made since L——, since Lermontov even. Stavrogin probably had more malice than the two of them put together, and it was a cold, calm and so to speak a rational malice, and that is the most repulsive and terrifying of all.[5]

Stavrogin's overwhelming sense of spite derives from that excessive consciousness which he shares with the Underground Man. His spiteful indifference to a world he knows too well as stale, flat and unprofitable is the equivalent of Baudelarian *ennui*. The greater the degree of consciousness, the harder it becomes to experience the surge of vertigo with which intensity overwhelms its subject.

Consciousness is the opposite of intensity. Dostoevskian consciousness, the 'disease' of the Underground Man, and the source of Stavrogin's monumental indifference, is the product of the new brain. Intensity is the sign that the old brain is momentarily in complete command. Under its sway the subject is taken ecstatically beyond the control of his consciousness into a paradisiac condition – the world of the *paradis artificiel*.

That the intensity addict aims for loss of consciousness can be seen in *The Gambler*. As the central character leaves the casino, his pockets bulging with gold, we can see that his experience has taken him beyond conscious thought:

> The alley was so dark that you couldn't see your own hand. It was half a mile to the hotel. I had never been afraid of thieves or robbers, even as a child; I didn't think of them now. In fact I don't remember what I thought about on the way home; there were no thoughts. All I felt was a terrible sense of pleasure, success, victory, power – I do not know how to describe it.[6]

When recalling his experience he describes it as a whirlwind. Its essential characteristic is a kind of vivid immediacy. All sense of rational framework, of any kind of context to the experience, is utterly lost, for intensity has taken him quite beyond the control of the new brain:

> . . . instead of thinking about what to do next, I live under the

influence of recent experiences, the influence of fresh memories, of all that whirlwind which snatched me into its vortex and tossed me out again. Sometimes I think that I am still spinning and that at any moment the storm will sweep by and snatch me up on its wing, and I will escape again from order and a sense of measure, to spin onwards . . .[7]

The whirlwind of intensity is opposed to consciousness, normality and restraint. It snatches the gambler away from *order* and *measure*, from the world of the Third Horseman and the planned environment of his reality.

We have seen that Dostoevsky, like Baudelaire, brings out the relationship between the craving for intensity and *ennui*. His characters simply oscillate between those two conditions, because the possibility of a meaningful and constructive existence in reality seems to be denied them. Thus, upon hearing that his erstwhile benefactor had become a Catholic, Prince Myshkin suggests that this kind of characteristic Russian extremism is the product of *ennui*:

Precisely, by boredom, by our boredom, it's not satiety, on the contrary it's thirst . . . not just thirst but an inflammation, a feverish thirst.[8]

Myshkin regards atheism and religious heterodoxy as the reflection of a craving. It is the motivation of such decisions, and even more the *mode* in which they are expressed, that concern us in our study of intensity. Myshkin makes it clear that the decision is made out of what is tantamount to a physical appetite: as opposed, say, to any metaphysical considerations. The age of intensity operates through appetites, and thus its satisfactions can only be short-lived.

Nevertheless its advantages are real enough while they last. Intensity of experience acts as a relief from tedium and has the effect of completely overriding any awareness of reality. For example, Rogozhin's obsession with Nastasya Filipovna, an obsession founded upon appetite, excites him sufficiently to make him forget everything, including his fear of his awesome father. He embezzles his father's money in order to buy jewellery for a woman he has never met. His gesture surpasses even that of Eugénie Grandet and her misuse of her gold to fit out her cousin, despite her fear of her own epic miserly father. It is the feeling of delirium which Rogozhin experiences, the vertigo with which the old brain asserts itself, bringing him to the brink of unconsciousness, that justifies his actions to himself:

We set off. What was under my feet, what before me, what beside me – I neither know nor remember.[9]

The same overriding sense of vertigo overwhelms Fedor Pavlovich

Karamazov, and brings about his death. He is a character of limitless cunning and duplicity, who has amassed a fortune through his shrewdness. His only weakness is sex, and Grushenka is his supreme blind spot. Just as his son Dmitri is so blinded by his own desire for her that he will stop at nothing to win her, so his repulsive father allows himself to be killed, for all his precautions, because at the height of his excitement he only believes what he wants to believe. His capacity for self-deceit under the burning, overriding promise of ultimate intensity makes him draw back the bolt and admit Smerdyakov – who has announced Grushenka's arrival:

> He started to tremble like a schoolboy. 'Where is she, here?' he sighs but he still won't believe it. 'Over there,' I say. 'She's over there, open up.' He looks at me through the window, half believing, afraid to unbolt the door. 'Now he's afraid of me,' I think. The joke is that I suddenly remembered to make those signals on the window-sill, announcing Grushenka's arrival, before his very eyes: he didn't seem to believe my words, but once I tapped out the signal he opened up immediately. I tried to go in, but he stood in the way, blocking it with his body. 'Where is she, where is she?' he looked at me, trembling. Well, I thought, it looks bad if he's that frightened of me, and my own legs nearly gave way for fear he wouldn't let me in . . . I whisper, 'Over there, there she is under the window, can't you see her?' 'You bring her in.' 'She's afraid,' I said . . . 'She's hiding in the bushes, go and call her yourself . . .' He ran off to the window, and put a candle on the sill. 'Grushenka,' he cried, 'Grushenka, are you there?' He called her all right, but didn't dare lean out, didn't want to move away from me for fear, because he had grown very frightened of me, which is why he didn't dare to move away. 'There she is,' I said . . . 'There she is in the bushes laughing at you, can't you see?' Suddenly he believed me, and really began to tremble, he was very much in love with her, and he leant out of the window. I grabbed the cast-iron paperweight off his table . . . and slammed a corner into the back of his skull. He didn't even yell. He just sort of sat down and I hit him twice more.[10]

Fedor Pavlovich seems to know that Smerdyakov is lying, that Grushenka is not there, that he is about to be murdered. But his desire is too strong. He is convinced that she has come because he hears the signal, regardless of the fact that he can see that it is Smerdyakov who is making it. His desire eventually overrides the warning messages of the new brain altogether, and, disregarding all the evidence, Fedor Pavlovich leans out of the window.

That is a key moment in the experience pattern of intensity: the moment of the plunge when the protagonist decides to commit himself and dive headlong into whatever may await him. The experience of intensity is not simply made up of a series of ecstatic moments. Each such moment is itself part of a cycle. It begins with a gradually growing feeling of anticipation which comes to a climax as the subject commits himself and takes the plunge. The ensuing period of ecstasy is then succeeded by a terrible mood of anti-climax which succeeds it. It must be said that, with few exceptions, Dostoevsky does not dwell on the latter condition. It is much more comprehensively chronicled by Baudelaire's account of 'Morning after' remorse. The same mood of exhausted staleness is captured by Rimbaud in *Une saison en enfer* and in the concluding stanzas of 'Le Bateau Ivre'. Dostoevsky prefers to concentrate upon the earlier phases of the cycle. In the following lines from *The Adolescent*, Dolgoruky, the would-be Rothschild, is about to start bidding at a sale:

> I looked on wondering what to buy . . . I wondered and waited, I felt as one does at the tables, just before you've placed your first bet, when you've come to gamble: 'I may bet, I may go away – it's up to me.' Your heart isn't thumping yet, but it is slower, beating gently – by no means a disagreeable sensation. But you rapidly begin to feel irritated by the indecision, and it's as if you go blind; you reach out and take a card, mechanically, against your will almost, as if someone else were moving your arm, and there is a different feeling altogether, a gigantic one.[11]

The prospective 'gambler' anticipates the surge of intensity that is about to come; he is about to be overwhelmed but is still sufficiently aware to be able to savour the experience. The actual plunge brings about the abandon of all self-control, all consciousness. It is an extravagant vengeance which the old brain wreaks upon commonsense. Above all else, it is the capacity to exult in the plunge which characterises the Karamazovs, and Dmitri in particular:

> . . . tomorrow I'll fall out of the sky, because life begins and ends tomorrow. Have you ever felt, ever dreamt of falling off a mountain into a pit? I'm falling now, and it's no dream. I'm not frightened and nor should you be. That is to say that I am frightened, but it's exciting. Not exciting exactly, ecstatic.[12]

Elsewhere Dmitri uses the same image of falling, and once more he seems to exult in his own undoing, sees it as a kind of heroism:

> . . . if I fall into the abyss, I fall straight, head first and legs out.[13]

Dmitri's attitude tells us much about the mentality of the intensity addict. He turns the dream of falling, which for most of us constitutes a grotesquely unnerving nightmare, into a metaphor to describe the peculiar pleasure that he derives from his own sense of his self-destruction. He wallows in the plunge, even though it will smash him when he hits the ground, because it is a source of fear so acute that it turns to ecstasy. Through his actions Dmitri reaches out for a totality of experience. He seeks to grasp all life in a single gesture, a gesture so complete, so definite, that it cannot but appear larger than life itself. It compresses the maximum of experience into the smallest possible compass. This need for concentrated experience is highly characteristic of Dostoevsky's characters, it is through it above all that their craving for intensity expresses itself. For example, Dmitri shares this quality with Katerina Ivanovna, he recognises it in her when she comes to ask him for money to save her father's honour:

> . . . she was not afraid to risk a terrible insult, in order to save her father. But look at her pride, her urge to take a risk, the challenge to fate, the infinite challenge.[14]

It is the sheer plenitude of such experience which Dostoevsky's characters prize, because they have lost any other sense of value. Completeness of sensation becomes a surrogate for psychic wholeness. This is the very essence of the intensity syndrome, an essence summed up by Dostoevsky in one casual phrase. He is referring to the quality of life in contemporary London:

> a passionate thirst for life and the loss of all higher sense of life.[15]

He points to the loss of a sense of whole meanings which he associates with appetite and a lapse into sensation.

Les Fleurs du Mal succeeded in isolating the intensity syndrome, where Dostoevsky merely sensed it as a mode of behaviour that was central to the contemporary personality. There is one area, in particular, in which Baudelaire's more comprehensive analysis throws light on an aspect of the Russian's treatment of intensity which, at first sight, appears somewhat confused.

Although Dostoevsky's treatment of intensity will take us into the darker corners of his world, it is a little surprising to find that it does not do so necessarily. Dmitri Karamazov is an intensity addict, and yet the Karamazov addiction is characterised by a tremendous vitality and love of life. Dmitri never loses his unflagging enthusiasm, he has none of the listless apathy of Stavrogin or Svidrigailov. His pursuit of intensity is almost at one with that simple and passionate love of God's creation, embodied, for example, in Zosima, which, for Dostoevsky, is that opposite of intensity – an ecstatic joy. But for all his vitality, Dmitri remains capable of single-minded obsessions that must be fed at all costs. He thereby takes the first step on a path that leads eventually to Stavrogin and Svidrigailov. This would seem to imply that there is a point at which it is scarcely possible to discriminate between intensity and its very opposite.

Reference to Baudelaire throws considerable light on this confusion, showing that it is not merely the result of sloppy analysis on Dostoevsky's part, but rather it is a vital aspect of the intensity phenomenon. Baudelaire bases his account of addiction upon man's sense of a need for spiritual fulfilment, in the first instance. Gradually, he becomes willing to meet that need not with spirituality, but with its opposite, the *paradis artificiel*. This willingness derives from the curious ease with which Baudelaire's man is able to confuse the experience of ecstasy with the experience of intensity. It is precisely through this confusion that he becomes an addict. The confusion is caused early in his development, by a tragic act of shortsightedness. Baudelaire's hero recognises in beauty the earthly reflection of a spiritual world. But he fails to see that beauty is fatally ambiguous, that it reflects both heaven and hell.

> Viens-tu du ciel profond ou sors-tu de l'abîme
> O Beauté. Ton regard, infernal et divin,
> Verse confusément le bienfait et le crime.[16]

Such is the hero's craving, however, that he elects to disregard this crucial moral ambivalence. He settles for beauty of any kind, regardless:

> Que tu viennes du ciel ou de l'enfer, qu'importe,
> O Beauté, monstre énorme, effrayant, ingénu!
> Si ton oeil, ton souris, ton pied m'ouvrent la porte
> D'un Infini que j'aime et n'ai jamais connu?[17]

With these lines the choice is made. In the ensuing poems we can see the poet turn away gradually from spiritual towards sexual beauty, and in that turning away the slow descent into the addict's hell begins.

Baudelaire views beauty as a blend of spirituality and intensity. The curious reluctance displayed by his character to distinguish between its two sides is partly a reflection of that coarsening of the ethical palate which Baudelaire suggests is a sign of his age. It is also the direct consequence of the general loss of a grasp upon whole meanings. We would suggest that the Baudelairian theme of the ambiguity of beauty is essentially the product of a particular age, the age which has lost its whole meanings. It is first encountered in the 'Satanic' aspects of Romanticism, but it is not until Baudelaire, and later Dostoevsky, that we actually find the theme of man's specific inability to cope with beauty's ambiguity. We would derive this inability from the loss of his capacity to make spiritual value judgments, from the loss, in fact, of whole meanings.

Baudelaire describes an age in which the faculties have been so dulled that man no longer finds it easy to discriminate between good and evil. There is a point where they appear utterly confused. This in itself casts light on the curious confusions of Dmitri Karamazov's character, his associations with both Zosima and Svidrigailov. The relevance of this aspect of Baudelaire's analysis to Dostoevsky is confirmed by the Russian's own treatment of the theme of the ambiguity of beauty. The relationship between spirituality, beauty and intensity, the enigma of beauty and man's inability to resolve it, constitutes perhaps the most important single piece of common ground between Dostoevsky and Baudelaire.

The theme emerges with a particular force in *The Idiot*. Myshkin believes passionately in a spiritual beauty that will save the world.[18] This belief in beauty as the last remaining repository of whole meanings is, indeed, highly characteristic of the age. It accounts for the 'aesthetic' bias of the nineteenth century, for Wagnerism and the various spiritual and artistic movements loosely grouped under the Symbolist banner. It is a belief shared by Flaubert. Although his novels represent the grim and sardonic account of a world in which there are no values left, Flaubert remained passionately committed to a belief in the aesthetic value of language as a source of whole meaning. Like Myshkin, Flaubert believed that beauty might save something of the world.

Myshkin's belief in beauty as a source of spiritual wholeness is shared more or less explicitly by most of Dostoevsky's positive characters – for example, Verkhovensky senior's belief in the Sistine Madonna, in contrast with the vulgar utilitarianism of the socialists. With his assertion that it will save the world Myshkin seeks to turn beauty into an ethic. But unfortunately beauty and goodness are not necessarily one. Dostoevsky, too, sees beauty as specifically ambiguous. Myshkin himself admits this. When the Epanchin ladies ask him to give his opinion of Aglaya he replies:

It is hard to judge beauty: I'm not ready to do so. Beauty is a riddle.[19]

Earlier he had observed, about the portrait of Nastasya Filipovna, that such beauty could turn the world upside down.

Aglaya both admits and mocks her admiration for Myshkin by linking him to Pushkin's Poor Knight, with his devoted Platonism. But Myshkin is only one side of the coin; on the reverse there is Rogozhin. His cult of beauty is no less intense than Myshkin's for its epic sensuality. The theme of the two faces of beauty, Aglaya and Nastasya Filipovna, lies at the centre of *The Idiot*. It is from the duality of beauty that we should derive the *Spaltung* that divided Myshkin and Rogozhin. Neither character alone is able to act as he should; each requires the participation of the other. But it is only through the destruction of beauty, and of sanity, that they are eventually able to come together. The beauty of *The Idiot* is profoundly ambiguous, *eros* or *agape*, and Myshkin finds himself in a hopeless situation torn between two women. Whatever he does one or both must be destroyed. Beauty itself is divided and hence to worship beauty leads not to wholeness but to destruction.

Beauty's ambiguity plays an equally important part in *The Brothers Karamazov*. Essentially, it is used as a comment upon the Karamazov character. This is proposed as supremely representative of the age, in that it is capable of every kind of extreme and excess from ascetic spirituality to the most violent debauchery. Moreover, the point at which the one tendency shades into the other is imperceptible. Dmitri is particularly aware of the congruence between his own personality and the ambiguity of beauty. Indeed his 'confession' to Alyosha is virtually a resumé of *Les Fleurs du Mal*. The cult of intense beauty can bring man to the brink of hell, precisely because beauty can be infernal or divine. Having told Alyosha that he too, as a Karamazov, is potentially exposed to the 'raging storm of sensuality', he links the Karamazov potential for extremism to the theme of the ambiguity of beauty itself:

> Beauty is a frightening, a terrible thing. Frightening because it is indefinite, cannot be defined, because God created nothing but riddles. The two shores meet here, all contradictions co-exist . . . Beauty! What I cannot bear is that a man with the noblest of feelings and great intelligence begins with the ideal of the Madonna, to end with the ideal of Sodom. More frightening still is the type who has the ideal of Sodom in his heart without rejecting the ideal of the Madonna; his heart yearns for it in all sincerity, in all truth, as it did when he was young and innocent . . . Is beauty in Sodom? Believe me, for most people it resides in Sodom . . . It is terrifying that beauty is not only frightening but an enigma. The devil and God fight here – the human heart is their battlefield.[20]

Both Baudelaire and Dostoevsky derive their account of man's susceptibility to the cult of intensity from this view of the enigmatic quality of beauty. Because man lacks the capacity to discriminate he can all too easily cultivate that aspect of beauty that leads not to Zosima but to Svidrigailov. This fundamental inability to discriminate is reflected in the otherwise puzzling ambiguities of Dmitri Karamazov's own character. On yet another level, it reinforces Dostoevsky's own complicity in the intensity cult. At the very heart of his creative conception there lies a certain confusion, an inability to distinguish between good and evil.

Dostoevsky's account of the intensity cult and its point of departure resembles that of Baudelaire. However, he lacks the latter's analytic clarity. He never really grasps the pattern of intensity as a whole. He is unable to describe the formation and development of the addiction, although he is all too aware of its nature. But what he loses in clarity he gains in texture. Baudelaire's work remains something of an abstraction, a psychological allegory. Dostoevsky's account is more concrete, more specific. He tells us how it has come about that 'l'action n'est pas la soeur du rêve' by exploring the new ideologies, where Baudelaire does little more than postulate that premise.

However, Baudelaire succeeds in isolating the intensity syndrome and analysing its nature. It is in the light of that analysis that the essential motivation of Dostoevsky's characters becomes clear. We arrive at an understanding of Dostoevsky through Baudelaire. This is because the former's understanding of the phenomenon is weaker than his intuitive sense of its importance. He fails to provide a coherent analysis; its elements remain scattered through the pages of his work, and at no time do they interlock. They remain embedded in the works as individual aspects of the overall theme. Dostoevsky's inability to bring them together into a single coherent whole accounts, finally, for the shape of his work, for the 'loose baggy monsters' of the novels themselves.

CHAPTER ELEVEN

Intensity and Time

> Il y a des moments de
> l'existence où le temps et l'étendue
> sont plus profonds, et le
> sentiment de l'existence
> immensément augmenté.[1]
> BAUDELAIRE

We suggested that the experience of time passing was a theme which focused the Romantics' rejection of their reality. It was essentially an experience of anguish. Correspondingly, escape into eternity becomes perhaps the supreme aspiration of Romanticism. Thus, it was a sense of its timelessness which reinforced the Romantic view of the value of artistic creation. Through art the Romantics aspired to an atemporal plenitude. The opposition of time to timelessness, itself a version of the opposition of horror at reality and escape from that reality, lies at the centre of Romantic experience.

It is no less important to Baudelaire. In poems such as 'L'Horloge' time becomes the very signature of Baudelairian *ennui*. Paradoxically, it passes both slowly, and with lightning speed. Each moment of *ennui* drags on indefinitely with no promise of release, but at the same time the river of time that sweeps man down to his death rushes on like a mountain torrent. Baudelaire's aspirations to timelessness are less ambitious than those of the Romantics. In writers such as Blake and Novalis there is a very real strain of mysticism, a profound belief in the possibility of achieving eternity. It is a possibility that Baudelaire no longer seems to believe in as such. He appears to feel that complete escape is not possible. This is, of course, a reflection of the increasing pessimism of the age. Instead his poetry celebrates not eternity itself but the super-privileged moment: this constitutes the contradictory notion of a moment of eternity which is short-lived, and hence, finally, within time. Baudelaire believes in the consoling experience of a sense of plenitude, and it is this that constitutes the signature of his idea of happiness. Poems such as 'Recueillement', 'Le Balcon', 'La Chevelure' are all celebrations of that experience. 'La Chambre Double' is another account of the temporary defeat of time – by means of laudanum – but it also describes the moment when the experience of time returns to the poet's consciousness.

141

The super-privileged moment, Baudelaire's ultimate aspiration, is also the ultimate objective of the intensity drive. Intensity aims at producing a moment so super-saturated with experience that the subject loses his self-consciousness in a surge of vertigo. Moments such as these are so intensely lived that the rest of existence appears flat and grey in comparison.

The slip from an aspiration to eternity to an aspiration to the privileged moment illustrates that essential degrading of values which is characteristic of intensity, substituting sensations for values and whole meanings. It is a reflection of that degradation of man's sense of spirituality which both Baudelaire and Dostoevsky see as characteristic of their age. The longing for eternity is reduced to a longing for plenitude of sensation. The aspiring intensity addict is content to oscillate between occasional moments of such plenitude and their opposite, a listless tedium.

Although Baudelaire treats of this oscillation, it is usually for him a relatively gentle process. Despite that Stavrogin-like moment in which Baudelaire, smashing the glazier's wares, opts for a moment of intense pleasure at the cost of eternal damnation, the poet usually savours his moments of plenitude more gently – with *luxe, calme* and *volupté.* His sense of happiness is based on the illusion of being in a state of grace and spiritual good order. The savage alternation between on the one hand violent and intense experience, on the other the desert of reality, is a rhythm that is more characteristic of Rimbaud, the supreme poet and victim of intensity. Witness the sad end of 'Le Bateau Ivre' and *Une saison en enfer*, and the rapturous sense of timelessness of 'L'Eternité'.

Violent oscillation is the base component of Dostoevsky's grammar of human behaviour. Virtually all his characters – with the exception of his 'holy men', Zosima, Makar Dolgoruky, and Sonya Marmeladova, partake of that rhythm. Characters such as Dmitri Karamazov aspire to the 'intensest possible moment'. That this should be, implicitly, the *summum bonum* of Dostoevsky's world, is that world's most telling indictment.

This suggests, as did Baudelaire in 'Le Voyage', that the modern age can offer nothing permanent, nothing to satisfy man's craving for wholeness. All it can propose is a series of isolated sensations, *paradis artificiels* which offer a pseudo-eternity.

The sense of disillusion at the impossibility of achieving a true plenitude, a genuine and lasting satisfaction within the world, is central to the experience of the age of intensity. Its importance is confirmed by the fact that it is this that forms the backbone of the last great novel to reflect this culture-pattern – *A la recherche du temps perdu.* Proust's novel describes the central character's growing awareness of disillusion in the face of the series of disappointments that negate the promises held out to him in his youth. It is the sense of a slow but ineluctable decline that forms Marcel's experience. He eventually acknowledges that his world will never yield that fullness of meaning which he had hoped to find. Proust's answer itself partakes of intensity's celebration of the super-saturated moment. By dint of Bergsonian pseudo-science he tries to manufacture wholeness of meaning out of memory. Marcel attempts to bring the isolated experience of certain supremely privileged moments of plenitude into a synthesis. He uses them to re-create that sense of wholeness, unity and meaning to which he aspires. But the only wholeness achieved is the purely aesthetic wholeness of a work of art. Ironically, the extraordinary significance which he is impelled to confer upon essentially trivial and discrete moments of experience provides the proof that Marcel is in a world in which whole meaning is not possible.

It is arguable that Proust is not conscious of this eventual inadequacy, although it may be said to be reflected in that irony which sets the tone of his novel. Needless to say, Dostoevsky's awareness falls well short of that of Proust. Again we find in him an instinctive intuition which senses the importance of the experience of concentrated time, but leaves it embedded in fictional situations without clarifying its significance on the conceptual level. The novelist simply isolates the privileged moment as the most important element of his characters' patterns of experience. It also constitutes the most important element in his own handling of fictional time.

Dostoevsky neither relates this theme to the intensity drive as such, nor does he surround it with any kind of semantic frame. We again encounter that peculiar lack of awareness and self-consciousness which distinguishes Dostoevsky from contemporaries such as Flaubert, Baudelaire or Henry James. There is a reason for this, one which can only be brought out in the course of the rest of this book, but which is introduced by his handling of the theme of concentrated time.

His treatment of all aspects of the intensity drive is the treatment of a reformed addict. His insight into the mentality of gamblers, perverts and alcoholics has about it a certain complicity. Dostoevsky, who tended to thrive on threatening deadlines and quasi-induced financial crises, was himself a victim of the craving for intensity. This is why his novels, which offer a critique of the intensity experience, are written in a language of sensationalism and melodrama, a language of aesthetic intensity. Dostoevsky's understanding of the psychic sickness of his age was won at the expense of his own health.

The degree of his personal involvement emerges in his handling of the theme of the privileged moment. *The Idiot* makes use of two aspects of his own experience, surely the two most important in a lifetime that was quite eventful enough. They were moments of an ecstasy so sweet that they possessed a power and an intensity utterly absent from everyday life. Both as an epileptic and as a political prisoner who had faced a firing squad, Dostoevsky was indelibly marked by his own experience of the super-saturated moment. It was this that gave him the insight and understanding which enabled him to recreate the experience of intensity and its opposite, this also which made him a compulsive gambler and the literary master of the cliff-hanger.

It was epilepsy that ensured that Myshkin, just as much as Rogozhin, was under the sign of intensity. His experience of ecstasy is quietistic rather than violent. It is the experience of Baudelairian *recueillement* in which the world appears that place of harmony, order and synthesis which, in reality, it is not:

> Meanwhile, he began to reflect that in his epileptic condition there was a phase, just before the actual fit . . . when suddenly, in the midst of all the misery, the dark night of the spirit, the depression, his brain would sometimes flare up and all his life-force would suddenly take on an unaccustomed energy. His sense of being alive, his self-awareness, would increase nearly ten-fold in the lightning flashes that were such moments. His intelligence, his feelings would light up with a rare light; all his worries, his doubts would be resolved into a kind of higher serenity, full of clear, harmonious joy and hope, filled with reason and final cause. But these moments, these flashes were merely the anticipation of that final second (sometimes no more than a second) which began the actual fit. Thinking back upon these moments, when he was well again, he often told himself that these flashes and glimpses of a higher self-awareness and self-knowledge, and hence a 'higher existence' were no more than a sickness, the disruption of a normal state, and hence not a higher existence at all, but, on the contrary, part of the lowest level conceivable. Yet he had finally reached the highly paradoxical conclusion: 'What does it matter if it is a sickness? . . . What does it matter if it is an abnormal stress, if the actual result, the moment of awareness, when 'recollected in tranquillity' [*lit.* remembered and examined in health] appears to the highest degree harmonious and beautiful, gives an unheard of, undreamt of, sense of plenitude, measure, serenity and an ecstatic prayerful oneness with the highest synthesis of life? . . . If in that very second, the final conscious moment before the fit, he would have time clearly and consciously to say to himself, 'Yes, for such a moment it is worth giving up one's life,' then of course the moment really was worth his life-time.[2]

Dostoevsky makes it clear that what Myshkin experiences is an illusion of whole meaning. It is of the utmost significance that he not only feels a higher and nobler degree of self-awareness, he also feels cosmic harmony, a 'higher existence'. The world ceases to appear absurd, and becomes a place of meaning and, in Dostoevsky's words, of 'final cause'. In fact, Myshkin's experience is strikingly similar to the Baudelairian experience of whole meaning in *Correspondances*. In each case the world is re-experienced in terms of unity and synthesis. It becomes meaningful, part of a higher order. But it is important to understand that this is an essentially nineteenth-century experience of pseudo-mystic ecstasy and oneness, a kind of *paradis artificiel*, the consequence of mental aberration, and partakes of the fundamental ambiguity of beauty. As such it is totally characteristic of mid and late nineteenth-century experience of spirituality. The culture of that age presents mystic ecstasy as something that is yearned for and dreamt of, but which cannot be experienced as such. Nothing happened on the road to Damascus in the age of cast-iron. However, De Quincey, Baudelaire, Rimbaud all treat of the state of pseudo-ecstasy, the surrogate which is artificially induced. Baudelaire's account of taking hashish both describes and condemns what he refers to as the attempt to 'atteindre le paradis par la pharmacie'. That modern man had to resort to drugs to achieve a condition of pseudo-ecstasy was itself a telling sign of the times. It reflects the attitude of the poet-hero of *Les Fleurs du Mal* who ignores the moral ambiguity of the sensation of ecstasy, and is prepared to accept any kind of experience that produces the desired effect.

In the passage quoted Myshkin comes perilously close to settling for a *paradis artificiel;* although he distinguishes his experience from the 'visions' procured by stimulants, his reason for so doing – namely, that he could recollect the experience in tranquillity – is unconvincing: witness Baudelaire's own reconstructions of his 'pipe-dreams'. At the very least his view of his experience is full of that irony which Lukács has suggested is central to the experience caught by the nineteenth-century novel. The passage suggests that this beatific vision of harmony and synthesis can only be experienced by a half-witted epileptic who knows it to be an aberration of his disease. Myshkin affiliates himself, almost, with the pack of Gadarene swine who will run over the cliff in their gallop after intensity. For he is tempted to disregard the illusory nature of his experience. By deciding that ecstasy is a legitimate experience *per se*, one which does not require the authentication of a truth test, Myshkin aligns himself with a paradigm of Dostoevskian characters that reaches down to Svidrigailov. He faces, then dodges, the problem that was to break Rimbaud. *Une saison en enfer* reflects the poet's despair at his discovery that the magic worlds which he believed himself to have created through poetry and auto-induced hallucination were illusions, mere literature, nothing but a set of words. Artificiality had invalidated the paradise, and the drunken boat was sober again.

Dostoevsky's other experience of the super-privileged moment, the firing squad, was also an artificial stimulus; artificial both in the sense that it was the product of external circumstance, and, much more important of course, in that the whole episode was an elaborate charade. It is not a far cry from this to the setting up of one's own charade – for example the erotic psycho-dramas of Genet's brothel in *Le Balcon*. After all, the pomp and ceremony of the masochist's paraphernalia merely serve to whip up a state of induced intensity designed to re-enact an initial experience of real cruelty. It was not a great distance from Nicholas's firing-squad to the moral masochism of Dostoevsky and his characters.

Be that as it may, the story of the appalling experience of the last minutes of one's life is again told by Myshkin, who 'heard it from a friend'. The five minutes that remained before the execution were lived with an intolerable degree of intensity:

> those five minutes seemed an eternity, riches beyond belief; he felt that he would live so much life in the course of those five minutes, that it was as yet pointless to think about the final moment . . .[3]

Literally the whole of his life was concentrated into this brief span; more important, he believed that were he to survive, every moment thereafter would be savoured as an eternity. That is to say that *he expected to continue to live with the degree of intensity which he had just experienced*. But, of course, one does nothing of the sort. Once the external stimulus is removed, one reverts to normal. Unfortunately, the memory of that level of existence, a level infinitely stronger, richer, more real than everyday reality, remains as something never to be forgotten. The result is that normal reality comes to appear intolerably flat. The moment of heightened experience is looked back to with intense nostalgia, and its victim risks being driven to recreate its feeling-tone as best he can.

It is this quality of experience larger than life which is captured in moments of concentrated time. It is at these moments that Dostoevsky's characters perform their decisive actions; and because of their author's complicity in their addiction, it is then that they are most completely themselves. One such moment is the court-room scene in *The Brothers Karamazov* in which Katerina Ivanovna, going against all her professed intentions, produces the letter which completes the case against Dmitri Karamazov:

> Of course you can only speak and confess like that once in your life, before death for example, mounting the scaffold. But Katya was her supreme self, her supreme moment come. It was the same

impulsive Katya who had once rushed to the young rake in order to save her father; the same Katya who recently, in front of these people, proudly and chastely, sacrificed herself and her maiden's modesty, as she told of 'Mitya's honourable gesture', in order to mitigate his lot if only by a little. And now she sacrificed herself again, but for another, and it may be that it was only now, only in that moment, that she first felt and understood how precious the other man was to her.[4]

By mentioning the scaffold Dostoevsky places the episode quite specifically in the paradigm of supremely privileged moments. Characteristically, it is through the intensity of her experience that Katerina Ivanovna comes to understand the direction of her own feelings. One lives and feels more fully at such times: intensification heightens self-awareness.

Because Dostoevsky's characters more or less all function through intensity, and the privileged moment is intensity's distinctive feature, they are exceptionally prone to moments of ecstasy that clarify their entire existence. Not only does this reflect the author's own Myshkin-like moments of intense clarity, it also reflects the creative process working itself out in him. Dostoevsky used to proceed by a series of intuitive leaps, as he gained more and more insight into characters and situations which gradually fell into place for him. *The Adolescent* features one such moment, as the hero spends a night in the cells:

> I won't begin to describe my emotions; . . . but I'll say one thing: I may never have experienced such joyous moments as those, in the dead of night on a plank-bed in the cells . . . It was one of those moments which may well happen to all of us, but only once or twice in a lifetime. At such a time you decide your future, divine your values, and say to yourself once and for all, 'That is where the truth lies, and that is how to reach it.' Yes, these moments were the light of my soul.[5]

However, the privileged moment more usually takes the form of an intense concentration of excitement that is regularly described as being worth the price of a lifetime. Dostoevsky echoes Baudelaire here. When Katerina Ivanovna comes to him for money, Dmitri Karamazov is terribly tempted to smash her with the most vulgar rebuff:

> You see, I'd have lost everything, she'd have run away, but it would have been 'diabolical', spiteful, well worth everything. I'd have writhed in remorse for the rest of my life, but oh! the pleasure of doing it.[6]

Dmitri has not yet reached the stage at which remorse is itself a pleasure, he is less far gone than Baudelaire – or Marmeladov. But he is ready to sacrifice everything in return for a moment's sensation: witness the moment when Grushenka decides to get drunk and dance, the moment he knows he has her:

> Mitya followed her like a drunk. 'Let it all happen – I'll give the world for this moment.'[7]

We suggested that the need for intensified experience, a need shared by Dostoevsky himself, is reflected in the aesthetics of his fiction. Such is his sense of melodrama that moments of intensified experience play a vital part in his works. No other novelist of his stature, not even Balzac, makes a more frequent or more successful use of the most vulgar devices of melodrama.

One of Dostoevsky's favourite tense situations, in every way characteristic of his kind of fiction, is notably rich in intensified excitement, more particularly in intensity derived from a very particular kind of embarrassment. Like Hitchcock, Dostoevsky often makes embarrassment and murder go together. There comes a moment when the prospective killer must declare himself; the moment when both victim and murderer know what is going to happen, and the murderer knows that the victim knows. The situation is, to say the least, embarrassing. In *The Landlady* the narrator decides to kill Murin, an evil old man who has a *jeune fille fatale* in his thrall. He approaches with a knife in his hand. Just as he is about to insert it he realises that the old man is looking at him, laughing, and the knife falls from his hand. Raskolnikov is similarly embarrassed. He catches Lizaveta's eye just before he sinks his axe into her skull. In another version of the situation in *The Eternal Husband*, Velchaninov finds Trussotsky bending over him in the dark with an open razor in his hand. A desperate struggle takes place, but it takes place in silence. The protagonists are too embarrassed to make a sound; to talk to each other, to acknowledge verbally what was happening, would be an intolerably embarrassing recognition of the reality of their encounter. As it is, the fight comes to an end when the would-be assassin asks his host for a glass of water. The next morning he leaves the flat in such a way that they can both pretend that the events of the night had never happened.

Perhaps Dostoevsky's supreme exploitation of this situation as a source of concentrated experience which adds the intensity to be derived from embarrassment to the intensity derived from the prospect of imminent execution is to be found in *The Gentle One*. The narrator, the pawnbroker husband, is lying in bed one night when he suddenly senses his wife standing over him with a revolver. He catches her eye, feels the muzzle pressed against his temple and . . . closes his eyes again as if to go back to sleep. He hopes that his behaviour will signify such moral strength that his wife will not dare to pull the trigger. As

Dostoevsky makes his character lie back feigning sleep and indifference, he is, in essence, reworking the death-sentence situation yet again:

> Yes, it is improbable, I know. But she might guess the truth – that too flashed through my head in the self-same moment. What a whirlwind of thoughts and feelings swept through my head in less than a flash . . . If she were to guess the truth and know that I was awake, then I'd already smashed her with my willingness to accept death, and her hand might lose its steadiness . . . They say that standing on a high place you feel drawn down to the chasm below. I believe many suicides and murders happen because the revolver has already been grasped. Here, too, there was a chasm, a 45 degree slope which you could not help sliding down, which called on you to pull the trigger. But the knowledge that I had seen it all, knew it all and was silently waiting to die at her hand – that might stop her sliding.[8]

The pawnbroker's mental activity is vastly intensified by his sense of tottering on the brink. The key expression signifying such intensification is 'whirlwind'. Dostoevsky uses the word elsewhere – in *The Gambler*, for example, to render that feeling of vertigo which lies at the heart of the experience of intensity.

It is a short step from such moments to an extended notion of concentrated time, a concentration lasting not for a moment, but for hours, days or even weeks. One of Dostoevsky's principal means of stepping up the action of a novel, increasing its pace, is by describing a day or days that are essentially overfilled with event. They become 'super-saturated solutions', a means of packing the action into an inordinately short span. Indeed, Dostoevsky's novels actually lose verisimilitude by the excessive deference they pay to the notion of unity of time. In their intensifying treatment of time, the novels themselves become the embodiment of the concentrated moment. Thus the author regularly reminds his readers that the complex set of events forming his narrative occurred within the shortest time-span. The hero of *The Gambler* writes:

> Perhaps I will stop spinning, if I give, for my own benefit, the clearest possible account of everything that happened in that month.[9]

The major novels are equally dotted with remarkable periods, days in which everything comes to a head and all the characters' fates are decided. Thus the narrator of *The Devils* describes a certain day as:

> . . . one of the most remarkable days in my chronicle. It was a day of surprises, a day of old and new dénouements, of violent explanations and even greater confusion.[10]

149

Another action-packed day occurs in *The Brothers Karamazov*. It is the day of Zosima's death. Alyosha 'looked back on that day as one of the saddest and most fateful days of his life.'[11] We find the same notion of a short span into which much action is crammed transposed onto a different time-scale when Shatov slaps Stavrogin:

> The whole scene took no longer than ten seconds. But all the same in those ten seconds a great deal happened.[12]

What Beaumarchais termed 'la folle journée' is a device that is central to Dostoevsky's narrative strategies. Its importance is a reflection of the importance of the intensity drive itself; showing the extent to which the author's creative vision is penetrated by it. It is interesting to compare the structural rôle of the privileged or concentrated moment in Dostoevsky with its equivalent in Baudelaire. Although many of his poems are specifically about the privileged moment, the latter plays an even more important part in the actual construction of *Les Fleurs du Mal*. In that work each individual poem is, itself, a privileged moment. Each poem imposes its own mood as an absolute condition. That is to say, that at no stage in the course of the work, until the final poem 'Le Voyage', does the protagonist display any awareness of the fact that the particular condition or state of mind captured by any given poem is impermanent. He is never able to compare what he feels with what he felt, or understand that whatever he may feel, he will not be feeling it for long. Each poem is experienced as a moment of eternity, an enduring condition, a moment freed of the passage of time, for better or worse. *Les Fleurs du Mal* consists of a string of such moments, each one entirely self-sufficient. It is not until the final poem that the protagonist has acquired a sufficient degree of consciousness to look back, compare the various elements of his past experience and make of them an attitude with which he will look to the future. This is the respect in which 'Le Voyage' differs from every other poem in the book with the exception of the first, 'Au Lecteur'. The sense of overwhelming permanence with which the mood of each individual poem imposes itself is a reflection of the notion of the super-privileged moment, a notion that creates the structural backbone of *Les Fleurs du Mal*.

Baudelaire's work differs from Dostoevsky's in that, although it comes close to the form of a novel, it remains founded in lyricism. It is the supreme characteristic of lyric poetry that the poem constitutes an act of immediate intuitive apprehension, synthetic rather than analytic. This quality is reflected in the all-embracing immediacy of Baudelaire's individual poems, the book becoming a string of privileged lyric moments. As a novelist, Dostoevsky can do nothing of the sort. Time is the stuff that the novel of the nineteenth century is made of. Dostoevsky is obliged, for all his obsession with the privileged moment, to place such moments within a temporal context. He can speed time up into the action-packed day, the five minutes before an execution, but the nature of his medium is such that he can never escape time itself.

The nearest that Dostoevskian characters come to escape from time is the *paradis artificiel*, the illusion of that escape, relieving monotony through moments of white hot intensity. However, they do, specifically, long for the actual abolition of time. Ippolit asks Myshkin if he recalls the passage from the *Apocalypse* in which the angel announces that 'There shall be no more time'.[13] Kirillov refers to the same passage. He professes a belief in intense moments that can be tantamount to an eternity – the theme of the degraded substitute – and continues:

'I do not believe in a future eternal life, but in eternity on this earth. There are minutes, you attain minutes, in which time suddenly stands still and becomes eternal . . .'
'*It's scarcely possible in our age*' answered Stavrogin, without any irony, slowly and thoughtfully, 'In the *Apocalypse* the angel swears that there shall be no more time.' 'I know. It's very true, clear and true. When the whole man attains happiness there shall be no more time, because it will not be needed.[14]

Kirillov advances the possibility of attaining a full sense of plenitude in this world: the plenitude of the whole man, and hence of whole meanings. Kirillov's aspiration is similar to that of the Romantics, particularly Novalis. Like the Romantics he associates plenitude with timelessness, confirming our assertion that time was seen as the signature of incomplete existence. However, Stavrogin qualifies Kirillov's aspiration by pointing out that they live in an age in which such ambitions can never be realised, since action is not sister to the dream. Just as Stavrogin's brand of intensity and metaphysical spite compared unfavourably with the mood of the Decembrists, and even Lermontov, so escape from time was not possible in the age of the Third Horseman and the star Wormwood. It was precisely because modern man was unable to achieve such plenitude unaided that he settled for the *paradis artificiel* of intensity, or sought in Baudelaire's terms to try to reach paradise through *la pharmacie*.

It is to the abolition of time that the supercharged moment aspires, but the only thing such a moment can achieve is the illusion of abolition. True timelessness lies beyond its grasp. This is why the cult of intensity is doomed. Baudelaire describes the destruction of a poet-hero who sets out in pursuit of whole meanings, is deluded by the essential ambiguity of beauty into settling for intensity instead, with fatal consequences. Baudelaire describes his fate as that of an 'âme sensible qui s'est trompée de route'. In Dostoevsky's world also, those who aspire to plenitude through intensity are doomed. The two characters who discussed the possibility of achieving timelessness in the passage quoted above, Stavrogin and Kirillov, both die by their own hand. The other character who referred to the abolition of time, the consumptive Ippolit, tries to bring his own death forward, but his failure to commit suicide is no more than a stay of execution.

Once again we find that Dostoevsky's intuition has reached further than his conceptual awareness. It was suggested that the intensity of experience that was enjoyed under sentence of death might lead to the self-induced intensity of masochistic psycho-drama. Dostoevsky's intuition senses that there is a link between the longing for timelessness, a longing worked out through intensity, and suicide, which is perhaps the greatest of all sources of self-induced intensity. Thus the steadily increasing suicide rate, which we saw Dostoevsky describe as a sign of the moral bankruptcy of the age, is also a sign of the intensity addiction itself. The last poem of *Les Fleurs du Mal* ends with the poet welcoming death, setting off gladly:

Au fond de l'Inconnu pour trouver du *nouveau*![15]

In the same way, Dostoevskian intensity ends with the trip to death as the final thrill. Cultivation of intensity in the self must lead inevitably to that self's destruction.

CHAPTER TWELVE

Modes of Intensity: Gambling

Baudelaire properly devotes one of his 'Tableaux Parisiens' to gambling, for gambling institutionalises the cult of intensity. The casino represents the official acknowledgment of society's craving for excitement. Baudelaire's poem, 'Le Jeu', describes the poet-hero envying the gamblers' capacity to feel such excitement:

> Et mon coeur s'effraya d'envier maint pauvre homme
> Courant avec ferveur à l'abîme béant,
> Et qui, soûl de son sang, préférait en somme
> La douleur à la mort et l'enfer au néant![1]

Gambling is one of the purest expressions of the need for intensity at all costs. The compulsive gambler, like other victims of the cult, is an obsessive. He is the sort that bookmakers refer to as a 'mug-punter': the sort who never wins, who appears to be in the game in order to make money for the house. Indeed, his motive is purer than the mere pursuit of profit. The experience of gambling, win or lose, is its own reward; it is an experience which he is prepared to pay for.

Gambling, which in the eighteenth century had been an essentially aristocratic pursuit, had been popularised by the Napoleonic armies and, by the middle of the nineteenth century, was very much a middle-class activity.[2] Dostoevsky, Baudelaire, and Balzac before them had come to regard it as the very image of the dissipated energies of contemporary man. Ludwig Borne describes it as follows:

> If one were to collect up all the forces and passion . . . which Europe dissipates annually at the tables, they would suffice to build a Roman people and a Roman history. But that's just it. Because every man is born a Roman, bourgeois society seeks to de-romanise him, hence our games of chance . . .[3]

Gambling is an excellent medium for the pursuit of intensity, because, as an activity without content, without an end-product, it can offer an unlimited and essentially meaningless excitement. The gambler has nothing to show for his activity, he neither acquires nor creates anything, for the house always wins in the end. However, he enjoys a considerable immediate return in instant excitement. Gambling is such a rich source of intensity because it functions entirely through the super-charged moment. The compulsive gambler plays in a kind of eternal present. He loses all sense of past or future: each race, each spin, each deal are completely absorbing. So self-sufficient, so independent of context are they that the gambler remains in a condition of vastly intensified reality that lasts as long as his money. While he plays the world has all the extra vitality, all the excitement and the colour that it takes on for any addict. Walter Benjamin recognises that gambling is a narcotic like any other because 'it invalidates the standards of experience'. He continues:

> The narcotic effect that is involved here is specified as to time, like the malady it is supposed to alleviate. Time is the material into which the phantasmagoria of gambling has been woven.[4]

He goes on to quote a gambler who asserts that his mania is the 'noblest of all passions'. This is precisely because he is not interested in making money.

> 'If you think I see only profit in the gold that falls to my share you are mistaken. I see in it the pleasures that it gets me, . . . They come too quickly to make me weary, and there are too many for me to get bored. I live a hundred lives in one.'[5]

Benjamin emphasises the all important point that gambling, like other forms of intensity, represents an escape from time. It also concentrates experience, packs a lifetime into a single spin of the wheel. It is precisely this sense of the super-saturated experience which is the definitive characteristic of the intensity cult.

We have described gambling as a *mode* of intensity. This is because there can be no such thing as the naked experience of intensity as such. It must always be experienced through something, it requires a medium, one which the addict can believe in. That is to say that ideally he must be able to persuade himself that he cultivates his particular version of the vice for the sake of the medium, not just for the essentially abstract excitement which it provides. Like rhetoric, intensity is at its most effective when one is not entirely aware that it is working on one, when it makes its impression just below the threshold of consciousness. This is why the best kind of sexual psycho-drama leaves the protagonist unaware of the artificiality of the set-up.

Gambling is such an effective medium for intensity because whereas, on the one hand, it is virtually an activity without content, the gambler is able to delude himself into believing that he does not play for the excitement, he plays to get rich.

Dostoevsky's own addiction to gambling is the perfect illustration of his involvement in the intensity cult. *The Gambler,* which is such a penetrating analysis of the punter mentality, derives its authority from the author's status as an addict. He composed the book in the wake of one of his disastrous tours of the casinos of Europe. Consequently, he displays tremendous insight, tremendous sympathy with the phenomenon which he is also criticising. Not until William Burroughs will we find such an understanding analysis of addiction.

Dostoevsky is very aware that this particular version of the intensity cult, though interesting enough in itself, also has a wider significance. It is a characteristic mode of experience, the experience of modern man in search of shallow sensation: Borne's dissipation of energy. Dostoevsky was not just trying to portray the archetypal punter, he also wished to depict a certain type of personality:

> . . . the work reflects in general the current state of our inner life . . . I take a genuine sort, but one who is broadly developed yet incomplete in every respect, having lost his faith and not daring not to believe, rebelling against authority and fearing it . . . The main thing is that all his life-force, his strength, his violence, his courage are devoted to roulette. He is a gambler, and no ordinary one, as Pushkin's Miserly Knight is no ordinary miser. He is a kind of poet, but the point is that he is himself ashamed of this poetry, since he is deeply aware that it is vile, although he is ennobled in his own eyes by his need to take risks.[6]

This is a fascinating analysis of a character who cultivates intensity. It stresses his shallow, rootless quality, his lack of a sense of values which might support him, and his reluctance to acknowledge his own sense of nihilism. The account is strikingly close to Baudelaire's analysis of the vacillating religiosity of his poet-hero. Dostoevsky also brings out the fact that his intensity addict is essentially disinterested. He is not driven by greed but, like Pushkin's character, by a purer motive, by a thirst for sheer excitement. That is what is meant by his 'vile poetry'. The passage also brings out another characteristic of the addict, his sense of heroism. Baudelaire admires the dandyism of his characters – 'Don Juan aux Enfers', or 'Delphine and Hippolyte', the *lamentables victimes*. Here, Dostoevsky has caught the gambler's admiration of his capacity for reckless waste, which, finally, resembles the drug addict's admiration for his own capacity for self-destruction. Moreover, like Baudelaire's hero, the gambler retains an awareness of his predicament, *la conscience dans le mal*, which is itself a source of intensity. Addiction is not allowed to obliterate the consciousness, for this would deny him the stimulus of remorse. He is both proud and ashamed of his vile poetry, of the wasteful dissipation of his energies.

There is something in this combination of pride and shame in Dostoevsky himself. He was, for a time, totally addicted to roulette, and there is, indeed, something heroic about the sheer scale of his loss of self-control.

His letters abound in hair-raising tales of a gambler's self-delusion. On one occasion, he writes,[7] from a casino town, to the bride he has left behind, informing her that although he misses her terribly, he is, alas, obliged to play roulette. Subsequent letters are a self-indulgent chronicle of disaster. Time and again he thanks her for the sums of money she has managed to raise. Unfortunately, he lost it all within the day, so could she try touching so-and-so for another loan.

He seems, seriously, to have been able to believe that roulette would make him rich. He looked to gambling for a solution to his financial difficulties. This in itself testifies to the scale of his self-delusion. In all his correspondence the word 'odds' never features once, there is no suggestion that they might be against the gambler. His attitude to the game is purely psychological, there is no hint of mathematical calculation. He maintains that a gambler cannot lose if he keeps his self-control; it is just that he always loses his.

For Dostoevsky gambling was essentially a struggle between the old and the new brain. If he was to win, the new brain must remain in control, but inevitably intensity would take priority over winning. The old brain would come surging through and Dostoevsky, throwing caution to the winds, would wallow and exult in a manic plunge that would wipe him out in both spirit and pocket. The essential Dostoevsky comes out in the following gambler's chronicle:

I got your letter yesterday, and was both terribly gladdened and quite horrified by it. What is the matter with you, Anya, what kind of a state are you in? Crying, unable to sleep, torturing yourself. What do you suppose I felt reading your letter? All this after five days, and what are you like by now? My dearest, my priceless angel, my treasure, I'm not reproaching you; on the contrary, you are dearer, more priceless to me feeling as you do. I know you can't help it, if you really are unable to bear my absence and are so over-concerned about me (I repeat I don't blame you, that I love you twice as much for it if possible, and that I really do understand); but at the same time, my love, admit that I must have been mad to come here without having sorted out your feelings, work it out for yourself, my dear: in the first place my missing you so much is seriously stopping me from coping successfully with this wretched gambling and coming back to you, so that I feel depressed; secondly, how am I to remain here knowing you feel as you do! Forgive me, angel, but I'm going to go into a few details about my enterprise, about this gambling business, so that you'll understand what it's all about.

Some twenty times, approaching the tables, experience has shown that if you play in cold-blood, *calmly* and using your head, *there is no possibility of losing!* I promise you, not even a possibility. It's blind chance on their side, but I have calculation, so it follows that chance is on my side. But what usually happens? I tend to begin with 40 gulden, took them out of my pocket, sat down and staked one or two at a time. Within quarter of an hour, usually (always) I'd won twice that amount. That was the moment to stop and leave, at least until the evening, to rest my over-excited nerves (I observed that I could remain calm and cold-blooded for *no more than half an hour at a stretch*). But I would just go out and smoke a cigarette and would immediately run back to the game. Why did I do so, knowing that I would certainly weaken, *i.e.* lose? Because, every day, getting up, I would decide that this was my last day in Homburg, that I would leave the next day, so that I couldn't play the waiting game. I was in a hurry, quickly, with all my might, to win as much as possible, all at once in a single day . . . I lost my detachment, my nerves grew irritated, I started taking risks, lost my temper and started to bet without thinking, lost and got cleaned out (because anyone who plays without thinking, haphazardly, is a lunatic . . . After I posted the letters asking you to send the money, I went to the casino; all I had left was 20 gulden (for emergencies) and I risked 10 gulden's worth. I employed virtually superhuman efforts to stay calm and collected *for a whole hour*, and I ended by winning 30 Friedrichsdore, *i.e.* 300 gulden. I was so happy and so utterly overcome by the wish to get it all over that day, double my winnings once more and leave, that I didn't give myself a moment to rest and regain my self-possession. I rushed off to the roulette table, began to bet with gold, and lost the lot, all of it, down to the last penny. All I had left was two gulden's tobacco money. My dear Anya, my love, you must understand that I have debts which I have to meet, or they'll call me a scoundrel . . . I had to win. *I had to!*

I do not gamble for fun. You realise that it was the only way out, and now I've lost it all through stupidity. I don't blame you, I curse myself; why did I not take you with me. Playing for modest stakes, daily, you can't *fail* to win; it is true, true, I've proved it twenty times, and here I am, knowing it as I do, leaving Homburg out of pocket; and I know that if I were to accord myself a limit of even four more days, I'd get it all back. But it's finished, I won't gamble any more.

Dear Anya, please, (I beg you again) understand that I'm not blaming you; no, I blame myself for not taking you with me.

NB. If by chance last night's letter goes astray, I resume its contents: I asked you to send me, *at once* twenty Imperials, by banker's transfer . . . I asked you to be quick as possible and send them by return. [8]

All Dostoevsky the addict is here. So oblivious is he to everything but gambling that he practises the most monstrous emotional blackmail. Anya must not feel guilty at worrying about him; she is not altogether to blame for his losses. Moreover, he has the addict's belief that he cannot lose, the punter's touching faith in his ability to recoup, to 'get himself out', if only he could stay on.

He presents gambling as a direct conflict between the old and the new brain; between calculation and the sheer ecstasy of plunging. There comes a moment, which every gambler knows and should fear, when a run of bad luck lasts so long that the gambler is terribly tempted to abandon the hopeless business of trying to win, and, instead, to align himself with the run of the game by seeing just how much he can lose. This is a moment of masochistic intensity when the old brain takes complete command. The gambler has come to feel that he can do nothing right, and is driven to plunge, to bet like a lunatic, in the attempt to try and lose as much as possible, if only to prove that he can still succeed at something.

This is the mood that drives Dostoevsky to stake gold by the handful. No longer driven by the prudent need to pay off his debts, he sucks in heady drafts of intensity, and keeps tossing his money onto the table until there is nothing left.

This kind of experience is its own reward. Dostoevsky's characters are prone to exult in the sheer extremity of their despair. In *Crime and Punishment* the hopeless drunk Marmeladov wallows in the joy he derives from utter hopelessness, from having literally nowhere to go. He is intoxicated by despair as he is by alcohol.

Dostoevsky's understanding of his age as a time of dreadful psychic disfigurement begins in his recognition of the sweetness of this kind of intoxication. It is a sweetness that he had learnt at first hand, in the gambler's experience of being cleaned out. His letters frequently describe situations in which he finds himself staking his last coin. Indeed it is almost as if the chief purpose of foreign travel, for him, was to provoke crises: situations in which he found himself down to his last rouble and a thousand miles from home. The following lines might have been penned by another unlucky gambler, Gogol's Khlestakov, as he sat, starving in the inn, before being mistaken for an inspector general:

Meanwhile my situation had deteriorated beyond belief. No sooner had you left than, early the next morning, the hotel informed me that they had orders not to serve me lunch, tea or coffee. I went to explain and the fat German proprietor told me that I hadn't 'earned' lunch, and that he would only allow tea to be sent up. So from yesterday I have no meals, I live off tea, and the tea is disgusting . . .

they don't clean my clothes or my shoes, they don't come when I call, and the servants treat me with indescribable German scorn. The German knows no greater crime than being broke and failing to pay on time. It would all be funny, but it's all very awkward. So if Herzen does not send me anything I expect considerable unpleasantness: I mean they might impound my things and turn me out, or worse. It's sickening.[9]

Dostoevsky was not sickened; he revelled in it. The gambler loves to take the ultimate risk: witness the hero of his story. Usually under the exclusive influence of the old brain, as he makes his final stake he enjoys the additional luxury of a moment's lucidity. As one grasps the note of hysteria running through the following lines, one comes to understand how their author used to lose every penny, far from home, with such regularity:

I was as if in a fever, and pushed the whole pile of money onto red – and suddenly, I came to! And for the one and only time in the whole session, fear sent a cold shiver through my limbs. Aghast I sensed and realised for a second what it would mean if I lost. My whole life was at stake![10]

The gambler comes to admit to the pleasure he derives from taking such a risk. Although the author makes it clear that these are the words of a pathetic addict who had no life away from the tables, he displays an understanding of the situation which suggests that he had learnt about addiction the hard way:

Really there is something unique in the feeling, when you are alone, in foreign parts, far from your homeland and your friends, not knowing what you will eat to-day, and you stake your last coin, the very very last![11]

The gambler thrives on risk; the higher the stakes the bigger the thrill. Unfortunately, like other modes of intensity, gambling is subject to the law of diminishing returns. The gambler can never be satisfied, because he is trying to satisfy an essentially metaphysical longing for a mysterious kind of perfection, by means of sheer sensation. As a result he can never satisfy his longing, only aggravate it. Supply can never meet demand, it can only step it up:

. . . I wanted to amaze the onlookers, by taking a mad risk, and, terrible feeling, I clearly remember that all vanity aside, I was myself overwhelmed by a terrible thirst for risk. It may well be that, undergoing so many sensations, the spirit is not satisfied, but merely irritated by them, and demands more and ever stronger sensations until it is exhausted.[12]

This, the essential moral of *Les Fleurs du Mal*, is the lesson that the Gambler learns.

Dostoevsky's account of gambling goes well beyond the mere establishment of the activity as a mode of intensity. He takes his readers right into the gambler's world, and tries to convey the feeling tone of the gambler's experience.

One of the essential characteristics of the intensity addict is the way in which his vice colours his fantasies. Gambling haunts the imagination of the gambler, even when he is not at the tables. He has gambling day-dreams that are the precise equivalent of the erotic day-dreams of the libertine. Every gambler has elaborate fantasies in which he pulls off the most fantastic series of coups, and 'breaks the bank at Monte Carlo'. Alternatively, an occult power affords him a glimpse of next year's racing results and he designs a multiple bet which takes him hours to work out, and which, for an insignificant stake, will drive the entire bookmaking industry into the bankruptcy courts. It must have been just such a day-dream, turning, in this case, into nightmare, which inspired Pushkin's *Queen of Spades*. In the following passage the hero of *The Adolescent* enjoys such a fantasy:

> All that night I dreamt of roulette, gambling, gold and calculations. I kept trying to work something out, as if at the tables, some kind of bet, some kind of odds, and it weighed on me like a nightmare all night. To be honest, all the day before, I kept recalling my win at Zvershchikov's, I put the thought from my mind, but could not do as much for the feeling, and the memory was enough to set me trembling. That win had hooked me. Was I really a born gambler? I certainly, at the very least, had gambler's characteristics. Even now, as I write this, I like to think about gambling for minutes at a time. I can sometimes spend whole hours, sitting quietly, working out gambling calculations and day-dreaming about the course of play, about betting and collecting my winnings.[13]

Along with his grasp of gamblers' day-dreams, Dostoevsky also understands gamblers' myths. In the following passage he pours scorn on system punters, because, as every addict knows, a system, which is designed to reduce uncertainty, reduces intensity too. But at the same time he has the born gambler's conviction that there is a kind of pattern, a run of the numbers, which one has to sense, rather than deduce; that this is a mathematical impossibility has never shaken any punter's conviction, the punter's motto is *credo quia absurdum est*. The passage reveals another of the gambler's traits: the sheer pleasure he derives from watching the fall of the results, regardless of whether or not he has a bet:

> . . . it struck me that actual calculation meant remarkably little

and certainly did not have the significance which many gamblers attached to it. They sit with bits of paper covered in scribbles, note the *coups*, count, work out odds, calculate, eventually bet and lose, like us mere mortals who play without calculating. However, I came to one conclusion which I believe to be true; in the course of blind chance, there is really, if not a pattern, at least a kind of order – which is of course most peculiar. For example, it can happen that after the middle twelve numbers, you get the twelve high ones; let's say that twice you get the high-range and then the low. After hitting the low-range it goes back to the middle-range for three or four times, and then to the high-range, which comes up twice, then to the low, once, then the middle-range for three in a row, and so it goes on for one and a half or two hours. One, two, three; one, two, three. It's fascinating . . . Some days or mornings for example, it happens that red or black come up more than 22 times in a row, and so it goes on for a whole day sometimes.[14]

We also see the gambler in action, when the intensity is flowing sweetly and the protagonist is quite drunk on it. For example, he describes the moment when the gambler is overtaken by a strange sense of absolute certainty, by the knowledge that on this particular *coup*, however long the odds, he simply cannot lose. At such times one can play the longest shots, be on the most improbable outsiders, draw three cards to complete a flush or straight, and know that you must win. Against all the odds you are certain that your combination will come up, and when it does the effect is overpowering:

> Yes, sometimes the wildest thought, the most apparently improbable thought imposes itself so powerfully that you end up by accepting it as perfectly feasible . . . No, more, if the thought is accompanied by a powerful, passionate desire, you may sometimes accept it as intended by fate, inevitable, pre-ordained, as something which cannot not happen! Perhaps there is something here, some combination of premonitions, some unusual effort of the will, or infection by one's fantasies – I don't know; but that evening (which I shall never forget as long as I live) something magic happened. Although it may be perfectly explained by arithmetic, it still seemed magical to me. And why, why did that confidence instill itself in me so deeply and firmly . . . For I really thought about it, I repeat, not as an odds-on bet (which might not come off) but as a literal certainty.[15]

He goes on to describe the greatest of all sources of gambler's intensity – the feeling that you are riding in on a run of luck. This is not an event; it is a condition, a state of grace in which you can do no wrong. One of the finest descriptions of the sensation is to be found in Norman

Mailer's *The American Dream*. His hero describes an episode during the war in which he stormed a hill single-handed. He knew that no bullet could touch him, just as he knew, as he ran between two machine-gun nests, that the grenades he threw with each hand, blindly, were bound to reach their targets: like the Zen archer who hits the gold without aiming. In this paradisiac condition, in Benjamin's terms, the standards of experience are invalidated. The natural laws that make everyday reality seem grey and narrow have been suspended for the gambler's sole benefit, and he basks in a paradisiac state of ecstasy. As zero comes up for the fifth time in succession, the gambler, who has had the maximum on each time, has won a victory over the laws of chance, over reality itself, to the tune of 37^5 to one. The winning run that defines all odds also defies the values that number and order represent – the values of the actuary and the accountant who know that gamblers never win. It is when he first sees such a run that the hero of *The Gambler* understands that he is an addict. His employer's grandmother, of whom more later, gets her first taste of blood at the tables:

> 'More, more, more, put on more!' yelled grandmother. I no longer argued with her, and, shrugging, staked another 20 Friedrichsdore. The wheel turned for a long time. Grandmother was trembling as she followed it.
>
> 'She can't seriously expect zero to come up again?' I thought, looking at her in astonishment. An overriding belief that she would win radiated from her expression, the unqualified expectation that, at any moment, they would call 'Zero'. The ball came to a halt. 'Zero,' cried the croupier.
>
> 'You see,' grandmother turned to me in wild exultation. I was a gambler! I knew it then. My limbs were trembling, my head reeling. Of course it was unusual for zero to come up three times out of ten, but it wasn't that unusual.[16]

When he starts his own run of luck everything melts into a dream. Gambling completely alters the value of money, and it is the sheer meaninglessness of winning – or losing, as he plays that, more than anything else, creates the mood of dream. The parameters of reality have melted away into timelessness, and the gambler is so much under the influence of the old brain that he plays like an automaton:

> 'Rouge' cried the croupier and I breathed again . . . They paid me in bank notes; I must have won 4000 florins and 80 Friedrichsdore (I was still counting at that stage).
>
> Then, I remember putting 2000 florins on the middle-range. I lost. I put on my gold and the 80 Friedrichsdore, and lost. I went

mad with rage; I snatched up my last 2000 florins and put them all on the low-range, just like that, without thinking! Actually there was a moment's pause, that must have been like Mlle Blanche, her feelings as she fell out of a balloon, in Paris.

'Quatre' cried the croupier. Together with my stake I had 6,000 florins again. I already felt like a winner, I no longer feared anything, anything at all, and tossed 4000 florins onto black. Nine or ten people rushed to follow me. The croupiers started to whisper among themselves. Around me conversation buzzed as they waited.

Black came up. I can no longer recall the size or order of my bets. I only remember that, as if in a dream, I won about 16,000 florins. Suddenly, with three bits of bad luck, I lost 12,000. Then I put the last 4,000 on *passe* (but without feeling a thing; I just waited mechanically without a thought) – and won again; then won four times more in succession. I just remember collecting thousands; I also remember that the middle-range came up most often and I stuck to it. They kept coming up steadily – three or four times in a row, then disappeared once or twice and then came up again three or four more times . . .

I don't think I could have been there more than half an hour. Suddenly the croupier informed me that I had won 30,000 florins and as the bank could no longer guarantee payment on any one turn of the wheel, the tables were closing till the next morning.[17]

He goes on to break another bank, then starts playing *trente et quarante*, where he makes a series of even money bets in the course of which red comes up 14 times in a row. He finally realises that he has won more than 100,000 florins. As he plays he grows less and less aware, less able to cope as the run goes on, until he becomes a kind of zombie, with neither consciousness nor control over his actions. So great has been his dosage of intensity that it has destroyed his capacity for sensation, numbing him into feeling nothing.

Corresponding to this state of all-absorbing present, when one is totally under the influence of the old brain, is the terrible let-down, the *post coitum triste* when the gambling has to stop. Naked reality seems unbearably flat in comparison with the world that the gambler has just left. Moreover, his sense of emptiness is aggravated by the fact that, like the alcoholic or the libertine, the gambler has no memories. The price he has to pay for his paradisiac condition of eternal present is zero recall. Intensity is an emotion that it is impossible to recollect in tranquillity. The abolition of time also means the abolition of recollection. Neither the gambler nor the libertine are able to live on their memories. They are thus chained to a treadmill: since they are unable to recall the quality of their experience, their only recourse is to go back for more. But, in the meantime, the moment of coming-round is extremely painful. There is an unbearable sense of let-down, and of waste, that is tantamount to the characteristically Baudelairian mood of recrimination and impotent remorse. One is left in the cold light of consciousness, quite unable to justify what now appear to be wasted hours, since one is unable to reconstruct their feeling-tone. Because gambling is so much an affair of the old brain, of sensation, it lies beyond conscious memory. Once again, incidentally, we find an echo of Proust here. The whole point of his Bergsonian view of *mémoire involontaire* was that, in our terms, it was able to tap the memory store of the old brain directly, recreate not mere consciousness, but sensation itself, and thereby reach into that area of past experience which Baudelaire has described as being *interdit à nos sondes* – beyond the reach of consciousness.

Although the gambler is overcome by this sense of self-disgust regardless of whether he has won or lost, there is no denying that losing, and *a fortiori* plunging, exacerbates that particular mood of self-recrimination. It has been suggested that the compulsive gambler is a masochist who really likes to lose. Certainly there are times when he can do nothing right, when the gambler does appear to court loss – Baudelaire has shown us that the intensity addict would rather feel anything than feel nothing. But, be that as it may, it is certainly true that the gambler prefers to win. The sense of somewhat heroic pain felt by a gambler as he 'goes down the drain' may provide intensity of a kind, but it is a kind which he would, on the whole, prefer to do without. But when all else fails, he will plunge:

> As for me, I was quickly cleaned out. I put 12 Friedrichsdore on *pair* and won, put on 5, and won, and this went on for two or three spins. I think I must have won about 400 Friedrichsdore, in about five minutes. I should have left, but a strange feeling came over me, a tempting of providence, an urge to defy it, stick out my tongue at it. I staked the maximum, 4000 guilders, and lost. Then growing furious, I took out all I had left, made the same bet, lost again, and left the table in a daze. I didn't even understand what the matter was . . . I just staggered about in the park until lunch.[18]

The author has left this character in the condition of highly disagreeable catharsis that comes after the plunge. This state of mind is no different in kind from any other post-gambling mood. It is simply that the sense of waste, of loss of self-respect, is infinitely stronger than usual.

Dostoevsky has suggested that his gambler was a character representative of his age. It is his addiction to intensity that makes him so.

Dostoevsky, himself a victim of that cult, is never lucid enough to be able to isolate the notion of intensity as such, as the distinctive feature of his manic characters. Although he describes the phenomenon, he remains unable to analyse it. Thus what he finds characteristic about the gambler is his belief that his vice will make him rich. He regards as typical of his age this tendency to opt for the instant, violent result, to be achieved overnight – as opposed to 'long haul' solutions. This lure of instant wealth makes the addiction to gambling symptomatic of a more general malaise. Both Dostoevsky and his character looked to the tables to solve their financial plight:

> However peculiar it may appear that I cherish such high hopes of roulette, it seems to me that the cliché that everyone accepts, namely that it is absurd and stupid to expect anything from gambling, is even more peculiar. Why should gambling be worse than other ways of making money such as trade? It's true, of course, that only one in a hundred wins – But what do I care?[19]

Dostoevsky also ascribes to other characters this same readiness to take risks in order to achieve instant results. It is just such an impatience, such a flash-in-the-pan attitude, that makes Raskolnikov act. He wants all his money at once. Indeed the last passage quoted might apply to Raskolnikov directly, with a small adjustment—for 'gambling' read 'murder'. He explains that he abandoned teaching because there is no money in it. What good are pennies:

> 'And you have to have all your capital at once?' He looked at her strangely.
> 'Yes, all the capital at once.'[20]

This same note of impatience, the need for immediate returns also plays its part in the Karamazov psychology. Not in Dmitri alone; Alyosha also manifests this need for intensity:

> Add to this, that he was in part already a young man of our times, that is to say, an honest young man whose nature craves, seeks for and believes in truth, who, while believing, requires instant participation with all his spirit, requires immediate action, with the overwhelming desire to sacrifice everything for this action, even his life. Unfortunately these young people do not understand that to lay down your life is perhaps the easiest sacrifice of all, and to sacrifice, say five or six years of your youth in difficult, arduous study, if only to multiply your power to pursue the truth and to act tenfold, such a sacrifice is beyond the strength of most people.[21]

Baudelaire agrees with Dostoevsky in seeing in this need for the instant result one of the chief characteristics of modern man. *Les Paradis*

Artificiels are an indictment of man's recourse to artificial stimulants in order to create a surrogate mystic experience. Man's readiness to resort to drugs is characteristic, for Baudelaire, of his readiness to settle for instant illusions; intensity of experience justifying all means. Man's willingness to take drugs, and damn himself in the process, is ascribed to his desire to:

Emporter le paradis d'un seul coup.

Although *d'un seul coup* is an adverbial expression which has the force of a somewhat emphatic 'immediately', it is tempting to see another layer of meaning, on which *coup* is the *coup* of the gambler.

The essential ambiguity of Dostoevsky's attitude towards intensity, the quality we refer to as his complicity, comes out very strongly in his treatment of gambling. He is an addict, but one who looks on his vice with nostalgia, not revulsion. He may condemn it, and yet it remains for him a means of getting rich without allowing oneself to be contaminated by the pecuniary ethic. Unlike the tradesman or the banker, the successful gambler can get rich and keep his hands clean in the process.

He makes this point in a passage that associates gambling with the Russian national character. His treatment of the theme of quint-essential Russianness, the Russianness of the Karamazovs or Rogozhin, is itself a reflection of his ambivalent attitude towards the pursuit of intensity. He finds something admirable, heroic almost, about it, when it takes the form of the characteristically Russian love of excitement, that throws all caution and calculation to the winds. It is an utterly aristocratic approach to experience, one that champions conspicuous consumption of every description, in contrast with the penny-pinching cautiousness of an age subservient to the pecuniary ethic.

The Russian character never lost that generosity of spirit which both Stendhal and de Tocqueville found lacking in the Europe that they knew. Thus, in *The Gambler*, a horrid little Frenchman, all greed and vanity, named des Grieux, in ironic contrast with the supremely generous lover of Manon Lescaut, observes that Russians cannot play roulette:

'I believe, on the contrary, that roulette was made for Russians,' I replied, and when the Frenchman sneered scornfully at my retort, I pointed out that truth was, of course, on my side, since in referring to Russians as gamblers I was insulting rather than praising them, so that he could believe me.

'On what do you base your assertion?' he asked.

'On the fact that in the catechism of modern Western man's virtues and accomplishments, over the years the ability to make money has almost taken pride of place. But not only is the Russian incapable of amassing wealth, he even disperses it wastefully and in a disorderly fashion. Nevertheless, we Russians need money too . . . so we are all too happy and prone to ways of making it such as roulette, at which you can get rich in a couple of hours, without having to work. We are enormously attracted by it; but since we play wastefully, without concentrating, we go down the drain! . . . it's hard to say which is the more disgusting; Russian chaos or the German ability to get rich through honest toil.'[22]

Dostoevsky is proud of his nation's helpless inability to cope with the pecuniary ethic. A passion for instant results, strong sensations and getting rich quick might produce its crop of killers and sex-maniacs, but anything was better than the virtues of the shop-keeper.

The fascination roulette held for the Russian temperament emerges in one of Dostoevsky's most glorious creations: the grandmother of the hero's employer in *The Gambler*. At the very time when her family are hoping at any moment to receive the news of her death, she arrives to join them in the German spa of Roulettenberg. She is a notable contribution to the great portrait gallery of Russian literature's grandmothers. She represents the national character at the tables of Roulettenberg more than adequately. Headstrong and eccentric, she sails in, quite oblivious of the petty protocol of casino manners. The first time she plays she hits a rich vein of beginner's luck, and emerges triumphant in the face of the anxious disapproval of her prospective heirs, whose spirit is meaner than her own. On her next visit to the tables, however, first she loses, then she plunges:

'Grandmother, the 12,000 have all gone,' I announced.
'I can see they have,' she stated with a kind of savage calm . . .
'I can see, I can see,' she muttered looking straight ahead as if in thought.
'I can't bear it, put on another 4,000.'[23]

She plunges and plunges—her family appalled at the speed with which their inheritance is disappearing. She makes constant plans to depart, and keeps going back to the casino to recoup, until she has lost every penny she can raise. Before she leaves, her reputation as an eccentric and compulsive gambler has swept through the town, and she suffers what is for Dostoevsky, the ultimate humiliation of being roundly cheated by a bunch of hangers-on who are, inevitably, Poles. As she continues to plunge, her family make despairing plans to have her certified, and they lose all trace of dignity in their despair. She finally gets through 100,000 roubles, and is obliged to borrow the money for her return journey from a worthy and taciturn Englishman. She leaves, as she says, a poorer woman, but one who no longer believes foolishness to be the exclusive privilege of youth. For all her foolishness, the picture Dostoevsky paints of her, notably through her violent, direct and unaffected language, remains one of the most attractive pieces of character drawing he ever did.

Gambling, then, is the perfect medium for intensity. It is an activity that is almost totally self-justifying. However, it can never satisfy the craving for more excitement. It can only exacerbate or numb it. Because it is society's institutionalisation of the intensity drive, both Baudelaire and Dostoevsky single it out as representative of their age. The gambler is an addict in the full sense of that term. The hero of Dostoevsky's story is finally ruined by roulette, ruined in the sense that he cannot break his habit, and remains chained for ever to the German spas.

Yet for all his condemnation of gambling, Dostoevsky writes about it with deep understanding. It is as if he may have been cured, but his imagination is still with the compulsive gambler riding his run of luck. His attitude to gambling smacks of a certain *nostalgie de la boue*. He has the 'academic' interest in the vice reminiscent of a reformed alcoholic's interest in liquor.

This complicity in a particular brand of intensity goes deeper than a personal nostalgia for roulette. His suggestion that roulette is peculiarly suited to the Russian character raises the subject of his distinctly ambiguous attitude to the intensity drive itself. Whilst condemning it on the one hand, he cannot help acknowledging that the despairing cultivation of sensation for sensation's sake is a response to a mean-spirited civilisation given over to the pursuit of profit – to the world of Luzhin. Just as Flaubert makes it plain that, for all her capacity for self-delusion, Emma Bovary was finally better than the appalling petty bourgeois world of provincial Normandy, so Dostoevsky cannot help admiring the Russian's reckless capacity to abandon all caution in the pursuit of intensity. He associates it with a love of life and excitement which represents much that is finest in the Russian character.

The double standard by which Dostoevsky judges the Russian gambler, and the way in which he is obliged to admire his pursuit of intensity for its rejection of a world of cautious mediocrity, confirms, in miniature, our analysis of the basic motivation of the intensity syndrome. It represented a flight from an intolerable reality, an escape into sensation. In *The Gambler* Dostoevsky contrasts the self-destructive and exultant plunge of the Russian with the world of the German shopkeeper. There is no doubt which he prefers.

We can now begin to see why it is that Dostoevsky, despite his situation on the fringe of European culture, was able to create a fictional world that probed so deeply into the mythology of his age. For him, his national character was intensity-prone. His Russian grandmother of *The Gambler*, who had never been into a casino in her life, became an addict within five minutes. A craving for *sensations fortes* was, for him, the supreme distinctive feature of the Russian character. Small wonder then, that his portrait of the Russia of his time was to become the portrait of an age.

CHAPTER THIRTEEN

Modes of Intensity: Masochism

> Il serait peut-être doux
> d'être alternativement
> victime et bourreau.[1]
> BAUDELAIRE

> Soyez béni, mon Dieu, qui donnez la souffrance
> Comme un divin remède à nos impuretés,
> Et comme la meilleure et la plus pure essence
> Qui prépare les forts aux saintes voluptés![2]

The protagonist of *Les Fleurs du Mal* reaches a point in his moral decline at which he will accept any sort of sensation which might act as a relief from his state of empty indifference. Even pain, moral or physical, will serve. He comes to seek out and cultivate pain, and finally inflict it upon himself. It is self-inflicted sensation that motivates lines such as these from 'L'Héautontimorouménos':

> Je suis la plaie et le couteau!
> Je suis le soufflet et la joue!
> Je suis les membres et la roue
> Et la victime et le bourreau![3]

The pursuit of intensity operating as it does by the law of diminishing returns, the addict requires ever stronger sources of stimulus, and suffers a corresponding decline in their effect. His acceptance, and indeed his cultivation of pain, is the most telling indication of the straits to which he has been reduced by his habit. Intensity has turned him into a kind of professional loser.

Dostoevsky's view of the inadequacies of his culture virtually obliges him to portray its subjects as losers. His world is fundamentally a world of victims, because it is essentially one in which it is impossible to win. Hence he moves failure and weakness to the foreground of his fiction. But so affected are Dostoevsky's losers by their pathetic attempts at escape into intensity that they tend to become psychological cripples. Masochism and the exultant acceptance of pain and humiliation become their characteristic attitudes. So permeated are they by masochistic intensity that their only reply to those who bring them their pain is 'More, more'.

170

This response is an elaboration of the losing punter's compulsive plunge. If he is to be a loser anyway, the Dostoevskian character derives a sense of bitter intensity by compounding the magnitude of his loss. He acquires a taste for the sheer extremity of his situation, a taste which the hero of *The Gambler* displays, even away from the tables:

> I delight in being your slave. You can, you really can delight in the ultimate degree of submission and insignificance. The devil knows, perhaps you can delight in the knout, when the knout falls on your back, and tears the flesh to shreds.[4]

Viewed through the focus of the Baudelarian approach to sensation, the compulsive masochism of Dostoevsky's characters can be seen to be another manifestation of the intensity drive and their collective Gadarene personality.

One should perhaps distinguish between passive and active masochism. The passive masochist is content to exult in inflicted pain, the active masochist is prepared to bring that pain about, alone or with the assistance of others. However, he attempts to keep his pain under some degree of control. But if the sensation is to be at its most effective, the fact of that control, the self-induced element of the situation, must be conveniently forgotten. To arrive at maximum intensity the active masochist must suspend disbelief. If he is too aware of the contrived quality of the situation, the pain which is the source of his pleasure ceases to be pain.

The balance to be struck between pain and pleasure emerges in the following pen-portrait of a masochist. The father of Netochka Nezvanova was once a talented musician. Over the years he has allowed himself to lapse into a weak and self-indulgent loser, a type that will realise its definitive version in Marmeladov:

> In the first place he is mad; in the second this madness has caused three crimes, because he has wrecked two lives besides his own: that of his wife and of his daughter. I know him; he'd fall dead on the spot if he were to become convinced of his crimes. But the terrible thing is that for the last eight years he has been *nearly* convinced. For eight years he has been wrestling with his conscience, to admit it to himself not nearly but completely.[5]

The Underground Man is a masochist of a subtler and more perverse kind. One of his characteristics, one which is positively Baudelairian, is his ability to turn his sense of remorseful self-disgust into a source of pleasure. This emerges in the following passage, which is also important for its association of this kind of masochism with the kind of dualistic response to both good and evil that so disturbed Dmitri Karamazov. The Underground Man has just suggested that his sense of his own occasional 'heroism' is such that he can reconcile himself to more despicable behaviour:

> It is remarkable that these surges of 'everything beautiful and lofty' would even find me in my little moments of depravity, precisely when I had reached rock bottom, coming to me in little flashes, as if to remind me they were there, but without destroying the depravity by their onset; on the contrary, they seemed to enliven it by the contrast, and came in the proportions needed for a good sauce. The sauce consisted of contradiction and suffering, painful self-analysis, and all this suffering, great and small, gave a certain sharpness, a point even to my little moments of depravity, in short fulfilled the function of a good sauce.[6]

This is Dostoevsky's version of the Baudelairian habit of deriving pleasure from remorse. The Underground Man abuses what Dmitri Karamazov has described as modern man's capacity to retain a sense of idealism in the midst of Sodom, to provide himself with little stabs of guilt; dualism is put to good use as a source of masochistic intensity. The Underground Man, as the product of circumstance, urban culture and the excessive development of the new brain, is one of Dostoevsky's 'significant cripples'. He has grown so twisted that he can only have relations with others along an axis of violence and pain. He tortures a prostitute he visits savagely, by preaching to her and providing a graphic description of her eventual plight; as he tortures her, he feels a genuine compassion for her predicament and is tremendously guilty about the distress he brings to her. He can only relate to his erstwhile friends, whom he despises, but longs in his loneliness to embrace, by actions which oblige them to reject him with an even greater violence than they might otherwise have employed. That the Underground Man was directly responsible for his own rejection permitted him to console himself with the thought that, had he not behaved as he did, his friends would have welcomed him with open arms. He thereby avoids having to face up to the possibility that he is disliked absolutely. Moreover, he enjoys dwelling upon the intensity of his humiliation, as one enjoys biting upon a bad tooth – at least the pain is of one's own making and lies within one's control. In the following lines the Underground Man wallows in the thought of what his friends would do to him:

> Yes, let them beat me . . . Trudolyubov will beat particularly hard, he's so strong; Ferfichkin will grab me from the side, by the hair of course. Let it all happen! That's why I started it all. Their sheeps' heads will be obliged to see the tragic side of it all. As they drag me to the doors I'll yell at them that basically they're not worth a hair of my head.[7]

Masochism, like intensity of every description, begins with a plunge. In this case the plunge is almost identical to that of the gambler who, feeling unable to win, decides to lose instead. It is important to realise that Dostoevsky presents such characters as cripples, victims of their cultural circumstances. This emerges in a thumbnail sketch of a potential addict. In *The Idiot* Ippolit tells of his meeting with a couple of starving provincials, eking out their savings and waiting for something. These characteristic Petersburg figures live in squalid circumstances, and that squalor brings them close to the brink:

> I could see at a glance that they were both perfectly decent people, but they were reduced by poverty to that humiliating situation where disorder finally defeating all efforts to combat it, one is driven to the bitter necessity that derives from that very disorder which mounts daily, a kind of bitter and vindictive sense of pleasure . . . There are people who really enjoy the angry chip on their shoulder, particularly when it takes them (which it always does very quickly) to the end of their tether; at that moment they would rather, I think, feel insulted than not.[8]

The most striking example of the plunging cripple is Marmeladov of *Crime and Punishment*. He drinks out of despair, destroying his family and driving his daughter onto the streets, because he feels that, whatever he may do, his position is hopeless. If he should make it worse, he can at least feel that he is partly in control, partly responsible. His plunge maintains for him the illusion that he is to some extent master of his fate – like the compulsive gambler, before the first bet, who tells himself that he is still free to go away. This sense of responsibility, this illusion of control is of the greatest significance to Dostoevsky's characters. They are all finally imbued with a respect for metaphysical order and discipline, and are constitutionally unable to contemplate the possibility that their world is indeed without whole meaning: valueless and absurd. In a sense, a Marmeladov creates for himself an illusion of meaning by making his situation worse. Were he not to feel responsible for his plight, he would be obliged to recognise that he lived in a world in which the fall of a Marmeladov mattered still less than the fall of a sparrow.

Moreover Marmeladov, like the musician of *Netochka Nezvanova*, positively thrives on his exultant sense of humiliation and on the intensity of his awareness of his own guilt. His dependants can hope for nothing from him, for he has reached the stage at which the more they reproach him, the greater his sense of guilt and the greater the resultant thrill. In order to enjoy his situation to the full, he must descend as low as possible. It is for this reason that he married Katerina Ivanovna in the first place. She was a lady, and the nobler she was, the more humiliated he would feel by her. His view of her as a lady, himself as a pig, is the definitive Dostoevskian erotic relationship. Like that of Baudelaire, Dostoevskian eroticism is invariably twisted by the need for intensity. Instead of two hearts beating as one, the lovers tend to act out their respective intensity cravings upon one another – witness Marmeladov's view of his wife:

> Well, I may be a pig, but she is a lady! I am made in the image of an animal, but Katerina Ivanovna, my wife, is a person of education, born the daughter of a staff-officer. Yes, I may be rotten, but she is full of nobility of spirit and feeling.[9]

He derives an even stronger charge of intensity from his knowledge that he has driven his daughter to prostitution. He is all too happy to steal her last coins, the money she should devote to ensuring her cleanliness, in order to drink it, while fully aware of her need for personal hygiene.

Marmeladov is insistent that he is not looking for pity, as indeed he is not. He wants a good tongue-lashing that will activate his sense of guilt:

> 'Pity, I don't need pity!' Marmeladov exclaimed suddenly, rising with arm half-extended in a state of extreme excitement . . . 'Why pity you ask? Yes! There is no call to pity me! I should be crucified, nailed to the cross, not pitied! But judge, then crucify, and having done so take pity on him! . . . I'll go willingly to crucifixion, for I thirst not for pleasure, but for grief and tears! Do you suppose, innkeeper, that this small carafe of vodka went down pleasantly? Sorrow, sorrow is what I sought in its depths, sorrow and tears, and I tasted and I found them.'[10]

This passage, and others like it, in which Dostoevsky's characters exult in their awareness of their own inadequacy by plumbing its depths, can only be understood in the light of the intensity cult. The Marmeladovs of this world are both better and worse off than they appear: better because they thrive on their sense of their guilt; worse because their craving for sensation has so distorted their psyches that they are sicker than they could ever suppose at their most tortured moments of self-examination.

Perhaps Dostoevsky's most sophisticated and delicate masochist is Trussotsky, the hero of *The Eternal Husband*. Discovering by chance that his late wife used to take lovers among their mutual acquaintance, he seeks one of them out. Velchaninov is one of Dostoevsky's minor libertines, with the libertine's charm and with his sense of emptiness and lack of values. Trussotsky, the eternal husband, plays a game of cat and mouse with him. He is familiar, over-affectionate, and then drops hints about cuckoldry. As the story unfolds, he gradually imposes himself as the husband deceived. It emerges that in all probability the ailing daughter he has brought with him to the capital is Velchaninov's child. The nature of the relationship, Trussotsky's essential dependence on the man who had wronged him, emerges when Trussotsky attempts to cut Velchaninov's throat. He is unable to see the deed through because he needs him. Velchaninov provides him with a stimulus, the perpetual reminder of his humiliation as a cuckold. While he has Velchaninov he is able to re-activate his pain. Instead of his awareness remaining a passive memory – he only discovers his wife's infidelity after her death – he can recreate the details of his humiliation, by talking with Velchaninov about the old days. By biting on the bad tooth he is able to persuade himself that he is the master of his pain. But this most active of masochists takes his masochism even further.

Trussotsky plans a second marriage to a very young girl. He is insistent that Velchaninov meet her. It turns out, inevitably, that the girl already treats her husband-to-be as a bad joke, making merciless fun of him, while finding Velchaninov a charming and attractive man of the world. It is as if Trussotsky were quite determined to recreate the original triangle; he positively courts cuckoldry, as the mode through which his feeling is channelled. Supposing himself powerless to prevent cuckoldry, he prefers to plunge and precipitate the event. Thereby not only does he feel responsible for his destiny, he also ensures that he derives a sufficient and controlled charge of intensity from it.

The final meeting between Velchaninov and Trussotsky occurs some years later. The eternal husband is now married to a boisterous young lady who is anything but *farouche* – the triangle is completed by a handsome young officer whom she keeps in tow, while her husband does what he is told. Better the devil you know . . . might be Trussotsky's motto. But there is more to it than that. Trussotsky is another psychological cripple. Cuckoldry has become an emotional necessity for him: he has reached the stage when he positively requires someone to sleep with his wife, and more important perhaps, be seen to sleep with her, thereby humiliating him in public, in order to taste to the full the bitter joys of his particular brand of intensity.

Another of the more sophisticated modes of Dostoevskian masochism is that which derives its intensity from confession, private, or, more usually, public and collective. Marmeladov, Svidrigailov, Raskolnikov, the prince of *The Insulted and the Injured* and Stavrogin all confess their evil to others. Admittedly, their motives are various. Raskolnikov and Stavrogin really do appear to seek to purge themselves through confession, The other characters, however, regard confession as a mode of intensity, by exposing their evil they can enjoy the shocked reaction of their audience. For Svidrigailov, the prince and even for Marmeladov, confession is a means of re-activating, recollecting emotion in tranquillity, and making it serve a second time. A collective masochistic confession is the real pretext for the peculiar 'truth game' at Nastasya Filipovna's party in *The Idiot*. It will be recalled that each player undertakes to recount the most shameful event of his or her life. This peculiar parlour-game institutionalises the masochistic urge to seek humiliation through public confession. Confession is yet another form of plunging; an act of irrevocable commitment to public humiliation, it provides a degree of intensity proportionate to the enormity of the action confessed.

Masochistic confession in Dostoevsky is by no means confined to such specific set-pieces, although there are enough of these – other examples would be the murderer who confessed his crime to Zosima, and the long piece which Ippolit reads in *The Idiot*, a final plunge before he would attempt to take his own life. Dostoevsky actually sets entire works in a confessional tone. His narrators delight in revealing their own despicable behaviour. Thus *Notes from Underground* is a confessional monologue, in the course of which the narrator goes out of his way to make us aware of his despicable side. *The Adolescent* uses precisely the same narrative mode. The entire work consists of Dolgoruky's account of events through the focus of his own spite and meanness of spirit. He is perpetually drawing our attention to his own shortcomings. The same applies, albeit to a somewhat lesser extent, to *The Gambler*. In each case, the hero makes a clean breast of his weakness, and the narrative is actually shaped by its status as a masochistic confessional plunge.

The capacity of Dostoevsky's characters for self-inflicted punishment is as great as their capacity for intensity itself. Masochism is, perhaps, Dostoevsky's most generalised channel of intensity, as indeed it appears to have been in Baudelaire. When considering Dostoevsky's own relationship to masochism we again encounter the phenomenon of the author's personal complicity in the process he describes. We have seen how his gambling letters had something of the Marmeladov about them, as he castigated himself, chided his bride for over-reacting and urged her to stop at nothing in her efforts to provide him with a new stake. Moreover, his habit of pushing his financial circumstances to extremes while travelling abroad suggests that he wallowed in a certain kind of brinkmanship, on the borderline between love of risk and love of punishment.

More important than his personal masochism, as a manifestation of Dostoevsky's complicity, is his attitude to uninvited suffering. It is an essential element in the Dostoevskian credo that suffering is a burden to be shouldered. It must neither be resisted nor must it be avoided. It is imposed upon one as a peculiar kind of negative grace, and must

be accepted as such. Raskolnikov will only become capable of regeneration in so far as he accepts his guilt, his responsibility and purges
himself through suffering. *The Brothers Karamazov* is full of adjurations
to take on suffering, to accept rather than to resist it, and the sheer
scale of suffering becomes a measure of moral and spiritual stature.
This is the sense of Zosima's treatment of the inconsolable mother
whose young child had recently died (Dostoevsky wrote the passage
after having himself undergone such a loss). Dmitri Karamazov's
reaction to his sentence is, initially at least, also formed by a readiness
to accept suffering, almost on a Christlike scale. Indeed, it would seem
that Dostoevsky proposes the acceptance of suffering as his answer to
the appalling world in which he found himself. Passive acceptance of
suffering is advanced as the alternative to seeking to escape naked
reality through intensification of experience. Dostoevsky's acceptance of
suffering and the vale of tears as the alternative to escape would then
appear a direct echo of Baudelaire's assertion that 'tout homme qui
n'accepte pas les conditions de la vie, vend son âme.'[11] The acceptance
of life is the equivalent to acceptance of suffering. Baudelaire derives
addiction, in this specific instance addiction to narcotics, from a refusal
to accept the world as it is.

Now, of course, the Dostoevskian view that suffering must be
accepted without question, that it provides a path to purification and
ennoblement, is a vital part of his Christian metaphysics. His view of
universal guilt and universal atonement is the basis of a Christian
resolution of his culture's plight. He invites us all to take on, in so far
as our strength permits, the tiniest share of the burden which Christ
bore for all of us. Acceptance of suffering, as opposed to rejection and
an attempt to escape, is our immensely modest acceptance of our version
of Christ's destiny. It would be an unforgivable distortion of an aspect
of Dostoevsky's thought, which is not directly relevant to our analysis,
not to accord pride of place to this aspect of the theme of acceptance
of suffering and universal guilt.

Yet suffering in Dostoevsky has another side to it, one which is a
manifestation of his own complicity in the intensity cult. The clue is
provided by the behaviour of one of his victims, the 'Nellie' of *The
Insulted and the Injured*. She refuses to be comforted long after her
appallingly unfair treatment has been brought to an end:

> . . . she had been wronged and insulted,[12] her wound could not heal,
> and it was as if she deliberately sought to keep her wound open
> through that secrecy, that mistrust of us all; it was as if she enjoyed
> her own pain, that *egoism of suffering*, so to speak . . . it is a pleasure
> common to many offended and insulted people, who have been
> crushed by fate, and are aware in themselves of fate's injustice.[13]

Suffering seen through the intensity syndrome is not simply a means of purification. It has another dimension, and can lapse into egoism and the masochistic cult of one's own pain. The masochist precipitates and amplifies a situation which he is essentially powerless to prevent. In the same way acceptance of suffering might be thought of as Dostoevsky the stoic bowing his head before the inevitable, and positively welcoming the ills that he knew no man could avoid. But there comes a point at which the distinction between stoicism and masochism is lost. The two extremities touch – the phrase Dmitri Karamazov employed when talking about the ambiguity of beauty. The essential complicity between positive suffering and masochism, the ease with which one slips into the other, introduces yet another ambiguity—one, this time, which is not made explicit by Baudelaire— the *ambiguity of suffering itself*.

It is suffering's ambiguity that places it at the centre of Dostoevsky's world, where it features in its two manifestations of positive suffering and masochism. Although he is aware of the distinction, it is as if he is not always able to discriminate between the two sides of the coin. In the final analysis, this is a reflection of a greater inability, *the inability to tell good from evil any more*, an inability that derives from man's loss of grasp upon whole meanings. Dostoevsky himself had had a stoic rôle imposed upon him by circumstances which deprived him of both his liberty and his health. Small wonder that he finally arrived at the point at which stoicism turned to masochism, so that he could no longer distinguish between good and evil, pleasure and pain.

CHAPTER FOURTEEN

Modes of Intensity: Libertinage

> They say that Cleopatra . . . used to like
> sticking golden pins into the bosoms of her
> slaves, and enjoyed their cries and convulsions
> . . . we are still in a barbaric age,
> since people are still inserting pins.[1]
>
> DOSTOEVSKY

> Quant à la torture, elle est née de la partie
> infâme du coeur de l'homme, assoiffée de voluptés.
> Cruauté et volupté, sensations identiques, comme
> l'extrême chaud et l'extrême froid.[2]
>
> BAUDELAIRE

As a mode of intensity, sex, in Dostoevsky, plays a part almost as important as pure suffering. Like Baudelaire, Dostoevsky's view of sexual relationships is distorted by intensity, and operates along an axis of violence and pain. He would share the Frenchman's contention that cruelty and sexual pleasure are essentially identical, and would agree that a sado-masochistic component subtends every kind of sexual relationship:

> Je crois que j'ai déjà écrit dans mes notes que l'amour ressemblait fort à une torture ou à une opération chirurgicale. Mais cette idée peut être développée de la manière la plus amère. Quand même les deux amants seraient très-épris et très-pleins de désirs réciproques, l'un des deux sera toujours plus calme ou moins possédé que l'autre. Celui-là ou celle-là, c'est l'opérateur, ou le bourreau; l'autre, c'est le sujet, la victime.[3]

In Dostoevsky's world the object of one's desire tends to become a victim, to be tortured without mercy. The torturer derives his pleasure from the victim's suffering. Dostoevskian sadism is grounded in the cultivation of a sense of intensity sparked off by a distorted sense of compassion. It is essential that the sadist feel sorry for his victim. If he is incapable of pity he can derive no pleasure from the suffering of others. This is why, in literature at least, there is an intimate association between sadism and sentimentality. The association of sadism and sentimental compassion, sensitivity to the suffering of others, is an

179

essential feature of Dostoevsky's world. It accounts for the otherwise puzzling blend of Little Nell-type sentimental pathos with a talent for creating libertines so vicious and cold-blooded that they stand virtually alone in world literature, rendering the hysterical rhetoric of a de Sade or a Lautréamont jejune in comparison.

This aspect of Dostoevsky's personality and work emerges particularly in two letters, from admittedly somewhat suspect sources. The first is a letter of Turgenev's to Saltykov, dated 24 September 1882 (O.S.), shortly after Dostoevsky's death. Turgenev had little reason to love or even sympathise with Dostoevsky, and his understandable prejudices must be taken into account here. He begins by approving of an article which had termed Dostoevsky's 'a cruel talent', and continues on the theme of his complicity:

> [The author] correctly underlined a basic characteristic of his work. He might have recalled that there has been a comparable figure in French literature too – I mean the notorious Marquis de Sade. The latter even wrote a book entitled *Tourments et supplices*, in which he takes particular pleasure in insisting upon the depraved delights to be had from the infliction of exquisite torture and suffering. Dostoevsky also, in one of his novels, carefully describes the pleasures of a certain connoisseur . . .[4]

The second source also seems somewhat prejudiced. It consists of an open letter to Tolstoy from Dostoevsky's ex-associate Strakhov. The latter had just completed a biography of Dostoevsky at the request of his widow, and in his letter to Tolstoy he confesses to having whitewashed him. There is every reason to suppose that Strakhov was somewhat envious of Dostoevsky, and in this letter he also appears to be courting Tolstoy's favour. Certainly Dostoevsky's widow rejects his every assertion with indignation, and so she should. Nevertheless, something of the intensity addict comes through in Strakhov's letter, even though his actual accusations of personal depravity are probably without foundation:

> . . . I can neither deem Dostoevsky a good nor a happy man . . . He was bad-tempered, envious and corrupt, and spent his entire life in states of agitation which made him pathetic, and would have made him a joke had he not been so bad-tempered and intelligent . . . [The letter goes on to describe Dostoevsky treating a Swiss waiter very badly] . . . He was always having scenes like these, because he could not restrain his bad temper . . . once or twice I was really rude to him about them. But, of course, when it came to insults, he was above such things, and worst of all he used to enjoy the fact that he never felt any remorse for his shameful actions. He was drawn to shameful actions, and used to boast about them. Viskovatov

told me once how he boasted that he **** in a public bath with a little girl who was brought to him by her governess . . . The characters most like him in his novels are the hero of *Notes from Underground*, Svidrigailov in *Crime and Punishment* and Stavrogin in *The Devils* . . .

Together with that nature he was inclined to sugary sentimentality . . .[5]

There is every reason to suppose that the story of Dostoevsky and the little girl was invented by him to tease Turgenev; nevertheless, some of the mud thrown by Strakhov sticks. At the very least, he suggests that there was an aspect of his personality that was profoundly sympathetic to libertinage, an aspect that went hand in hand with 'sugary sentimentality' and a belief in his own righteousness. Strakhov very rightly compares Dostoevsky to Rousseau in this connection, a comparison that is peculiarly appropriate in the sense that Rousseau was the founding father of the cult of intensity.

Thus Dostoevsky seems to have a certain personal involvement in the sexuality of cruelty. He also echoes that taste for confessing their evil which we find in his libertines. Strakhov refers, moreover, to Dostoevsky's 'animal sensuality', another pointer to his complicity in the intensity drive. Strakhov and Turgenev cast a somewhat sinister light upon the nature of Dostoevsky's creative involvement in a world of child-rape and worse, although one must beware of accepting at its face value what Strakhov, in particular, had to say. However, it is perhaps this element of creative complicity that accounts for one of the most striking aspects of Dostoevsky's treatment of libertinage; namely its extraordinarily matter-of-fact quality. His villains are essentially creatures of flesh and blood, neither demonic Maldorors nor moustache-twirling Sir Jaspers. Far from being one-sided caricatures of humanity, it is from that very humanity that their sadism is derived. Thus it is because Dostoevsky's characters are creatures of feeling that they are also creatures of violence. The reconciliation of feeling and animal savagery is one of their most striking traits. Indeed, a sense of compassion is essential to the sadistic relationship, for this is dependent upon the torturer being able to find compassion for his victim. This is why sadism and sentimentality belong together. *Les Chants de Maldoror* advocate torturing a blindfold adolescent, and then removing the blindfold and appearing as the comforting rescuer. The plan reconciles torture, compassion and remorse in a strange blend of sentimentality and surrealistic violence.

We are afforded a fascinating glimpse of this aspect of the anatomy of sadism in a letter the French author Maurice de Guérin wrote to his friend Barbey d'Aurevilly:

Oserais-je lui avouer que j'ai dans mon âme les caprices d'une cruauté bien grande – Je me souviens que, dans un âge fort tendre, je goûtais un plaisir amer à battre les animaux que j'aimais . . . Leurs cris me procuraient un déchirement de coeur, je ne sais quelle volupté de pitié dont j'étais avide. Si j'étais empereur romain, je ferais peut-être donner la question à mes amis pour le désir de les plaindre.[6]

Although this confession comes from the sort of Frenchman who as a boy no doubt pulled the wings off flies for elaborate metaphysical reasons, it certainly provides an insight into the close association of cruelty and compassion. Of course, sadistic pity, like all versions of the intensity cult, only functions if the sadist can remain unaware of his true motives. Once he admits that he inflicts pain in order to stimulate his own sense of pity, he loses the illusion of participating in a real event, and intensity disappears with the return of disbelief.

The need to pity the victim accounts for one aspect of the vital rôle played by children in Dostoevsky's novels. No one can doubt that they were precious to Dostoevsky in themselves. His love for them is only equalled by that of Victor Hugo. Moreover, they have an innocence, a freedom from cultural contamination, that makes them hold out some promise of an alternative, of a better world. It is this that explains the otherwise puzzling sub-plot of *The Brothers Karamazov* – the story of Kolya Krasotkin and the Snegirovs. In his 'Speech at the Stone' Alyosha calls to the band of children to maintain, throughout their lives, that sense of organic unity which they were experiencing at that moment. It is through the focus of children that the author indulges his sense of hope.

But it is the very innocence of the child that casts it in the rôle of ultimate victim, notably the victim of sexual assault. Child-rape is the most villainous form of sexuality – witness its rôle in *Les Chants de Maldoror* – and hence, not only the favourite sport of the Dostoevskian libertine, but also a favourite topic for discussion, whenever the intensity aesthetic is operative. In an early story, *The Christmas Tree and the Wedding*, there is an episode in which a lustful and greedy middle-aged gentleman makes up to an eleven-year-old heiress. He begins by meditating on her fortune:

'Three hundred, three hundred,' he whispered, 'eleven, twelve, thirteen and so on. Sixteen. Five years. Let's say four per cent – twelve, five twelves are sixty, and what with compound interest it should be four hundred in five years time. But, my God, he doesn't just get four per cent the devil. He might get eight or ten. Five hundred, let's say five hundred thousand for certain, at least; what with dress allowances and . . .'

He makes up to the little girl, talking to her about her doll and becoming more and more aroused until he asks:

> in an inaudible voice that excitement and eagerness had virtually
> extinguished:
> 'And will you love me, nice little girl, when I come to call on
> your parents?'[7]

The Insulted and the Injured contains an attempt at child-rape in a
brothel. The little orphan girl Nellie is saved, in the nick of time, from
the clutches of a *madame* who had sold her, in advance, to some drunken
lechers. She had been dressed for a part which her rescuer only
understands fully as he tries to calm her:

> Elena seemed half-dead. I unhooked her dress, sprinkled some water
> on her and put her on the sofa. She was starting a delirious fever.
> I looked at her pale face, her colourless lips, her black hair which
> was untidy but which had been carefully combed out and covered
> in pomade, at her entire outfit, at those rose-coloured ribbons which
> were somehow still attached to the dress – and I understood the
> whole repulsive story.[8]

There is little point in compiling the whole catalogue of Dostoevsky's
accounts of sexual offences against children. But perhaps it should be
recalled that his publisher Katkov omitted a section of *The Devils*,
'Stavrogin's Confession', which tells of his seduction/rape of an innocent
child who was obsessed by him. She subsequently committed suicide.
It is implied that Svidrigailov had a similar crime upon his conscience.
During his last night on earth he has a nightmare featuring the fourteen-
year-old girl who drowned herself after receiving his attentions. He is
also engaged to a beautiful sixteen-year-old, and knows another young
girl, newly arrived in the capital, whose mother had taken her to a
dance-hall in the mistaken belief that it was a dancing-class. Svidrigailov is the first to admit that he is very fond of children.

Dostoevsky's children are not simply targets for rape. They are often
just neglected and maltreated, and this is offered by the author as a
sign of his times. It is also a source of intense and violent sentimental
pathos. It is precisely the suffering of children which compels Ivan
Karamazov to reject the divine creation as lacking order. He cites
some instances making his point with a heavy-handed irony. But
Dostoevsky uses his account of suffering in order to move his readers,
and himself, to pity – in a bid for an intensity of response itself not
far removed from sadism. This passage, which is distinctly disquieting,
revels in its understanding of the motivation of the sadist:

> I have better stories about children Alyosha. I've an awful lot of

stories about Russian children. A little five-year-old girl is hated
by her parents, 'highly respectable, educated and cultivated civil
servants'. You see, again I maintain that many members of the
human race have a strange characteristic – they love torturing
children, only children. These tormentors behave decently, warmly
even, towards other members of the species, as educated and humane
Europeans, but they really love to torture children, and in that
sense they actually love the children themselves. It is precisely the
defencelessness of these creatures that dazzles their tormentors,
the angelic trust of a child, who has nowhere to go, no one to go to –
that's what sets the vile blood of the tormentor on fire. Of course
inside every man hides a beast, the beast of rage, the beast whose
sensuality flares at the cries of the tortured victim, the beast of
unbridled license, the beast of the diseases of excess – gout, liver and
so on. These educated parents subjected that five-year-old girl to
every torture conceivable. They beat, flogged, kicked her, without
knowing why, made her body a mass of bruises; they eventually
grew quite sophisticated; they shut her in the outside lavatory all
night, in the cold and frost, and because she didn't ask to go in the
night (as if a five-year-old sleeping its deep angelic sleep, can learn
to ask at that age), they smeared her face with shit and made her eat
it, her mother, her own mother made her! And that mother could
sleep when she could hear her poor child groaning at night, shut
up in a foul place.[9]

Ivan suggests that we all have a potential for such behaviour, just as
Baudelaire warned his readers that they would read their own story
in *Les Fleurs du Mal;* as Lautréamont warns that his sado-erotic poetry
will explore the darker corners of his readers' fantasy world. Lautréamont, indeed, also writes of sadism in the family, at some length:
sadism is the image of family disintegration as it is in Dostoevsky.
Parents keep children confined in dungeons, mothers flog their sons
nearly to death for refusing to sleep with them. But the impact of such
scenes is mitigated by Lautréamont's Gothic rhetoric. They remain
mere masturbation fantasies. Dostoevsky treats the theme in the
documentary code of the case history and the result is much more
disturbing.

His sadists are, above all, aroused by helplessness. It is sexual sadism
that informs one of the most important of his devices of plot, the
humiliation of the defenceless. The intensity derived from such situations, both by his characters and by his aesthetic, is considerable.
Strangely, it is the selfsame feeling which underlies Dostoevsky's scenes
of 'punitive moralising'. The Underground Man preaches a sermon to
the prostitute, not in order to reform her, but for the sheer spiteful

pleasure of making her suffer. It is for the same reason that Raskolnikov drives Sonya Marmeladova to despair.

Even more or less normal sexual relationships tend to be founded in sadism. The Adolescent longs to annihilate and to humiliate the object of his desire. He wants a scandal that will wipe her out. Similarly, Natasha Ikhmeneva in *The Insulted and the Injured* loves her weak seducer because:

> Natasha felt instinctively that she would dominate, would rule him; that he would always be her victim. She tasted, in advance, the joys of loving boundlessly and torturing the one she loved to the point of pain, precisely because she loved him and because she had been in such a hurry to abandon herself to him.[10]

The most unlikely characters prove susceptible to this form of intensity, which Ivan suggested was a human universal. Thus Liza Khokhlakova is a sexual hysteric and an intensity addict who functions through sado-masochism. She can inflict pain upon herself – slamming her finger in a door. She also tries to pain Alyosha. She lives entirely for sensation, with a kind of cerebral sensuality. Dostoevsky makes it clear that she is capable of practically anything.

She is an intensity addict of a kind which anticipates real educated sadists such as Leopold and Loeb. Her sadistic fantasies are rendered through a language of sweetness. The eater of sweets is the laziest of sensualists, the utterly passive victim of a habit without heroism. (The Russian language reinforces the association of sweetness and sensuality with a lexicological motivation. Sensuality is *sladostrastie* – sweet passionateness, *sladki* meaning sweet.) Ivan Karamazov describes Turkish atrocities, shooting children in the head in front of their mothers, adding that Turks are very fond of sweets.

So is Liza. She tells Alyosha that she sends Dmitri sweets in prison. Virtually in the same breath she tells him that she longs to marry someone who would torment her, longs for disorder and violence. Finally, in a famous passage, she tells of a Jew who had tortured a four-year-old Christian child to death. It took four hours. She dreams of looking on and eating pineapple fruit salad.

For all these sadistic fantasies, Liza remains technically innocent. As a character she is finally overshadowed by the real Dostoevskian libertines. The Prince of *The Insulted and the Injured*, Stavrogin in his infernal aspect, certain sides of Versilov, all belong to a paradigm that has as its crowning glory Svidrigailov.

The libertine has come to a dead-end in his pursuit of intensity. In *Les Fleurs du Mal* Baudelaire describes a progressive degeneration as his hero gradually loses his capacity to feel, until nothing is able to move him: he simply exists, exhausted in the vacuum of *spleen*. No sensation has the strength to reach him any more; the needle can no longer find a vein. Dostoevsky's characters reach a comparable state of exhaustion. They come to exist in a wasteland, having drained all possible forms of sensation. Stavrogin has wrung every drop he can from vice, from his mocking marriage to a crippled half-wit, from acting on the savage spur of the moment, from duelling, from iron self-control – Shatov's slap—and even from condoning murder. The farewell note that he leaves Dasha is the work of a burnt-out case:

> I tested my strength everywhere . . . private tests, and in public, as always in my life, it turned out to be infinite . . . As I always could, I can wish to do something good, and derive pleasure from it; at the same time I can wish to do something evil, and get pleasure from that too. But as always, each sensation is too slight, it is never strong. My wishes are too weak; they can't lead me. You can cross a river on a log, but not on a splinter.[11]

It is this overpowering nihilistic indifference which gives to Dostoevsky's libertines their particular stamp. From Svidrigailov to Velchaninov, they all have in common an eventual indifference to virtually everything.

In one sense, they derive from the culture-heroes and nihilists of Romanticism, such as Lorenzaccio and Pechorin. They represent yet another stage in European man's enduring obsession with sensual indifference, as first embodied in Don Juan. But Dostoevsky's characters differ from the Romantics, differ even from Baudelaire's creation, in one important respect. They are without vanity, have no *M'as-tu vu?*. Romantic heroes derive a sense of self-indulgent intensity from the contemplation of their predicament, they enjoy their own self-awareness. Even Baudelaire's hero cultivates and dramatises his spleen, through the splendid rhetoric of his creator. The Dostoevskian libertine is neither vain nor self-conscious. He has reached far beyond such states. He can recount his own exploits, talk with a devastating frankness about his appetites, even discuss the impression he makes upon his listener. But he has no true sense of self; no sense of identity, and hence no capacity for self-recrimination or for guilt. Even that vein has been worked out. It would seem that the intensity cult has succeeded in burning away his old brain. That is to say, he has so over-abused his capacity for experiencing sensation, for instinctive response, that it is worn out, no longer able to respond. The nerves are dead, and the libertine has nothing left with which to pursue his libertinage.

This exhaustion explains the libertine's most devastating characteristic: a terrible matter-of-fact frankness. He is totally honest, quite ready to discuss what ought to be his secret self, the self which we all hide, and which he has more reason to hide than most. This frankness creates his most distinctive characteristic – a particular conversational tone. He is brazenly confiding, open, and yet dishonest and fundamentally shifty. He has his own motives for confessing, and these do not necessarily include the need to get it off his chest. Confession can also be a form of vice; for he loves a bit of dirt. Such characters choose to confess in squalid restaurants, midway between eating houses and *maisons de passe* – Nabokov talks of 'thumbscrew conversations in those stage taverns where Dostoevsky is at home' – they set up headquarters there, and enjoy surrounding themselves with trash. They revel in vice as they revel in frankness. In every respect they are characters with nothing to lose. It is this that distinguishes them from their fellow men. Everyone has something to lose except the libertine—he has nothing left.

Svidrigailov is the supreme incarnation of the type. He has been a profligate; not a gambler but a card-sharper. His future wife had bought him out of a debtor's prison. He went to live with her, on uneasy terms, in the country. There he had her peasant women – with her tacit consent, for a man is a man. He was probably responsible for a young girl's suicide, and for his wife's death. But Svidrigailov is not a satanic figure, no Melmoth or Maldoror. He has the manners and the appearance of a gentleman. He wears good, well-cut clothes, and is handsome, although his face, like that of Stavrogin, is somewhat expressionless. He has a genuine sense of humour, and likes to laugh. He has great charm and astonishing insight into the secret desires of others. Dostoevsky makes it clear, quite undramatically, that he is the kind of man about whom women of all classes can become obsessed. He is charitable, ensuring that Katerina Ivanovna Marmeladova has a decent burial, that her children's future is secured, and that Sonya can stop working. Charitable actions come as easily to him as they do to anyone, for good deeds are no monopoly of the virtuous.

Svidrigailov is pleasant but unfathomable. He is utterly frank to Raskolnikov about his attempts to seduce his sister. He nearly won by appealing to her reforming spirit, and by immense flattery. The combination almost brought about her undoing. Alas, at a critical point she read his expression a little too clearly, and virtue prevailed.

As he talks to Raskolnikov about his sexual exploits, reluctantly conceding that he did have a serf flogged to the death, he assures him that he no longer has designs upon his sister. Here we find another of the libertine's qualities – he would make a poker-player of genius. Svidrigailov seems to have put all his cards on the table, yet Raskolnikov is so confused that he can neither believe nor disbelieve. He is quite unable to read Svidrigailov, who could be anything. The more Svidrigailov shows him, laughing, the less Raskolnikov can cope. He is the kind of player who could show you all five cards face up, and still mesmerise you into doing the wrong thing.

As a voluptuary he knows exactly what he is doing, and has a fair idea of what he wants. He can look straight into that part of the self that is so secret that we do not even realise that it is there. He knows Dunya better than Raskolnikov, knows that there is a point at which he can get her. In the same way he knew how far he could go with his wife, how hard to punish her. He knows how to pick up sixteen-year-old girls, and how to charm them as he plays with them on his knee . . .

But Svidrigailov is the victim of a boredom so intense, so total, that he is beyond being bored. Libertinage has conferred upon the mysteries of human existence a kind of transparency that has taken all the savour from life. It is precisely this loss of ability to respond, this destruction of the metaphysical palate that Baudelaire describes when he writes:

Le Printemps adorable a perdu son odeur.[12]

So overpowering is Svidrigailov's sense of indifference that he is not even aware of being bored. His behaviour never signifies a sense of boredom or emptiness. On one occasion only does he give voice to it, casually, as he looks at his watch:

Honestly, I wish there were something; to be a land-owner, a father, a cavalryman, a photographer, a journalist . . . nothing, no speciality! Do you know, sometimes I'm bored.[13]

His list of possibilities is random-selected. He no longer cares sufficiently to have day-dreams about what he might have been. He is so indifferent that he simply reels off the first five occupations that occur to him, and then suspects he may be bored.

There is only one thing left for him. He returns to the capital to try once more for Dunya. He has a little wallow in some of his old haunts, but really his sense of emptiness has decided him on a trip—a *voyage* to America, as he calls it. He spends his last night on earth in a squalid *Biergarten*, and then in tying up loose ends. He makes a point of being orderly as the ironic culmination to a life of disorder. He sees Sonya, parts from his betrothed, aged sixteen, and gets wet in the process. He takes a room in a hotel which he discovers to his delight to be a brothel. Next door there are a couple of *louche* gentlemen. He has some tea and something to eat, goes to bed and has a terrible nightmare. He awakes before dawn and sets off to kill himself on a particular street, but half-way there he gives up and, in front of a protesting night-watchman, he sends a bullet into his brain.

Svidrigailov is the first and most complete existentialist hero. His total lack of any sense of whole meaning creates an indifference to himself and to everything else that makes Camus' *Etranger* appear an egomaniac. He believes in the possibility of an after-life, but paradise is a tiny country bath-house peopled by spiders. The image of paradise as an infinitely cramped and squalid spot reveals everything about Svidrigailov – and he makes no attempt to conceal it. Indeed, he is strangely favoured by a *rapport* with the beyond – both his late wife, and the serf he had put to death appear to him, but they have nothing but trivia to say.

We are also favoured with the picture of Svidrigailov in action. Dunya can still make his lust flare. He had reached the point of libertine obsession with her, when the very glimpse of her was enough to give him vertigo. He retains an infinite capacity for intensity in lust, and this is his tragedy. The capacity is there, but virtually nothing can realise it fully or sustain it.

He finally sets a trap in which he cannot fail to seduce or rape Dunya. Once again he enjoys paroxysms of intensity, which come to a peak as she threatens to shoot him in defence of her virtue. Of course he braves her revolver; the risk of death at her hand is an exquisite excitement as he walks toward her and a bullet creases his scalp. But then she ruins this, his supreme psycho-drama. She stops being the melodramatic victim, stops playing his game, throws the revolver aside and simply waits. He actually puts an arm around her waist, but she is quite indifferent to the sexual currents of the situation he is trying to create. She simply becomes a sack of potatoes, and by informing him that she could never under any circumstances love him, makes him feel that he would be making love to a corpse. He feels the intensity drain out of him:

> something suddenly seemed to leave his heart all at once, and perhaps it was not just the weight of the fear of death.[14]

Indeed not, Svidrigailov could feel the excitement leave him. He urges Dunya to go before he changes his mind; not because he might still rape her, but because he might murder her in retribution for her killing the last of his sensations and making him into a living corpse.

In his honesty, his calm, his control, his detachment, good humour and turn-out, the concern for physical comfort which he displays in the hours before his suicide, Svidrigailov is remarkably attractive. The ghosts he sees, his appalling nightmare of the lusting five-year-old girl in make-up, his paradise of spiders in a tiny bath-house, impart a metaphysical dimension that places him beyond sheer brutishness. He has all the courage and all the indifference of Baudelaire's 'Don Juan aux Enfers', all his *conscience dans le mal*. At the same time, he is a creature of flesh and blood in a way that the satanic creations of Romanticism were not. Dostoevsky has portrayed his supreme libertine through the conventions of realism, not through a Gothic code.

Svidrigailov is utterly plausible. We cannot dismiss him as a 'literary' figure. Moreover, unlike Don Juan, he is too big, too much a colossus of a burnt-out case, to have any vanity. He possesses all the superb defiant qualities of a Romantic Lucifer, but none of his trappings. Svidrigailov is too great, too empty, and too evil to smell of sulphur.

CHAPTER FIFTEEN

The Aesthetics of Intensity

Dostoevsky's complicity in the intensity cult is apparent in his choice of literary codes. The cult manifests itself in its emphasis upon pure sensation as a self-justifying activity. Baudelaire and Dostoevsky both describe this process directly, while Baudelaire also gives an oblique account of it through his rhetoric. *Les Fleurs du Mal* makes liberal use of the stock-in-trade of an earlier generation of hysterical and convulsionary Romantics. The work is steeped in the Gothic rhetoric of Romantic excess, the necrophiliac horror of the Romantic Agony. Yet Baudelaire always remains at a distance from his material. Gothic rhetoric is at one remove from its creator, representing the projection of his protagonist's state of mind, and specifically of his preoccupation with sensation. This aspect of the work constitutes a form of *oratio obliqua* which reflects the character's attitude to the situation even though that situation is apparently described by the author himself.

It is highly significant that Dostoevsky should have derived his own literary codes from what the French term *littérature à sensations:* the serialised *roman feuilleton*, the Gothic tradition of popular literature.

Until the third decade of the nineteenth century the notion of popular literature was essentially a contradiction in terms. Certainly the novel, in the hands of Mrs Radcliffe, or even Rousseau, had been regarded as an entertainment, but it was essentially an entertainment for the educated. The rapid increase in literacy and, above all, the rise, in the 1830s in both France and England, of the popular press, created a new type of readership for fiction, a mass readership, and the product was redesigned to meet the demands of the new mass market. Its production was streamlined – Alexandre Dumas allegedly ran a kind of novel factory – and the nature of its appeal was adapted to the taste of its new readers. The vast majority of these would consume the product in serial form, in the popular press. The 'sensational novel' might be described as publishing's first venture into the part-work.

The new brand of novel had certain definite characteristics. The most important of these was the nature of its appeal. Broadly speaking, the form has a single aim: to excite the reader at all costs, regardless of notions such as verisimilitude or historical accuracy. The popular novel was first and foremost a sensation machine. Thus the form is distinguished by the way in which it organises its appeal. Unlike more conventional novels it does not start slowly to build up tension gradually over some five hundred pages. It seeks to grip the reader immediately, and then to sustain a certain level of tension throughout. The emphasis on excitement at all costs is reflected in the popular novel's singular complexity of plot. Where the plot of *Madame Bovary* might be summarised in a sentence or two, an account of the plot of Soulié's *Les Elixirs du Diable* or Eugène Sue's *Les Mystères de Paris* would take several pages. Because all considerations of form and verisimilitude are sacrificed to immediate intensity, the plots are rambling shapeless affairs. They lack any one specific climax, abound in walk-on parts and make the most liberal use of coincidence. This is because coincidence is the sole device which permits the novelist to bring together into some sort of pattern series of episodes which would otherwise appear as totally unrelated elements in his plot structure. The discovery that the protagonists in various otherwise quite unconnected episodes turn out to be related to one another – a device which Sue and Soulié exploit and abuse beyond the point of mere excess – imparts to their work some pale semblance of unity. It is for this reason that the popular novel form positively abounds in unexpected encounters between friends of friends, and is full of discoveries of secret identities and relationships. For example, the prostitute Fleur de Marie, who is rescued from a life of vice by Prince Rudolf of Gerolstein in *Les Mystères de Paris*, happens to be the long-lost daughter whom he had come to Paris to seek.

Dostoevsky's debt to this literature is obvious at a glance and has been carefully explored. Why should he have based the forms of his fiction upon this essentially low literary tradition, rather than, say, upon the conventions of the *roman d'analyse* so successfully manipulated by Turgenev? The immediate and obvious answer was money. Dostoevsky employed the conventions of the popular novelist because that is what he was obliged to be; he actually lived by the pen. The critic has no right to criticise, from an aesthetic viewpoint, decisions made by a man who depended upon his work for his survival and the survival of his dependants. Dostoevsky had to sell books in order to eat, hence their sensationalism and their emphasis upon popular appeal. He simply could not afford the well-chiselled output of a patrician novelist such as Turgenev, Flaubert or Henry James. Indeed, his wife's memoirs frequently describe him envying the leisurely pace at which Turgenev and Tolstoy were able to work. He regularly complains of the violence which the pressures of the deadline do to his initial conceptions. Moreover, he finds it ironic that the publishers, knowing that he wrote from financial need, would therefore pay him as little as half the rate per sheet they would pay Tolstoy or Turgenev.

That being said, Dostoevsky's choice of form nevertheless throws a certain light upon his subject matter. That it was not solely a matter of economic choice is, in a sense, confirmed by the existence of comparable strains in *Les Fleurs du Mal* – which was certainly not intended to be a bestseller. Further confirmation is supplied by a third writer, Lautréamont. *Les Chants de Maldoror* are, among other things, the exploration of a certain sickness of the imagination, the perverted dream-life of an age addicted to sensation. In order to make this point the author informs us that he has made deliberate and liberal use of the forms of the popular novel. His very *nom de plume* echoes the name of one of Sue's heroes – Latréaumont. Like Baudelaire the author of *Les Chants* seems to have sensed that literary styles and fashions reflect the spirit of the age that created them, and that, in that sense, they constitute a comment upon that spirit.

Yet Dostoevsky's use of popular forms cannot be said to represent an ironic comment upon the age which generated them, the age of intensity. He espouses those forms not ironically but whole-heartedly, and as such they comment upon the author's own deep involvement in the intensity cult. His use of the conventions of sensational literature reflects his own undisputed sensationalism, as well as reflecting the world which his fiction describes. Dostoevsky's use of the codes of the *feuilleton* is appropriate to a world in which intensity is the supreme driving-force, for the *roman feuilleton* was the first aesthetic manifestation of the intensity cult.

It is in this rather special sense that art-forms, and particularly popular art-forms, provide a fascinating insight into the psyche of an age. The success of writers such as Soulié, Sue, Dumas, was itself evidence of a collective addiction to sensation, and hence it confirms the accuracy of the respective analyses of Baudelaire and Dostoevsky.

Dostoevsky's choice of form echoes Baudelaire in yet another respect. In his preface to *Les Fleurs du Mal* Baudelaire describes the 'state of the nation' concluding with a reminder to the *hypocrite lecteur* that he is as much a part of the analysis, as much an intensity addict as any character of Baudelaire's. Now, in as much as Dostoevsky's novels gratify the reader's own craving for excitement, they too bring him into the world which they describe. Dostoevsky's use of the aesthetic of intensity is its own comment upon the proliferation of the intensity drive. The novels are the perfect illustration of the proposition that the medium is the message.

Viewed in this light the form of Dostoevsky's novels can be seen to have a certain charge of meaning. His use of blatant coincidence, the multiplicity of secret relationships that subtend works such as *The Insulted and the Injured*, create a very specific atmosphere, the atmosphere of aesthetic intensity. This debt to the popular novel is reflected in the subject matter of his work as well as in its form. In the first place, he shares its interest in the more colourful aspects of the urban underworld.

Sue's *Les Mystères de Paris*, for example, opens with the account of a thieves' kitchen, portraying the manners and the speech of criminal types. Sue's work has a documentary dimension that makes it the forerunner of the private-eye realism of Dashiell Hammett and Raymond Chandler. Along with this there is a second strain – a sentimental philanthropy, a genuine if paternalistic concern for the victims of city life. It is this paternalistic attitude that inspired Marx's unique excursion into literary criticism, his attack on Sue in *The Holy Family*.

An interest in criminal types coupled with a sentimental concern for urban misery is precisely Dostoevsky's tone. His novels stand as proof that an obsession with vice, violence and sexual perversity is perfectly compatible with sentimental humanitarianism. Indeed, the blend is peculiarly characteristic of his age. Balzac, Dickens, Sue, Baudelaire and Dostoevsky are all capable of making pathetic and successful appeals to our social conscience at one moment, while appealing at the next to aspects of our secret selves which we would prefer to ignore. Dostoevsky's concern with libertinage, alcoholism, prostitution and murder in the big city represent a direct affiliation to the traditions of the popular novel. Indeed, it is this very aspect of the form which, the critic Walter Benjamin suggests, is the most significant manifestation, in the popular novel, of the climate of the age. Crime, violence and sexual excess are the price that must be paid for the new urban society of slum-dwellers. The very existence of the detective story is evidence of a certain degraded way of life. Benjamin quotes a certain Adolphe Schmidt:

> 'It is almost impossible to sustain a decent way of life in one of the densely populated areas, in which no one knows anyone else and cannot be embarrassed by them . . .'
>
> The masses here feature as a refuge, protecting the anti-social type from his pursuers. It is in their most threatening manifestation that they make themselves felt. It is they that constitute the source of the detective-story.[1]

Benjamin suggests that it is the anonymity and isolation of city life which is the cause of criminal themes and indeed criminal behaviour. Moreover, it is the general atmosphere of *obosoblenie* – isolation and insulation – that protects the criminal from detection: Raskolnikov was alone in the city, nobody recognised him at the scene of the crime. Thus the emphasis placed by the popular novel upon crime and detection is the aesthetic reflection of the isolation and trauma which informed the new urban society.

The suggestion that the city is the place of isolation gives a charge of meaning to what might otherwise appear one of Dostoevsky's narrative weaknesses, one which he shares with the popular novel form: namely, his unashamed use of coincidences. The rôle of coincidence becomes meaningful in that it suggests that the city is the place in which people only come together by chance. The brief encounter is the only possible kind of association, and it is this that forms the basis of relationships in the city. City life is so haphazard, disintegrated and dispersed that it is proper that meetings, the establishment of any kind of community or togetherness, should be seen to be the consequence of blind chance alone, and in no sense the result of a purposeful pattern which might reflect a more organically integrated community.

Dostoevsky is himself perfectly conscious of his affiliations with the tradition of the popular novel. In a letter he once described his purpose as being 'to create an impression' (*proizvesti effekt*)[2] and this is precisely the aim of *littérature à sensations*. The tension curve of Dostoevsky's novels is the single sustained level of intensity which we associate with that form. However, this is not to say that he treated his work lightly. He never considered that his books were mere entertainments, never lost his sense of high seriousness. The view he takes of his work emerges in another letter. He is writing a little discouragingly about a project to adapt *The Devils* to the stage:

> There is a certain secret of art whereby an epic form can never find a corresponding dramatic one.[3]

There is no escaping the connotations of high seriousness in the term 'epic'. At first sight, a view of his novels as epics might seem inconsistent with their affiliation to sensationalist literature. However, it is tempting to wonder whether it might not have been precisely the sensationalist aesthetic of the popular novel which represented for Dostoevsky the epic form of the nineteenth century. Although his use of the word 'epic' may well have been inspired by the tradition inaugurated by Gogol who described *Dead Souls* as a *poema*, that is to say a 'smaller kind of epic', it may also be an instinctive recognition that the epic of the age would not come from the revivalist poetry of a Hugo or a Tennyson; the recognition that it was the popular novel that was the true epic form. After all, its aesthetic and its values were as genuine a reflection of its time as were the Classical Alexandrine or the *laisse* of the *chansons de geste* of theirs. It is precisely this point that is made by Baudelaire when he suggests that Balzac is an epic writer, and that the heroes of the *Iliad* would scarcely reach the ankle of some of his creations.[4]

Besides Dostoevsky's general debt to the popular novel form, he develops certain aspects of the aesthetics of intensity which, although present in the popular novel are only perfected by Dostoevsky himself.

Perhaps his single most important contribution is a quality we have termed 'sadistic pathos'. This vital Dostoevskian device consists of an appeal to the reader's sense of pity that is overpoweringly and disagreeably strong. The response is one of unbearable pain, for it is a feature of the sentimental appeal of the *feuilleton* that there is no emotional release, no catharsis – why get rid of emotions that one has gone to such lengths to induce in the reader?

It is the anti-cathartic treatment of the emotions that makes for the gulf that separates the novels of Dostoevsky from tragedy proper. We know that a tragedy will end badly, because the whole situation has a dreadful aura of inevitability about it. We know that Dostoevsky's novels will end badly only if he tells us as much – and this he often does. The atmosphere of his novels is that of a *roman d'aventures* in which chance has taken over from fate as the force that drives the motor. Fate implies the existence of whole meanings, as does tragedy. Dostoevsky portrays a world in which tragedy as such is no longer altogether possible.

Tragedy imposes upon the emotions a discipline, a form of order which lends purpose to them. The appeal which Dostoevsky addresses, particularly to our sense of pity, is wildly undisciplined. He uses a rhetoric of 'emotional overkill' which is as different from the emotional world of tragedy as the popular novel was from tragedy itself. Dostoevsky's prime concern is with the sheer intensity of pity, and nothing else. Scenes such as Raskolnikov's dream of drunken peasants flogging a pony to death, beating it across its 'tender eyes', are unbearable. Although this scene in particular is a symbolic icon of a world 'où l'action n'est pas la soeur du rêve', the world of unrelieved suffering animal and human, it is also very much a part of the intensity aesthetic, and the sadist's part at that. The intensity of Dostoevsky's will to pity is a part of the sado-masochistic syndrome, itself a manifestation of the need for sensation at all costs. The pity that he wrings from us may take us beyond the threshold of pain, but anything is preferable to apathy and indifference. Dostoevsky takes a positive pleasure in stimulating both his and our own sense of pity.

It is not a far cry from this 'pure' or disinterested kind of violent appeal to the emotions to its applied counterpart – emotional blackmail. Although it is always a little absurd to talk of national characteristics, our own experience suggests that Russians are particularly prone to both the pure and the applied forms of sadistic pathos. Emotional blackmail seems to play a most important part in Russian family life, an impression recently confirmed by a comparative study of Russian and American methods of education, in which it emerged that where the American system employs punishment as a deterrent, the Russian system brings its young pioneers to heel with the threat of 'withdrawal of love'.

Dostoevsky is himself a past master at emotional blackmail and the irresponsible manipulation of the feelings of others. For example, when in a penal settlement in Siberia, and afterwards in exile, his letters have none of the cheerful stoicism of a prisoner anxious to spare his relatives the knowledge of what prison life was really like. There is none of that matter-of-fact acceptance of appalling conditions and ill-health which novels such as *The First Circle* and *A Day in the Life of Ivan Denisovich* have led us to expect as the proper way for political prisoners to behave. Dostoevsky's Siberian letters are a perpetual stream of complaint. He complains of bad health, and even fears for his sanity. He makes not the slightest effort to cheer his correspondents up. His sole concern seems to be that they should feel for him as intensely as possible. If not exactly emotional blackmail this is certainly sadistic pathos – we hear not a note of that hymn of joy which Dmitri Karamazov promised to chant in the salt-mines.

Dostoevsky uses emotional blackmail as such upon his nephew Isaev. If we are to believe Anna Dostoevskaya, Isaev was an unspeakable young sponger, and perhaps this should be taken into account when considering the way in which his uncle chides him for being a poor letter-writer:

> Your Mama is most unwell. Perhaps the thought that you may soon be an orphan will act as some kind of a check upon your casual behaviour, and make you take life seriously. Up to now, I have always said that you had a kind heart. If that too is untrue, what on earth will become of you?[5]

Thus we would be advised to take account of the author's capacity for sadistic pathos when examining his appeals to our own sense of pity. For example, the scene in which Ivan recounts to Alyosha the atrocities which parents perpetrate upon their children has already been compared to the sadism of Lautréamont. The sadism does not just reside in the actions themselves but in the loving detail with which Ivan recounts them. It is he who ensures that we get the picture, every bit of it; just as does Dostoevsky himself with the numerous atrocity stories of drunken husbands, parents and Turks that fill his *Diary of a Writer*.

It is sadistic pathos that informs the account of family life *chez* Marmeladov. The sheer extremism of their plight, of Marmeladov's alcoholism – he even pawned his wife's stockings and stole from his own daughter – is sadistic in its exaggeration. Similarly we are spared no detail of the death throes of Marmeladov's wife—but then Dostoevsky never spares his readers. As Katerina Ivanovna goes out onto the street, with her pathetic family providing an inept musical accompaniment, and the blood-stained handkerchief of the galloping consumptive pressed to her lips, the appeal becomes so strong that Dostoevsky unwittingly lapses into Gothic black comedy.

Netochka Nezvanova supplies another instance of this kind of drastic appeal. A hopeless, dissolute father is persuading his dutiful daughter to steal the last pennies from her sick mother, so that he can go to a concert:

> 'Netochka,' he began with a trembling voice, 'My dear, listen, give me the money and to-morrow . . .'
>
> 'Papa, Papa, I can't,' I cried, falling to my knees and beseeching him, 'Papa, I can't, I mustn't, Mama must have some tea. You must not rob Mama, you really mustn't. I'll get some another time.'
>
> 'So, you don't want to? You don't want to?' he whispered to me savagely. 'So that means you don't want to love me? All right! I'm going to leave you now, for ever. Stay with Mama, and I'll leave you both and won't take you with me. Do you hear, you bad little girl? Do you hear?'
>
> 'Papa!' I cried in terror, 'Here, take the money. What am I to do now?' I said, wringing my hands and snatching at the hem of his coat. 'Mama is going to cry! Mama is going to scold me again!'[6]

Before this passage is rejected out of hand as melodramatic extravagance, it should be pointed out that it is no more hysterical than the appeals that Dostoevsky addressed to his own wife, to let him have the remainder of their travel money so that he could carry on gambling.

Dostoevsky's novels positively abound in this mood of emotional blackmail. Here, for example, is Ippolit, the tubercular youth of *The Idiot*, visiting an influential school-friend in order to ask him a favour. He places him in a situation in which it is impossible to refuse:

> I was wracked by coughing again, sunk into a chair and could only just recover my breath.
>
> 'Don't worry, I've got TB,' I said. 'I have a favour to ask.'[7]

Ippolit did not have to inform his friend that he was to all intents and purposes a dying man, still less did he have to juxtapose the announcement with notice that he had a favour to ask. This is an example of emotional blackmail in its purest form.

The most striking and invidious of all examples of emotional blackmail is to be found in Mme Raskolnikova's letter to her son. It is a classic, containing all the typical ingredients. Thus it concerns the family, and is the account of conspicuous sacrifice – the emotional blackmailer's version of conspicuous consumption. It is totally successful in that neither victim nor perhaps blackmailer are aware that blackmail is intended. Finally, a peculiarly Russian trait, there is no question of blackmail for practical advantage, no manipulation towards an end. Raskolnikov's mother is not trying to make her son do anything, she is simply anxious that he should appreciate the nature of the sacrifices being made for love of him. This is a disinterested activity, blackmail for blackmail's sake. The letter is designed to make its recipient *feel* as strongly as possible by making him fully aware of the true extent of his sister's sacrifice.

It will be recalled that the letter describes how Dunya was first slandered by Svidrigailov's wife, who suspected her of having an affair with her husband, and then triumphantly and conspicuously vindicated when the truth emerged. Mme Svidrigailova proceeds to find her a husband in Luzhin. The letter describes the situation in such a way that it is clear that Dunya is sacrificing herself to a monster. Look how it qualifies every point advanced in Luzhin's favour:

> He's a reliable man, who is well to do, he holds two positions and already has money of his own. It's true that he's already 45, but he looks pleasant enough and is still attractive, anyway he's a solid, decent man, just a little gloomy and a trifle superior. But maybe that's just a first impression. By the way, be careful, dear Rodya, when you meet him in St Petersburg . . . not to make up your mind about him too quickly, as you tend to, in case there should be anything you don't like about him at first. I'm just saying that, although I am sure you will like him. Besides, if you are to get to know someone, you have to take things gradually and carefully, not to make a mistake or form prejudices, which are later hard to justify and smooth over. And, there is much more about Petr Petrovich which suggests him to be a most worthy man. On his first call he announced to us that he was a positive person, but one sharing in many respects 'the convictions of our younger generations', as he put it, and who was against all kinds of prejudice. He said a great deal more, because he wanted to show off a bit, and very much enjoyed the sound of his own voice, but there's scarcely anything wrong with that. Of course I didn't understand a lot, but Dunya told me that although he was not particularly educated, he was intelligent and probably kind. You know your sister Rodya. She is determined, sensible, patient and generous, although she is impulsive, as I well know. Of course there is no love on either side, but Dunya is a sensible girl . . .[8]

The letter continues with the suggestion that Raskolnikov may think his mother a silly old woman but that, although Luzhin was kindness and generosity itself, she felt that perhaps she had better not plan to live with them, that she was sure that he would suggest it, but that she would refuse . . . Finally she discusses plans to come to St Petersburg. Her future son-in-law was good enough to assist them. They would be travelling third class and would, fortunately, get a lift to the station, which, she reminds her son who must have known it anyway, was only 90 versts away, on a peasant's cart!

In short, the letter spares Raskolnikov nothing. It goes to great, if unconscious, lengths to point out the sacrifice that is being made for him. No wonder it is the receipt of this letter, written for the sake of intensity let it be observed, which finally clinches his decision to commit murder.

The invitation contained in the letter to Raskolnikov to read between the lines becomes clear when his mother's behaviour is compared to that of his sister. The latter makes every effort to persuade him that the marriage is really a good thing. She realises Luzhin's shortcomings, but sees him as the lesser of two evils, and sees no real obstacle to her happiness. There is no question of self-sacrifice. She claims to be acting out of enlightened self-interest. Raskolnikov's reaction, quite properly, is that she is a liar. Far from being the decent sort she makes him out to be, Luzhin is clearly unspeakable. Of course Raskolnikov is intelligent enough to have seen this for himself, but anyone could have seen it had they been suitably briefed by that letter. On meeting him, Raskolnikov never gives Luzhin a chance, because he knows all about him already.

Dostoevsky himself frequently exerts emotional blackmail of this kind upon the reader. A classic instance is the end of *The Brothers Karamazov*, with the Snegirov boy dying of consumption in the midst of his family of cripples, halfwits and drunks. One has but to reach a chapter entitled *U Ilyushenkin Postelki* – a virtually untranslatable piece of pathetic rhetoric (*lit.* At Little Ilyusha's Little Bedside) – in which the diminutives convey not size but intense *Schmalz*, to know that Dostoevsky has prepared yet another savage wrench at his readers' heart-strings. If his works employ an aesthetic of intensity, then for the sado-masochist sadistic pathos is the greatest source of intensity of them all.

Emotional blackmail, like other modes of intensity, only works properly when you are unaware of it. Once you realise that you are over-responding to a situation for the pleasure of the response, that pleasure is drastically diminished. This may account for Dostoevsky's own sublime ignorance of the very existence of such a thing as sadistic pathos and emotional blackmail. Dostoevsky always writes as an insider, he remains too much a successful blackmailer to be able to characterise the process. This is why he never does so in so many words; also why he never spares his readers, never makes any serious effort to exercise restraint or control upon his treatment of the emotions. There is never any irony or distance in his work, none of that detached quality which characterises Solzhenitsyn's treatment of the horrors. Dostoevsky always goes the whole hog.

That being said, it is the greatest testimonial to his genius that Dostoevsky should have been able to write novels that wallow in sadistic pathos and the aesthetics of cheap sensationalism, but which are never cheapened by their aesthetic slumming.

Dostoevsky seeks to capture the spirit of his age through an aesthetic code built upon the need to provoke a reaction at all costs. Its aim is neither beauty nor harmony of form, but sensation and intensity. In this respect, too, his work lies close to that of Baudelaire. In the latter's poetry we can see the beginnings of a shift of emphasis from a concern with meanings to a concern with art as a mode of intensity. Baudelaire was the first poet of his age who expressly cultivated shock and surprise for their own sake. He states that there can be no beauty without surprise. It is his emphasis upon the importance of aesthetic shock tactics that makes him the father of the modern movement in the arts.

It is the predominance of intensity over all other aesthetic values and considerations that is the chief characteristic of modernism. In that respect, the new aesthetics may be seen to be a direct reflection of the new age, the age of intensity. Twentieth-century aestheticians and artists put surprise and shock as their ultimate aesthetic aspirations. Apollinaire, both in his poetry and his art criticism, the Futurist aesthetic of Mayakovsky, the disruptive shock tactics of Dada and the Surrealists' enchantment with their own capacity to surprise themselves all reflect this. As late as the 1940s Picasso would still maintain that the value of his art was in its disruptive quality. The object of artists of earlier ages, say from the High Renaissance to the middle of the nineteenth century, may broadly be said to have been the rendering of a world-view which was, finally, founded on a sense of cosmic harmony that sought to make the divine creation meaningful, and which was, on a more modest level, committed to the articulation of meanings; whereas, from Baudelaire and Dostoevsky onward, we see artists beginning to turn their backs on meaning, reducing their work to the cultivation of mere meaningless sensation, a sensation which is described by twentieth-century aesthetics as a 'pure aesthetic response'. The desire of twentieth-century artists, such as the abstract expressionists, to eliminate all forms of reference or meaning from their work, because meaning was felt to compromise its essential purity, is a direct reflection of their concern with intensity of aesthetic experience and nothing else. The very possibility of meaning is rejected.

It is surely proper to regard this turning away from meaning as an abdication, itself a reflection of the intensity cult. Art turns its back on its traditional preoccupation with whole meanings to concern itself with 'freshness and intensity' – the qualities which C. Day Lewis suggested as the essential attributes of the poetic image. Art becomes reduced to sheer intensity of response – hence the flight from meaning in the arts of this century, a flight most perfectly expressed in the aesthetic nihilism of Dada.

Rejection of meaning, of the so called 'literary' and 'programmatic' elements in painting and music, has become a received idea of twentieth-century aesthetics. The rejection is finally a rejection of the universe of meanings which Western culture has inherited. It is a rejection which Baudelaire and Dostoevsky trace out, but, unlike, say, the Russian Futurists who also describe that rejection, gaily talking of 'throwing Pushkin overboard from the steamer of modernity', the earlier writers have an awareness of the reassurance once provided by meanings, an awareness which compels them to describe rejection of meaning as a loss.

Why this should be considered a loss can be illustrated by further consideration of the aesthetic of intensity. One of its most complete devotees was Rimbaud. His poetry is both a rejection of the traditional values of his civilisation and a quest for values through sensation. His poetic barbarism is essentially disruptive, while at the same time seeking to create its own universe of sweet sensations, a universe in which meaning has been replaced by naked intensity. Rimbaud reduces everything to the level of simple, concrete sensation: nothing exists for him beyond the 'kick' of language.

In his attempt to live through sensation alone Rimbaud nearly destroyed himself. Pure sensation cannot be sustained and we have seen that the moment when it drains away is utterly traumatic. This has been the message of our study of the intensity cult. Unfortunately it is a message that can, apparently, only be learnt the hard way. A. Alvarez, in *The Savage God*,[9] traces the fascinating relationship between suicide and artistic creation in this century. The suicide-rate among artists has been alarmingly high. Dostoevsky's examination of the way in which the cult of intensity can lead one straight to spiritual bankruptcy and suicide may help to tell us why this should be. In modern art's rejection of meaning and all other foreign bodies, in pursuit of an absolute chemical purity, it has destroyed its own *raison d'être*. In other ages, the intense excitement which any work of art should convey, was a means, harnessed to a concern with values beyond the limits of that particular work. That excitement became in this century an end in itself, the sole end. The result is a dreadful impoverishment. The artist who seeks to create a work of art which will be nothing but itself, ends by creating nothing. It is this that accounts, finally, for the virtual poetic sterility to which a Mallarmé or a Valéry eventually succumbs.

But perhaps those were the lucky ones. The concern with pure sensation, pure intensity cost others their lives. Dostoevsky's association of the intensity cult with sterility and self-destruction casts a strange light on the fate of one of the most gifted of all the practitioners of aesthetic intensity – the painter Jackson Pollock. Pollock is perhaps the intensity cult's definitive victim. His painting was quite unconcerned with statement and meaning, all its value lay in the thrill of making, the intense sensation of applying paint to canvas. In this respect his art is the end of the line: one could go no further in the attempt to purify art of its dross. It is the embodiment of total sensation: there is nothing beyond it, the sensation is all there is. It is said that neurology is now able to provide a subject with a direct means of stimulating the pleasure centres. The sensation is infinitely stronger than orgasm, and can be repeated indefinitely. The only drawback is that the subject would continue to stimulate his pleasure centres until he dropped dead.

Something of this kind seems to have happened to Jackson Pollock. His art found a mode of being which was pure, meaningless intensity, and nothing else: a dead end. Intensity seems to have proved finally as sterile to Pollock as it did to Svidrigailov. It is impossible, and unforgivably intrusive, to suggest that Pollock took his own life in the car crash that killed him; let us say that one can understand how he had grown to be a careless driver.

PART FOUR

The Age of Intensity: In Conclusion

CHAPTER SIXTEEN

The Public Synthesis

Dostoevsky develops the themes of Romantic literature and goes on to record a particular state of culture – the moment before it comes apart. He is, above all, concerned with offering a study in depth of the Gadarene swine, as they break from a trot into a canter. He describes the divided society in which every man is out for himself, determined to secure, at whatever cost to himself or to others, those rights which utilitarian reason informs him are inalienably his for the taking.

In Dostoevsky's world harmony, the organic unity of the group, cannot be achieved. Families only exist in order to be split asunder by the pressures of urban poverty, sexuality and parricide. The divided state of society is reflected in the divided state of the individual; Dostoevsky's doubles, Myshkin and Rogozhin, the younger Verkhovensky and Stavrogin, Versilov's split personality, the inner divisions of the Underground Man, and Raskolnikov, the very embodiment of schism.

The nineteenth century seems to have its very being in turmoil and confusion, deriving from the rapid rate of technological and cultural change, the increasing importance of the pecuniary ethic, the tantalising possibilities of an open society regularly glimpsed from 1789 onwards, but never achieved. Old values were patently useless, the experience of one generation without relevance to the next. Small wonder that the typical reaction of the Dostoevskian character was to withdraw into a divided self.

This sense of division and lack of organic wholeness is reflected in the rise of the novel form. The novel becomes the supreme medium through which to render the nineteenth-century experience, and not just because it is the form of absolute sinfulness. It is particularly suited to the expression of the dispersed, piecemeal experience of that age. The narrative form – Stendhal's 'mirror that moves along a road' – does not need to reflect unified experience. It is able to portray the haphazard succession of incidents which fail to come together into any meaningful pattern, that are random and absurd. It can handle such materials because the only formative element which it acknowledges is time itself; mere succession provides it with form enough. It is able to base itself upon the sheer meaningless succession of event upon event. Flaubert's *L'Education sentimentale* is a novel whose theme, precisely, is meaninglessness. The hero comes to accept that his life is without meaning or achievement, that it lacks any supremely privileged moment around which he could weave his experience into a meaningful and organic whole. A *madeleine* is but a *madeleine* to him. All he has to show is a set of trivial memories, because he moved in a world essentially without value.

Traditional literary forms such as the epic, tragedy, pastoral or even lyric poetry were all based on the recognition that there exist crucial moments which could shape the whole life of a man, or indeed of a culture. It is with such essentially meaningful moments that they concern themselves. The very status of their subjects as subjects is a recognition that they are meaningful. Whether it be the founding of Rome, the erection of a monument more permanent than bronze or being kissed by Jenny, the work of art in question asserts the supreme validity of the experience it relates. The novel denies the validity of such experience, almost by definition it constitutes its negation. This explains why the attempts of novelists to portray organic wholeness have proved so singularly unsuccessful. The form is unable to handle such topics, which is why, for example, Gogol found the regenerative Parts Two and Three of *Dead Souls* impossible to complete. Narrative fiction as he knew it could not portray the resurrection of Chichikov without aesthetic disaster. Similarly, the aesthetic success of *Oblomov* is probably despite Goncharov, and certainly despite Belinsky. That it is aesthetically disastrous for the novelist to portray a world of positive values and organic wholeness is confirmed by the writing of Tolstoy. The organic unity of the Rostovs' world is only acceptable because it is shown to be doomed, lapsing eventually into the sour, gritty epilogue. Whatever the virtues of Levin's development in *Anna Karenina* as a spiritual communication, aesthetically it is a disaster.

Unlike epic or lyric forms, the novel cannot portray unity and wholeness. It is formed by its representation of dualism and division. It is this that accounts for the thinness and for the shortcomings of Dostoevsky's handling of the theme of synthesis. As a novelist he has remarkably little to say about this, the supreme aspiration of nineteenth-century culture. Synthesis, the restoration of a divided world to a state of Edenic unity, was the most important of all Romantic aspirations. It is one to which Dostoevsky's novels do scant justice, when compared to their treatment of destruction, because the novel as a form perfectly adapted to the representation of destruction was the form in which the devil had the best tunes. It is no coincidence that it is only outside the novels themselves, in his *Diary of a Writer* and in his *Pushkin Speech*, that Dostoevsky deals at any length with the theme of synthesis as such.

Dostoevsky has based his analysis of collapse upon the disappearance of whole meanings, and the consequent readiness in contemporary man to gratify appetite at all costs. Absolute need is the sole categorical imperative. Dostoevsky seeks to recreate a universe of meanings and values through religion, more specifically through the Russian Orthodox Church. Religion was the only institution that took full account of man's spiritual needs, that recognised that he was more complex than the organic machine which behaviourist planners and architects of the Crystal Palace would have him be. Religion alone would create meaning; the proof of this proposition for Dostoevsky was that the decline in belief had made for a corresponding increase in a sense of aimlessness. Like Baudelaire, Dostoevsky ascribes the irritated consciousness, the *spleen* of modern man to the loss of his sense of religion:

> . . . with great speed, a complete lack of faith in the soul and its immortality takes root. It's not just that this disbelief becomes a conviction . . . there also takes root a peculiar and universal indifference to this noble sense of human existence – an indifference that can be almost comic . . . to everything that is alive, to the truth of life, to everything that confers health upon it and destroys corruption and decay.[1]

It is this view of religion that directs Dostoevsky towards the Russian Church as a medium for synthesis. This explains the otherwise obscure discussions in *The Brothers Karamazov* about the relation between Church and State, and also the lengthy discourse of Zosima on 'The Russian Monk'. It is not just a spiritual synthesis that is aspired to, but ultimately a social one:

> at first spiritual union of mankind in Christ, and then through the strength of this spiritual union of all in Christ, and inevitably deriving from it, a proper political and social union.[2]

There is nothing ecumenical about Dostoevsky's religion. His rejection of Western forms of Christianity is total. Protestantism he regards, anticipating Max Weber, as a mere mandate to commerce, whereas Catholicism has sold out to the socialists. Religion has vanished from the West. As Zosima puts it,[3] there is no church left in the West, only ecclesiastical architecture. Russia alone has preserved the image of Christ, and only through her people will salvation and synthesis be achieved.

This introduces the second element in Dostoevsky's plan for synthesis: his advocacy of Russianness. His mode of resistance to individual self-seeking and the consequent cultural collapse is a reaffirmation of traditional cultural values. Although this is a fairly conventional Russian attitude, when viewed in a European context it gives Dostoevsky somewhat sinister co-religionaries. He aligns himself with conservatives such as Barrès and Daudet, and the whole ignoble band of anti-Dreyfusards. They too sought to withstand the universal dis-integration of values by re-affirmation of cultural grass-roots.

But Dostoevsky's attitude cannot be lightly dismissed as *fin de siècle* chauvinism. It is true that *Diary of a Writer* devotes thousands of words to tiresome, sabre-rattling disquisitions on the Balkan problem. (It is incidentally ironic that Dostoevsky, who made such efforts to stop the cultural rot, should have made his small contribution to the apocalypse of 1917 by reinforcing attitudes which would turn the Sarajevo assassination into a flashpoint.) However, his affirmation of Russian values makes more sense than the cultural archaeology of Barrès and Daudet. Culturally speaking, Russia was in a unique position in Europe. It has been one of the purposes of this book to show how Western culture contained within it the seeds of its own destruction. The roots of the process can be traced back to some of its most distinguished figures such as Bacon and Montaigne. For a Westerner to resist the process of development which originated in the empirical tradition would be tantamount to resisting oneself. Russia's situation was different. There European culture was the result of a transplant. True the operation had been relatively successful, and rejection symptoms were never dangerously acute. Nevertheless, up to 1917, there had remained a second culture relatively unaffected by the Petrine reforms. Enough of the folkways and patterns of traditional Russian culture had survived to Dostoevsky's day to provide him with the possibility of a genuine conceptual alternative, a way of thought about culture which did not necessarily embrace the Western frame of reference. The educated Russian of the later nineteenth century was not obliged to maintain that wholehearted commitment to the European tradition which imposed itself upon his Western counterparts.

It is the existence of an alternative that enabled Dostoevsky to analyse the collapse of Western culture so accurately. It is certainly this that informs his belief that his own civilisation, different in kind from the rest of Europe, might succeed where Europe appeared to have failed.

Diary of a Writer and *The Brothers Karamazov* describe Russia's ideal rôle as defender of the faith and the eventual medium of synthesis. Elsewhere both Shatov and Myshkin express the intimate association of religion with national culture. Shatov, in particular, almost reaches in his ideas the point when each nation must have its own gods, the point, in fact, of Rousseau's civil religion. That it is incumbent upon Russia, as the only nation to have preserved the image of Christ, to transcend the materialism of the age, is a point made by Versilov, one of Dostoevsky's most important spokesmen on this subject. That Dostoevsky should have used the cosmopolitan and divided Versilov is characteristic of the oblique way in which the novelist is obliged to

advocate positive values. Dostoevsky's advocacy is at its most effective
when he uses essentially flawed vessels such as Versilov, Shatov and
Myshkin. Their flaws serve to colour the views they express with that
particular irony which is *the* dominant tone of the nineteenth-century
novel, the literature of *illusions perdues*.

Versilov's plan for synthesis is based upon a combination of nationalism, religion, a rejection of socialism and advocacy of a peculiar version
of the *thèse nobiliaire*. He considers that egalitarian trends and the
aristocracy's abdication of responsibility in favour of Rothschild
delivers his country into the hands of shop-keepers and mountebanks.
Versilov is close in spirit, if not in analytic detail, to de Tocqueville.
He too felt that so-called democratic institutions had simply served
to increase the power of the central government over a nation of sheep
who believed in institutionalised mediocrity and voted Napoleon III
to power. Such democracies were essentially the raw material of dic-
tatorships. This is why, for all his awareness of the shortcomings of the
ancien régime, de Tocqueville could see the advantages of a hereditary
aristocracy, free from the moral pressures of the pecuniary ethic,
independent of the central authority and open to the call of honour,
a class with moral responsibility that was prepared to stand up and
be counted.

Through Versilov, Dostoevsky expresses a similar view. He believes
passionately in the potential rôle of the Russian gentleman. The
Russian upper classes alone were still a possible source of moral
authority, in a position to check the mindless rush into aprioristic
and tyrannical egalitarianism. Only an aristocracy could preserve a
sense of honour – an ethic of human behaviour which used to play
an important part in European culture. It asserts that there exist
standards and values which are held to be desirable although they
have nothing to do with making money or gratifying the senses.

In order to check the decline, Versilov calls for a selective aristocracy
which, he felt, Russia was uniquely qualified to create. He thereby
avoids the possibility of the Russian aristocracy following the French
example and, as de Tocqueville put it, degenerating from a class into
a caste. Versilov proposes an honour-based class of potential leaders:

Our gentry could, even now, without its privileges, remain an upper
class, as the defender of honour, enlightenment, knowledge and
spiritual values, and this, most important of all, without hardening
into a separate caste, which would be fatal to the conception. On
the contrary, we have always kept the door to the class open; the
time has come to open it wide. Let every honourable or courageous
action, every advancement of knowledge, confer entrance to our
highest social category. In that way the class would automatically

become an association of the best, in a true and literal sense, as opposed to a privileged class.[4]

Underwriting this class of leaders is the stability conferred upon Russia by her native culture. 'The people' have a strength and a confidence which ensures the survival of their cultural values:

> they conduct their affairs better than we do. They can continue to live in their own way in the most unnatural situations, in the most unfamiliar situations they remain completely themselves. We do not.[5]

Dostoevsky's sentimental championing of the strength of the 'Mighty Russian People' contains its fair share of chauvinist nonsense. Yet time and again, through the civil war, the purges, the siege of Leningrad, it would seem that history has proved him right. It is the ability to absorb sustained punishment that makes him look to his country as a champion, a source of future stability, this that makes him echo the Gogolian view of Russia's historic mission, and provide his own contribution to that moving patriotic commonplace:

> The main thing is, it scarcely needs saying, they'll take it. Of course they'll take it, they'll take it without our help, with or without support. Russia is strong and has taken plenty already. Her purpose and goal will not permit her to turn vainly from her ancient path, she is too big for that. Whoever believes in Russia knows that she'll take it all, even doubt, and will remain essentially the same holy Russia of ours, and however she might change her countenance one need have no fear ... Her purpose is so noble, her inner sense of that purpose so clear ... that whoever believes in that purpose must transcend his doubts and forebodings.[6]

At the heart of Dostoevsky's hopes for synthesis and resolution lies this unoriginal, jingoistic but stirring belief in the real likelihood of his country's survival. It is this also which creates that Russian/foreign opposition so important in his work.

As part of the path to synthesis, he celebrates the 'essential Russian-ness' of characters such as Mme Epanchina and Rogozhin. They express themselves in a vivid, no nonsense Russian idiom that might have come straight from Gogol. Their language celebrates their solidarity with their native culture. By the same token 'abroad' is associated with disaster. Stavrogin's suicide follows on his intention to take up Swiss citizenship, and as he dangles he is referred to as the 'citizen of the canton of Uri'. The disintegration that ends *The Idiot* sees the Epanchins living abroad. Mme Epanchina, miserable and homesick, ends the novel as follows:

'We've had enough fun, it's time to be sensible. All this, all this abroad, all this Europe of yours is just one long fantasy, and all of us, abroad, are just a fantasy – mark my words, you'll see.[7]

Accordingly, Dostoevsky does not suffer foreigners gladly – the ridiculous German-Russian Kapernaumova of *Crime and Punishment*, the no less ridiculous card-sharping Poles of *The Brothers Karamazov* are just the head of a long paradigm of satirised foreigners and xenophiles. Indeed Dostoevsky takes his dislike of foreign culture beyond the point of absurdity. There is a passage in his *Diary of a Writer* which condemns the teaching of French in schools, a practice he deems as pernicious as masturbation – irregular verbs make you blind.[8]

His loathing of xenophilia is based on his view of Russian radicals, who turn their faces to the West, as cultural apostates:

[The liberal] hates popular customs, Russian history, everything. If there's an excuse, it's that he doesn't know what he's doing, and believes his loathing for Russia to be the most productive liberalism. . . . It was not so long ago that some of our liberals believed almost that this hate for Russia was a sincere love of the fatherland . . .[9]

Dostoevsky's case for his culture is resumed in a letter he writes to the Tsar in which he explains the theme of *The Devils*. It emphasises Russia's rôle as an organic centre, and the loss of stability that arises from a rejection of traditional values:

My view is that this is not a chance nor an isolated phenomenon. It is a direct consequence of the gulf that divides Russian progressives from the native autochthonous roots of Russian life. Even the most talented representatives of our pseudo-European enlightenment have long since concluded that it is positively criminal for us Russians to think about our cultural autonomy. The worst thing is that they are perfectly right; for once we have *proudly* called ourselves Europeans, we have thereby refused to be Russian. In our fear and dismay at the fact that our intellectual and scientific development lags so far behind Europe, we have forgotten that . . . as Russians, we may hold the power to bring a new light to the world.[10]

Unfortunately, like all Dostoevsky's sources of positive value, Russia and Russianness prove profoundly ambiguous. History has shown that qualities of essential Russianness are not incompatible with the *Shigalevshina*, the terrorism and political paranoia of twentieth-century Russia. One of the most intense and aesthetically successful assertions of native cultural values in the most jingoistic of contexts was Eisenstein's remarkable *Aleksandr Nevsky*. His images, together with Prokofiev's score and indeed his subsequent cantata, are one of the greatest celebrations of grass-roots and patriotic values ever to emerge from

Russia. Its values were in no sense in conflict with those of Stalin's régime. Indeed, the 'Russia can take it' attitude, which Dostoevsky finds central to his image of his country as Christ-bearer, was precisely the attitude which ensured the success of the *Shigalevshina*. Thus, autochthonous cultural values were not a sufficient barrier for the Gadarene swine. Once again we find the point acknowledged by Dostoevsky on an instinctive level. We have seen that he establishes a profound relationship between Russianness and the cult of intensity. Gambling was described as a form of conspicuous consumption well suited to the Russian sense of *razmakh* – the gesture with which Rogozhin presented the earrings to Nastasya Filipovna – it is also the supreme medium for intensity.

Dostoevsky recognised that his national character suffered from a profound moral ambiguity. It was this that explained its potential for dualism, its ability to sustain mutually incompatible moral attitudes. In *The Adolescent*, the hero detects in himself at one and the same time both 'the soul of a spider' and a profound and sincere desire for spiritual good order. It is a condition that he considers to be typically Russian:

> . . . there was an intense longing for good order, certainly, but how could it exist with longings of a different kind – God knows how different – that was a mystery. It always has been, a thousand times I have wondered at man's capacity (especially Russian man's) to nourish in his soul the most intense ideal together with the most intense meanness of spirit, and this in all sincerity. The point is, is this an extraordinary breadth of character in Russian man which will take him a long way, or is it simply meanness of spirit![11]

The passage focuses the whole issue of Dostoevsky's complicity in the intensity cult, the way in which his characters try to sustain completely conflicting attitudes, and, above all else, the sheer difficulty of coming to any valid conclusions on such issues. The most important of all the consequences of the loss of a sense of whole meanings now begins to emerge. Without the support these used to provide, man is no longer able to make meaningful value judgments. Dolgoruky cannot determine whether Russian man is rich in potential, or spiritually evil. The essential consequence of the loss of whole meanings is that man cannot tell good from evil any more. It is this that accounts for the all important rôle in Dostoevsky's works of moral contradiction and ambiguity.

Here we see Russian man offered as the archetypal source of moral ambiguity. He plays a part somewhat similar to that of beauty itself in *Les Fleurs du Mal*. The profound capacity for ambiguity and contradiction which Dostoevsky advances as characteristic of Russian man in particular can be seen, through the focus of ambiguity in Baudelaire, to be a more general characteristic of nineteenth-century man. It is this emphasis on ambiguity which explains, in the final analysis, why Dostoevsky's novels provide such an effective account of the state of nineteenth-century culture. He sees as characteristic of Russian man, those very qualities of dualism, division and internal contradiction which we have suggested to be the distinctive features of post-Romantic European culture as a whole. Small wonder that his myth-making has a relevance that transcends the city limits of Skotoprigonevsk.

Dostoevsky's concern is identical to Baudelaire's. Dualism, contradiction, paradox and the inability to make value judgments are the result of the loss of whole meanings and the consequent cult of intensity in the course of which ethical considerations are swept aside.

Dostoevsky derives the resulting breadth of character, the capacity to derive intensity from both vice and virtue, from quintessential Russianness. This view of Russianness as something potentially flawed accounts for the essential inadequacy of his belief in his native culture's potential for future synthesis. It accounts for more sinister and, on the surface, more puzzling phenomena, such as the popularity of Stalin's régime, and the personal popularity which that great and good man, or rather his memory, enjoys to this day among many of those who had the good fortune to survive him.

Russian broadness is embodied by the Karamazov brothers. The point is made by the public prosecutor:

> . . . we are broad characters, Karamazov characters, and, this is the point, able to combine all possible contradictions and to contemplate two infinities [*lit.* both abysses] at the same time – the infinity above us, the infinity of the highest ideals, and the infinity below, the infinity of the basest and foulest degradation . . . Two infinities, two infinities, gentlemen, at one and the same time – we would otherwise be most unhappy and dissatisfied, our existence found wanting. We are broad, broad as mother Russia.[12]

The speech is important for its association of mother Russia with a more general condition, that described by Baudelaire in some of his best known lines:

> Il y a dans tout homme, à toute heure, deux postulations simultanées, l'une vers Dieu, l'autre vers Satan. L'invocation à Dieu, ou spiritualité, est un désir de monter en grade; celle de Satan, ou animalité, est une joie de descendre.[13]

Dostoevsky can be seen to understand that the Russian character, to which he looks for the eventual synthesis and salvation which he hopes for, is the meeting place of extremes, of Myshkin and Rogozhin. The Russian susceptibility to intensity emerges in Ivan Karamazov's observation that Russians have a particular inclination towards sadism. In the Russian capacity for extremism and the sustaining of mutually contradictory attitudes, Dostoevsky glimpses the troubles to come. Here again, his vehicle of positive value can be seen to be eroded by those very forces which Dostoevsky was seeking to withstand.

Dostoevsky's novels are positively permeated by his understanding of the Russian complicity in the intensity cult, of its love of extremes. But as a thinker, as the author of *Diary of a Writer*, he prefers to ignore them. He only seems able to grasp them intuitively, allowing them to emerge as mythic elements in the texture of his fiction. He cannot give any kind of conscious recognition to these qualities, which is why they lie well below the surface of the novels, and never feature much, if at all, in the rest of his writing.

The fiction alone recognises the dark side of Russianness, the qualities of *tyomny narod* – the dark people. Together with its enthusiasms the national character has a boundless capacity for darkness and suspicion. It is, for example, this quality of paranoid suspicion that shapes the image of Ivan the Terrible – from the correspondence, apocryphal or otherwise, with Prince Kurbsky, down to the claustrophobic sets of Eisenstein's films. Another, no less powerful treatment of the 'spider-like' qualities of the national character is Solzhenitsyn's inspired evocation of the half-crazed Stalin, in the privacy of his own apartments, in *The First Circle*.

Dostoevsky captures these very qualities in the paranoid suspicions of Rogozhin, embodying it in the description of his home. It features, less intensely, in the infinite cunning and duplicity of Lyagavy, the peasant with whom Dmitri Karamazov tries to do business. It is the dominant quality in the personality of Murin in *The Landlady*. The strain is a familiar one, and Dostoevsky frequently associates it with images of religious heresy.

That heresy plays a vital symbolic rôle in Dostoevsky's novels has long been apparent. Murin, Raskolnikov, Versilov, Rogozhin all have obvious links with the Old Believers. But the true extent to which Dostoevsky loads his novels with references to the sects has only recently been brought out by Richard Peace's fascinating and distinguished analysis.[14] He shows that these connotations have the most extensive ramifications, including characters as remote from one another as Stavrogin and Smerdyakov.

The theme of heresy is presented as part of the hysterical extremism of the intensity cult. Myshkin suggests on one occasion that nowadays even educated persons are joining the extremist sects. Through figures such as Rogozhin, and the lowering presence of his late father, it is also shown to be part of the darkness, the introverted suspicion and paranoia of the *tyomny narod*. Dostoevsky, who advocates synthesis

216

through religion, seems here to be aware that religion itself, like his other sources of positive value, is also potentially a source of fatal ambiguity and doubt. The rôle of his heretical connotations is to show just how deeply the very notion of the good is infiltrated by its opposite. At the same time this hostile treatment of heresy and sectarianism is quite consistent with his view of Orthodoxy – 'He that is not for us is against us.' Yet the enemies Dostoevsky brands with heresy are not xenophiliac outsiders. They partake of quintessential Russianness; but they also reflect an innate tendency to go against the light. The very existence of such 'deviationist' characters in his novels shows Dostoevsky to have been profoundly aware of the ambiguities embedded in his culture.

As a creative novelist, Dostoevsky understood those ambiguities well, indeed his fiction is created by them. As a thinker, he chose to ignore them: hence his jingoism and his championing of Russian culture as a means of checking the degeneration he saw about him. He adopts a position that is very close to that of Gogol. But the latter made the fatal mistake of attempting to express his position aesthetically, in the last two parts of *Dead Souls*, which were intended as a description of the 'positive Russian life'. Gogol recognised that the result was a disaster, and seems to have concluded that his word was poisoned. This is itself a fascinating anticipation of the phenomenon we have termed Dostoevsky's complicity. Dostoevsky is essentially under the thrall of the intensity which his work indicts. His aesthetics function through a code of intensity, his plans for social stability and synthesis are riddled with it. In the same way Gogol came to realise that he could only write about evil, that when it came to the depiction of the good he was aesthetically impotent.

As much is true of Goncharov, Turgenev, Flaubert, of Tolstoy even. It was an aesthetic impossibility for the novel to advocate a positive solution to the problems of the age, for the novel was born of those problems and reflected its origins in every fibre. In many respects Dostoevsky's word was as poisoned as Gogol's. The appalling jingoistic chauvinism of *Diary of a Writer* is his version of Gogol's *Selected Passages from Correspondence with Friends*. The assertion that Russianness would provide an eventual solution has proved a lamentable mistake, for Russianness survives, thrives even, in a police state. Everything we have seen in Dostoevsky helps us to understand that Russianness and political terror are in no way incompatible.

CHAPTER SEVENTEEN

The Living Life

Dostoevsky's assertion of religion and national culture has its equivalent on the personal plane. A series of associations links the two levels. Through characters such as Shatov and Myshkin, Dostoevsky expresses a passionate love of the very soil of his country. This is, in turn, linked with Orthodoxy. Patriotism and religion come together in a peculiar conjunction which takes a form described by Dr Peace as 'earth worship'.[1] His study carefully reveals the presence, in the heart of Dostoevsky's positive values, of an almost pagan cult of the earth. It is around this cult that Dostoevsky builds his accounts of personal fulfilment and ecstatic joy. Zosima combines it with Christianity, Dmitri, whose very name evokes Demeter the earth-goddess, also celebrates it. Dr Peace links this cult with Zosima's quoting from the Scriptures about the grain of corn that must die to bring forth fruit. He also detects the theme in other positive characters, such as Marya Lebyadkina, Shatov, Alyosha, and in Versilov and Ivan.

Closely associated with this cult is the all important Dostoevskian theme of *zhivaya zhizn'* – the living life. He uses the term to describe a particular kind of exultant joy at God's creation: it is close to Christ's 'the waters of life', and has the sense of an immediate experience of the sheer plenitude of existence. Zosima first encounters it in the joyful ecstasy of his dying brother, Alyosha finds it too in the chapter entitled 'Galilean Cana'.

To attain the living life is the ultimate Dostoevskian experience: to taste paradise on this earth. Unlike the world of intensity, this is not a *paradis artificiel* to be achieved by denying life, but the genuine article to be reached through its acceptance. It is this quality, indeed the very desire for it, that the Underground Man believes to have been destroyed by the new culture:

We have grown unaccustomed to life, we all more or less limp along. So unaccustomed, that at times we feel strangely disgusted by the real 'living life', and so we cannot bear to be reminded of it. We have reached the point when we almost regard the real 'living life' as a burden, a duty, and secretly we all agree that it is better to go by the book.[2]

This is his version of 'alienation'. Civilisation has destroyed our capacity for authentic experience. It is this familiar view that forms

218

Dostoevsky's central thesis. Individuals who have been more or less untouched by civilisation, who are integrated rather than alienated, still achieve it. Versilov is at least able to talk about it:

> ... I only know that [the living life] must be something terribly simple, most ordinary and obvious, every day and every minute of the day, so simple that we cannot believe it could be so simple, so of course we've missed it for thousands of years.[3]

The simplicity is actually achieved by Makar Dolgoruky. He describes the extraordinary joy of sleeping out, on a pilgrimage, and waking to a dawn like the dawn of creation. He embraces God and nature together, as if seeing them for the first time.[4] His joy resembles that of Zosima's brother. The serene experience of nature, although directly linked to Christianity, has a feeling tone that is remarkably close to certain passages of Rousseau: for example, the famous *nuit à la belle étoile* in the fourth book of the *Confessions*.

Ivan Karamazov shares this potential love of life, which, significantly, he opposes to logic. But Dmitri is its greatest devotee. It is his capacity for joy that saves him:

> Even in the midst of degradation I begin a hymn. May I be damned, may I be base and mean, but I may still kiss the hem of Your garment, in which my God is clothed; may I follow the devil, but I am still Your child, oh Lord, and I love You, and feel joy, without which the world cannot survive.[5]

When about to leave for Mokroe he announces that he loves life too much to contemplate suicide. The living life stands in absolute contrast to the burnt out victims of intensity such as Svidrigailov.

Or does it? In prison Dmitri craves for a plenitude of experience:

> Alyosha, you have no idea how much I want to live now, what a craving I have for existence and awareness, it was within these bare walls that it actually took root in me.[6]

The distinction between thirst for life and thirst for intensity is not easily made. Although the two extremes of, say, Zosima and Svidrigailov have little enough in common, Dmitri is midway between the two of them, partaking of them both. The slip from 'living life' to 'dead life' is imperceptible.

Dostoevsky is all too aware of this. Thus, there is more to Zosima than mere serenity. As Dr Peace puts it:

> ... there is something of the Lermontovian guards officer about him ... he is prey to the Karamazovian vice of sensuality.[7]

Zosima too was once a devotee of the intensity cult.

Similarly, both Ivan and Kirillov are capable of a Zosima-like love of life. They both respond, in particular, to the sticky green leaves of spring which so delighted Zosima's brother. But Kirillov kills himself; and Ivan goes mad.

Once again, and for the last time, we are confronted by the problem of Dostoevsky's complicity. There can be seen to be an osmosis between intensity and the living life itself. In an age which has lost its grasp of whole meanings and is no longer able to make confident value judgments, they become too easily confused for comfort. What may begin as a love of life may all too easily end in a death wish. Once again, we find at the centre of Dostoevsky's world a terrible ambiguity— the most vital ambiguity of all. The gulf between Zosima and Pechorin is less great than it appears, and Alyosha is a Karamazov, not a saint.

We have seen that Dostoevsky described beauty as a riddle. We have shown that apparently positive Dostoevskian values, such as suffering, and religion itself, are presented as ambiguous. The same quality applies to the living life and to the notion of living authentically. In Dostoevsky's world the difference between the ecstatic joy of the living life and the artificial ecstasy of intensity can become virtually imperceptible. Both Zosima and Kirillov believe in earthly paradises; which of the two is the artificial one?

These multiple ambiguities are, in the final analysis, to be derived from that loss of whole meanings which is responsible for the cult of intensity. It would almost appear that Dostoevsky himself suffered from that loss more acutely than any of his characters. Hence his life-long wrestling with the problem of atheism. It is almost as if he himself has arrived at the stage when he can no longer tell good from evil. His account of human behaviour suggests a continuous and uninterrupted spectrum of personalities, extending from the radiant Zosima, right down to Svidrigailov. Between those two poles there is no absolute divide, any more than there is in the spectrum: one type of personality shades off into another, and perhaps it is Dmitri who stands in the precise middle of the range. But the tragedy, for Dostoevsky, is that good and evil do not exist on a sliding scale, they constitute an absolute and uncompromising division, which makes no allowances for shades of grey. The continuous spectrum from Svidrigailov to Zosima will be divided into sheep and goats, and Dostoevskian man would seem to have lost the ability to tell which is which.

The ambiguity of Dostoevsky's notion of the living life emerges when this is placed in a wider context. The reference to Rousseau was something more than a casual echo. Rousseau was the first major writer to treat of the alienating quality of modern culture, of the way it deprived man of a mode of being that was rightfully or naturally his. The alienated state of culture is opposed to a mythical state of nature, and the opposition is crucial to his thought. It is only in nature that an authentic mode of existence is possible.

Something of this has filtered down to Dostoevsky. He opposes nineteenth-century culture both to nature and to an older, more 'natural' tradition. It is only in nature and in Russian culture that an authentic, unalienated existence may be achieved.

But Rousseau is not just the first thinker to condemn modern culture. He is also the founding father of the intensity cult. While placing as his supreme good the notion of authenticity of experience, he suggests that it is intensity of emotional experience that provides the means of authentication. Authenticity and emotional intensity are inseparable.

The quest for authenticity becomes one of the essential themes of nineteenth- and early twentieth-century literature. In the midst of an essentially inauthentic culture, heroes set off in various directions in pursuit of the real thing. 'Nous vivons contrefaits,' says one of Gide's characters. The positive characters of Dostoevsky experience their own version of that immediacy of joy in direct contact with their world which represents victory in the struggle against alienation. Unfortunately, that joy is all too easily confused with defeat. When is a *paradis* authentic, when is it *artificiel;* are the super-saturated moments of ecstatic perception that precede an epileptic fit a glimpse of the living life or the creation of intensity?

Dostoevsky's advocacy of authentic living, as opposed to living in the alienated state of culture, is, of course, close to the position of Nietzsche. His affinities to Nietzsche's thought, notably in his conception of the new man, have been described in detail elsewhere.[8] Less apparent, perhaps, is their common rejection of the falsifying culture-pattern in favour of an intense and authentic experience of nature, ecstasy, and joy. The message of *The Anti-Christian* and *Thus Spake Zarathustra* is that man must free himself of the constrictions of his culture-pattern, shake off his past, and only then will he find joy.

A concern with authenticity of experience which could only be found beyond cultural convention is the essential element in the thought and indeed the life of André Gide. *Les Nourritures Terrestres* is a sub-Nietzschean celebration of the rediscovery of immediate contact with nature. The joyful experience it celebrates is not unlike Dostoevsky's idea of the living life. The parable of the dying seed, moreover, was to prove quite as important to Gide as Dr Peace[9] has shown it to be to Dostoevsky: *Si le grain ne meurt*. Finally, Gide's fictions are a perpetual exploration of the falsifications imposed by culture, falsifications that must be overcome if authenticity of existence is to be achieved.

It is no criticism of Dostoevsky to link him with Nietzsche and Gide.

To suggest that his notion of the living life fits into the important Romantic and post-Romantic paradigm of authenticity is not to diminish its meaning but to clarify it. But, in their various ways, both Gide and Nietzsche contributed not to stability but to dissolution. They make strange bed-fellows for Dostoevsky, the cultural conservative. They encouraged their readers to grow over-aware of a quality of experience which they suggested was theirs by right, but which eluded them and which they should stop at nothing to attain. That this has a familiar ring should come as no surprise. Both Gide and Nietzsche variously made the fatal error of confusing authenticity and intensity. Gide encouraged the rejection of cultural convention in favour of a personal quest for authenticity which placed a premium on personal fulfilment. Despite cautionary tales such as *L'Immoraliste*, the tenor of his work invites the reader to liberate and develop his self, whatever the cost. Gide's declaration of emotional rights encouraged a whole generation to take their needs too seriously, creating a climate of unenlightened self-interest, which, it has been suggested, contributed to the fall of France in 1940.

An excessive concern with authenticity has strange consequences. Dostoevsky associates it both with Christianity and with the cult of the earth; but one does not necessarily imply the other. Nietzsche and Gide expound a cult of the earth that is anti-Christian – *Les Nourritures terrestres*. Indeed the concern with living authentically will subsequently be developed into the pagan humanism of Camus – what is *L'Etranger* about if not this? – and to the commitment of Sartre, who will contrast authentic living with his notion of *mauvaise foi*.

It is desperately ironic that Dostoevsky's meditations on the living life should lead to Nietzsche, Gide, Camus and Sartre. His plans for synthesis and the mending of the broken halves of the modern psyche, the repair of dualism and division reflect, in a way that is genuinely tragic, that despairing quest for experience at all costs which had so distorted that psyche: his solutions reflect the very conditions which they seek to cure.

As a novelist, Dostoevsky seems to have been uncomfortably aware of the shortcomings of his plans for synthesis. The awareness is reflected in the phenomenon we have described as his complicity. His novels admit the extent to which the cult of intensity has become all pervading: no aspect of his world is entirely free from sensationalism. As a novelist, he understood that if his work was to be aesthetically successful, it must actually minimise the theme of synthesis and positive values. This is why he renders the theme through characters such as Shatov, Makar Dolgoruky or Zosima who are, in a special sense, weak characters: weak in the sense that they do not really belong in the world of Dostoevsky's fiction. Zosima and Dolgoruky, in their positive aspects, are essentially outsiders, interlopers who can form no real relationship with Dostoevsky's more characteristic creations. Their irrelevance is acknowledged by the fact that they are killed off.

Dostoevsky's awareness of the problems of portraying positive values is reflected in his conception of a 'positively beautiful person'.[10] He can only portray such a man in the guise of an impotent half-wit who is driven out of what remains of his mind by his contact with Dostoevsky's reality. His world is one in which the good are killed off or destroyed, in which the regeneration of Raskolnikov cannot really be described, in which Sonya Marmeladova has to sell her body and Alyosha Karamazov has a rich, if untapped, vein of sensuality.

Dostoevsky's world is indeed tragic, not in the exalted sense that it re-expresses chthonic myths of incest and parricide, but in the sense that it is a world in which victory is not possible. So all pervading is the craving for intensity that victory itself must be described with the language and the values of defeat.

CHAPTER EIGHTEEN

The Heritage of Intensity

> My painting is direct . . . the
> method of painting is a
> natural growth of a need.
> JACKSON POLLOCK

Twentieth-century culture has been shaped by insecurity, change and terror. The relevance of nuclear fission extends beyond physics and military strategy; it offers a metaphor for the disintegrative forces that function on every level from the militant radicalism of minority groups to the casual violence which we are coming to accept as a fact of everyday life. What began in the 1790s as the rise of nationalism and individualism has culminated in such terrible absurdities as the Black September movement and Hell's Angels.

One of the consequences of this general process of what Dostoevsky would term *obosoblenie* has been the disappearance of any vestige of whole meanings, universally accepted certainties. Any sense of overall meaning or purpose has been traded in for concepts such as 'the absurd'. This can be all too clearly seen in the arts. From the poetic barbarism of Rimbaud's artificial paradises onwards, the artist has increasingly come to maintain that his concern no longer lies with meanings or moral high seriousness, but with acts of individual self-expression. Art becomes reduced to mere personal gesture.

In other words, statement is rejected in favour of intensity. The rejection of whole meanings is paralleled by a steady rise in artistic terrorism. Dada, the Russian Futurists who made Pushkin walk the plank (Nadezhda Mandelstam calls Petr Verkhovensky the first Futurist), the even more drastic rejection of language itself by the poets of *zaum* (trans-sense) who reduced their poetic statements to a series of meaningless syllables, all bear witness to this assault upon art as meaning.

The arts also testify to an ever-increasing preoccupation with violence. Marinetti doubled as a poet and war-correspondent. He exultantly describes the effect of automatic weapons on serried ranks of dust-biting Turks. André Breton advised the would-be Surrealist to to go down into the street, a revolver in each hand, emptying them into the crowd. It is not such a far cry from these poetical tropes to current events in the Middle East, and no cry at all to that essentially twentieth-century phenomenon the violent intellectual: Malraux's celebration of the thinking man of action and the political terrorists of Sartre and Camus.

The intellectual killer is a far cry from Coleridge's clerisy. That the expression is not a contradiction in terms is itself a telling enough indictment of the age. The readiness to opt for violent, 'radical' solutions cannot be entirely unconnected with a readiness to opt for intensity rather than harmony and stability. Like Alyosha the world has come to prefer immediate action to the long haul.

This century has of course seen attempts to create new meanings, systems of synthesis and integration. But these attempts have been hopelessly contaminated by intensity and rooted in violence. Marxism-Leninism, Maoism, German and Italian fascism were all attempts to find alternatives to the chaos of the capitalist world. They all grew 'out of the barrel of a gun', and, like the socialism of Dostoevsky, they entailed oppression or denial of the freedom of the spirit. Twentieth-century attempts at whole meanings have turned ideals into ideologies.

Inevitably, one is obliged to see the present as the creation of its pasts. The ideas which have made us what we are have a pedigree. They can be traced back to the Renaissance 'spirit of inquiry'. This can be seen gradually to have destroyed an earlier sense of wholeness, of a world in which every part stood in significant relation to every other part of the cosmos, microcosm echoing macrocosm. In place of this coherent and meaningful world-picture we have acquired an advanced technological culture with a genius for piecemeal solutions at the expense of whole meanings. The French Revolution saw the moment when European man began to reap the whirlwind of this set of transformations. He has not yet finished getting that harvest in.

Baudelaire captures the final loss of whole meanings as his character turns his back on *correspondances* and lowers his sights, settling for mere sensation. Dostoevsky also describes the trading-in of meaning in return for a narrower, intenser universe. It is true that he attempts to maintain a hold upon whole meanings – hence his advocacy of synthesis, yet for all that advocacy, it is the Grand Inquisitor and Ivan Karamazov who are given the best tunes. Ivan's rebellion, his refusal to accept a divine creation founded upon the suffering of children, is infinitely more threatening than the Satanism of Baudelaire or even Voltaire's anguished response to the Lisbon earthquake. The fundamental lack of creative conviction in Dostoevsky's case for synthesis points up the impossibility of advancing whole meanings in a civilisation that had already lost its sense of wholeness.

It is this very loss that accounts for the disappearance of meaning from the arts. Anton Ehrenzweig's *The Hidden Order of Art*[1] has attempted an account of artistic creation in approximately Freudian terms. For all the limitations that this necessarily imposes, the work is full of fascinating insights. It suggests that the creative process begins with a phase of disintegration and 'scattering', which, in a complete cycle, is succeeded by a stage of re-integration, the re-creation of a new organic whole. It is a testimony to the incomplete, disintegrative and schizoid quality of our culture that the twentieth-century artist seems to find scattering more important than wholeness – hence the disintegrated planes of analytic cubism, the harmonies of twentieth-century music, and finally the moving, intense but meaningless canvasses of Jackson Pollock.

By the same token, any attempt at the rendering of harmony or of balanced forms must needs be divorced from reality, shown to be without reference. Harmony and reality are felt intuitively to be incompatible, one excludes the other. The abstract expressionism of the Ecole de Paris, de Staël, Poliakoff, Soulages, consists of form without reference; representation of reality is considered meaningful, hence destructive, corrupting or absurd. Formal harmony can only be sought somewhere out of this world.

Dostoevsky and Baudelaire anticipate not only the death of high art but the death of high seriousness in the arts. Baudelaire abandons Delacroix's painting to champion Constantin Guys and his sketches, to praise the High Spirituality of Fashion, to write a Eulogy of Make-up. The quality of modern life was only to be grasped by substituting trivia for traditional iconography, violence for serenity, intensity for meaning: 'Voici le temps des assassins.'

Dostoevsky's penny dreadfuls catch the same mood. The quality we have termed his complicity is finally a creative complicity in the spirit of his age: the age of intensity. It may come as a surprise to learn that this, our own age, dates from the middle of the last century. We tend to assume that the craving for bigger and better sensations is essentially a twentieth-century phenomenon. We blame our hardware – cars, supermarkets, advertising, drugs and trade-unions – for the discontented world of the intensity-freak. That Dostoevsky should have described the syndrome long before the coming of the hardware suggests that the paraphernalia of the consumer society are not themselves responsible for Western man's billion dollar a day habit. They only feed it. Nor was Soviet Russia built in a day. Stalin could never have succeeded if it had not been for Shigalev.

Strangely, one of the very few voices in recent years to speak of a civilisation of whole values, one which believes in the vitality of tradition and cultural heritage, in humanism in the best possible sense of that term, and which, in a manner quite free from complicity, is able to make genuine creative use of those beliefs, is the voice of a Russian – Aleksandr Solzhenitsyn. He is free both of the fashionable pessimism of the West, and its mirror image, socialist optimism. He is able to write about positive values without sounding like Kipling's 'Jelly-bellied flag-flapper', or even like Dostoevsky in his sabre-rattling aspect. He believes passionately in the possibility of the humanist values which he champions. In his lament for the decaying churches of the Russian countryside, in his account of the yobboes pressing round the faithful at midnight on Easter Sunday, he brings Christian values alive, making us realise that they have long since died in the West, as a result of the attempts of the Western churches to 'meet the challenge of the twentieth century' (a newspaper recently reported that an Anglican priest had resurrected an ancient prayer for the blessing of chariots in order to intercede with God on behalf of his parishioners' motorcars).

Half a century of Shigalev has not made Solzhenitsyn lose hope. He is still able to turn back to his cultural heritage, or in *August 1914* to discriminate between mediocrities and 'the good soldier'. It is this fundamental sense of hope and human dignity, together with a great love of his country, that shapes both the form and the conception of his novels. In this particular respect, his complicity-free accounts transcend the achievement of Dostoevsky, but transcend them because Solzhenitsyn has come out of the other end of the tunnel which his predecessor saw looming. Compared with Dostoevsky, Solzhenitsyn's work lacks intensity – and this is perhaps the greatest possible praise. It may in part be this lack of intensity which accounts for the somewhat patronising attitude adopted to his work by Western critics, who find the novels 'tremendously moving but technically naïve'. Technical naïvety, like the other kind, stems from a belief in whole meanings. The belief is here professed by someone who, more than any Western person of letters, has had every reason to have written off the possibility of wholeness of meaning many years ago. Perhaps Zosima was right after all, and finally something other than the rough slouching beast will come out of the land which, alone, has preserved the image of Christ.

Notes

All references to the works of Baudelaire concern his *Oeuvres Complètes* published by Editions de la Pléiade, Paris, 1963, my translation.

Unless otherwise stated, quotations from Dostoevsky are from the Moscow edition of his works, Volumes I–X, published in 1956, my translation.

Introduction

1. Richard Peace, *Dostoevsky*, Cambridge, 1971.
2. Robert Lord, *Dostoevsky Essays and Perspectives*, London, 1970.

One   La Douceur de Vivre

1. Our fathers lacked this word *individualism*, which we have forged for ourselves, because in their time there was in fact no individual who did not belong to a group, and who could think of himself as utterly alone (A. de Tocqueville, *L'Ancien Régime*, Oxford, 1927 edition, p. 103).
2. Robert Mauzi, *L'idée du bonheur au 18-ème siècle*, Paris, 1960.
3. a benign circle of friends, a select and choice set (Robert Mauzi, *op. cit.*, p. 36).
4. *Ibid.*, p. 71.
5. *Ibid.*, p. 441.
6. They are too happy, they cannot be guilty. Evidence of pleasure becomes the moral criterion of the action (Quoted by Mauzi, *op. cit.*).
7. . . . since in civilised societies all kinds of social conditions are necessary in order to ensure that lasting mutual dependence without which societies would lapse into a state of anarchy that would destroy them, it follows that there must be persons destined to serve others, and that if such persons . . . were to discover the terrible nullity of their situation, they would, most certainly come to loathe their lot, and seek to escape by death or some other means from their miserable condition, and thus they would destroy the harmonious constitution of society (Blondel, *Loisirs philosophiques*, Paris, 1752, pp. 38–42).
8. . . . even the idea of a violent revolution played no part in our fathers' intellectual life. They did not talk about it, it had not yet been conceived (de Tocqueville, *op. cit.* p. 149).
9. There was only one people. That jealous class called the bourgeoisie in France, and which is beginning to be born in England, did not exist; there was nothing to come between the rich landowners and the labouring class. In those days the manufacturing professions were not ruled by machines, the privileged classes not governed by extravagant follies (Chateaubriand, *Mémoires d'outre-tombe*, Paris, 1967 edition, Vol. I, p. 385).

Two   Romantic Agony

1. Robert Mauzi, *L'idée du bonheur au 18-ème siècle*, Paris, 1960, p. 167.
2. The craftsman, parched by the fire he stokes, who makes iron bend and the anvil groan; the farmhand in the evening, armed with a goad, leaning on the plough to open a furrow; the worker, deep in the bosom of the earth, looking for metal or cutting stone; the author whose labour is the result of his indigence . . . These various

pictures of a thousand different conditions present to my eyes, equitably apportioned, pleasure at all times and for all ages.

3. Robert Owen, *Observations on the Effect of the Manufacturing System with hints for the improvement of those parts in it which are most injurious to health and morals, dedicated most respectfully to the British Legislature*, London, 1815, pp. 5, 10–11.

4. John Ruskin, *Stones of Venice*, 1899 edition, Vol. II, Ch. VI, p. 165.

5. William Morris, *The Aims of Art* in *Selected Writings*, Nonesuch Press, London, 1934, p. 527.

6. William Morris, *Art and Socialism* in *Selected Writings*, p. 635.

7. Thomas Carlyle, *The Works of Thomas Carlyle*, London, 1897–9, Vol. II, p. 233.

8. The men of the eighteenth century scarcely knew that passion for well-being which seems to be the mother of servitude, a flabby passion, but one which is persistent and enduring, which readily blends and, as it were, mingles with several private virtues, love of the family, moral rectitude, a respect for religious beliefs, and even the lukewarm and assiduous observance of the established religion, which permits honesty and prevents heroism, and excels at creating docile men and craven citizens. They were better and worse. In those days the French loved fun and adored pleasure; perhaps they were more disorderly, less restrained in both passions and ideas than they are to-day; but they did not know that moderated and decent sensuality which we see now. In the upper classes more time was devoted to embellishing one's life than to rendering it comfortable, to distinguishing oneself than to getting rich. Even the middle classes were not totally given over to the pursuit of material well-being; the pursuit was frequently abandoned, in order to run after more delicate and noble pleasures; everyone valued something else beside money (de Tocqueville, *op cit.*, p. 125).

9. George Lukács, *The Theory of the Novel*, London, 1971 edition, p. 64.

10. We seek the infinite everywhere and always find only finite things (Novalis, *Werke*, Hamburg, 1953 edition, Vol. I, p. 310).

11. . . . another madman . . . a sad man of feeling not without wit or talent, but whose experience of the foolish vanities of the world have gradually disgusted him with real life, and *who readily consoles himself for his lost illusions with the illusions of a life of the imagination* (C. Nodier, *Contes*, Paris, 1961 edition, p. 170, my italics).

12. A. Béguin, *L'âme romantique et le rêve*, Paris, 1937, Vol. II, p. 289.

13. I have kept myself a child because I scorn to be a man (Quoted by Béguin, *op. cit.* Vol. II, p. 333).

14. *Ibid.*, pp. 63–4.

15. If I wish to portray spring I must be in winter; if I wish to describe a beautiful landscape I must be in town; and a hundred times I have said that were I ever shut up in the Bastille, I would paint the portrait of liberty (J-J. Rousseau, *Confessions*, Book II).

16. Béguin, *op. cit.*, Vol. I, p. 140.

17. Quoted by M. H. Abrams, *The Mirror and the Lamp*, New York, 1958 edition, p. 215.

18. *Ibid.*, p. 127.

19. Thus poetry appears to be a response, the only possible response, to the elemental anguish of creation, confined within an existence in time (Béguin, *op. cit.*, Vol. II, p. 450).

20. Lilian Furst, *Romanticism in Perspective*, London, 1969, p. 136.

21. Quoted by Furst, *op. cit.*, p. 137.

22. Abrams, *op. cit.*, p. 65.

23. In antiquity each individual was a member of a living city . . . Nowadays it's the very opposite. The image of the *patria* is to be found neither in the temple, the gymnasium or the camp . . . The idea of government has grown increasingly abject.

There is no monarchy, aristocracy or even democracy. All there is is individualism and egoism. Will our concern for the free development of the individual oblige him to go through life alone, dazed by the absolute indifference of those around him? (J. G. Farcy, *Reliquiae*, Paris, 1831, pp. 118*ff*).

24. the great number of examples that he sees, the enormous quantity of books that deal with man and his feelings make him adept without experience. He becomes undeceived with nothing to show for it; he has desires left but no illusions. The imagination is rich, abundant and full of marvels; life itself is poor, dead and lacking in enchantment. In an empty world man lives with a full heart, and, without having made use of anything, he is disabused of everything (Chateaubriand, *Le génie du christianisme*, Vol. II, iii, p. 9).

25. See above, note 10, Novalis, *op. cit.*

26. Lukács, *op. cit.*, pp. 120–1.

27. Enid Starkie, *Petrus Borel*, London, 1954, p. 72.

Three   Baudelaire

1. The painter, the real painter will be the one who will manage to catch the epic aspect of modern life, and make us see and understand . . . how noble and poetic we are in our cravats and our patent leather boots (Baudelaire, *Oeuvres Complètes*, Paris, 1963 edition, p. 886).

2. . . . each century having expressed its own beauty and its own morality . . . If one wishes to understand by Romanticism the most recent and modern expression of beauty . . . (Baudelaire, *op. cit.*, p. 878).

3. a world in which action is not sister to the dream (*op. cit.*, p. 115).

4. In all men at all times there are two simultaneous postulations, one towards God, the other towards Satan. The invocation to God or spirituality is a desire to elevate oneself; that towards Satan or animality is the joy of degrading oneself (Baudelaire, *op. cit.*, p. 1227).

5. Theory of true civilisation. It does not consist in gas, steam or table turning, but in the reduction of traces of original sin (*op. cit.*, p. 1291).

6. The world is going to come to an end. The only reason it might survive is the fact that it exists. How feeble this reason is when compared to all those that suggest the contrary, especially the following: what has the world left to do, henceforward, under the heavens? For even supposing that it continue to exist materially speaking, would it be an existence worthy of the name . . . Machinery will so completely have americanised us, progress atrophied all our spiritual side, that nothing in the bloodthirsty, sacrilegious and unnatural daydreams of the Utopians will compare to what will actually come to pass. I ask any thinking man to show me what's left of life. There is no point in even talking about religion or looking for its remains . . . Property virtually vanished with the suppression of the right of primo-geniture, but the time will come when humanity, like an avenging ogre, will snatch the last morsel from those who suppose themselves the rightful heirs of revolutions.

. . . it is not through political institutions that universal ruin – or universal progress – will manifest itself . . . It will be through the increasing abjection of the human heart. Do I need to say that what politics there will be left will struggle hopelessly in the grip of a universal brutality, and that governments will be obliged, in order to survive and create for themselves a semblance of order, to have recourse to methods which would make even our contemporaries shudder, however callous they may have become. Then sons will run away from home not at eighteen, but at twelve, liberated by their precocious gluttony; they will run away, not in quest of heroic adventures, not to rescue beauties imprisoned in towers, or to immortalise an attic with sublime thoughts, but to start a business, get rich and enter into competition with their abominable fathers . . . Then anything which might resemble virtue, what am I saying, anything that is not the fervent adoration of Plutus, will be deemed a howling absurdity. The Law ... will banish citizens incapable of getting rich. Your spouse, o bourgeois, your chaste better half whose virtue is your idea of poetry, infiltrating the principle of legality with an irreproachable baseness, the vigilant and amorous guardian of your coffers, will quite simply be the perfect incarnation of the kept woman. Your daughter ... with childish nubility will dream in her cradle, that she sells herself for a million. And you yourself, bourgeois, even less of a poet than you are to-day, will have no complaints, no regrets. Because there are things in a man that grow stronger and flourish as others weaken and wither, and because of the way our age is progressing, you will discover that your entire inner life will be reduced to that of your digestive organs (*op cit.*, pp. 1262–4).

7. See D. Fanger, *Dostoevsky and Romantic Realism*, Oxford, 1965.

8. Eugène Sue, *The Mysteries of Paris*, London, 1864 edition, p. 1.

9. Swarming city, city full of dreams, where the spectre accosts the passer-by in broad daylight. Mysteries flow everywhere like sap, through the narrow channels of the powerful colossus ('Les Sept Vieillards' from *Les Fleurs du Mal*, *op. cit.*, p, 83).

10. In vain, my reason tried to take the helm; the playful storm thwarted its attempts; and my soul, that old hulk, danced and danced without masts, on a monstrous and limitless sea (*ibid.*).

11. In the sinuous folds of old capital cities, where all, even horror, becomes enchantment, I observe, obedient to my fatal moods, peculiar beings, decrepit and charming.

How many of these little old women have I followed. One, in particular, at the hour when the setting sun bloodies the sky with crimson wounds, sat down, pensive, on a bench ('Les Petites Vieilles' from *Les Fleurs du Mal*, *op. cit.*, p. 86).

12. What bizarre things does one not find in a great city, when one knows how to walk and look. Life swarms with innocent monsters. My Lord, my God ... take pity on mad men and women. O Creator, can there be monsters in the eyes of Him who alone knows why they exist, how they *were made* and how they *might not have been made?* (*op. cit.*, p. 303).

13. Whether you come from heaven or from hell, what matter, Beauty, enormous monster, terrifying and naïve, if your eye, your smile, your foot open for me the door of an infinity which I love but have never known. From Satan or from God, what does it matter? Angel or Siren, what difference does it make, if, fairy with velvet eyes, rhythm, perfume, light, my only queen, you make the universe less hideous and the moment weigh less ('Hymne à la Beauté', from *Les Fleurs du Mal*, *op. cit.*, p. 24).

14. Anyone who does not accept the conditions of life sells his soul (*op. cit.*, p. 384).

15. Allow, allow, my heart to grow drunk upon a lie (*op. cit.*, p. 39).

16. One must be always drunk. All is there; that is the sole issue. In order not to feel the hateful burden of time, which breaks your shoulders and bows you down to the ground, you must be drunk without respite.

But on what? Wine, poetry, virtue, as you please. Just get drunk ... It is time to get drunk. In order not to be martyred slaves of Time, get drunk, get drunk continually (*op. cit.*, p. 286).

17. No! there are no more minutes, no more seconds! time has disappeared; it is Eternity that reigns, an eternity of delights! ('La Chambre Double', *op. cit.*, p. 234).

18. Yes, yes, time has reappeared. Time reigns supreme now; and with the hideous old man have returned all his demoniacal procession of memories, regrets, fears, anxieties, nightmares, rages and neuroses. I assure you that the seconds are now powerfully and solemnly accented, and each, as it surges from the clock, says: 'I am Life, unendurable, implacable Life!' (*op. cit.*, p. 235).

19. And drunk on my madness, I cried furiously after him: 'La vie en beau, La vie en beau!' These neurotic jokes are not without danger, and they can be expensive.

But what does eternal damnation matter to him who has found, in a second, infinite pleasure (*op. cit.*, p. 240).

20. The vindictive man whom alive, for all that love, you could not satisfy, did he fulfil upon your inert and consenting flesh the immensity of his desire? ('Une Martyre' from *Les Fleurs du Mal*, *op. cit.*, p. 107).

21. For, as if from a fearsome drug, human beings are privileged with the ability to extract new and subtle pleasures even from pain, disaster and fate (*op. cit.*, p. 346).

22. I adore you as much as the vault of night, vessel of sadness, great silent one, and love you the more, beauty, that you run from me, and when, ornament of my nights, you appear with added irony to increase the distance which separates my arms from blue immensities. I advance and attack, climb in my assault, like a choir of worms swarming over a corpse, and I cherish, implacable and cruel beast, that very coldness which makes you more beautiful for me (XXIV from *Les Fleurs du Mal*, *op. cit.*, p. 26).

23. Bitter knowledge, which one gains from the voyage. The world, monotonous and small, shows us its face, today, yesterday, tomorrow: an oasis of love in a desert of *ennui* ('Le Voyage' from *Les Fleurs du Mal*, *op. cit.*, p. 126).

24. This life is a hospital in which every patient is possessed by a desire to change beds. . . . Finally my soul explodes, and, wisely, it cries to me: 'Any where, any where, as long as it's out of this world!' (*op. cit.*, p. 304).

Four   The City

1. Dostoevsky, Correspondence, in the Russian edition of the collected works of Dostoevsky, Moscow, 1956, Vol. II, p. 150.
2. *Winter Notes Upon Summer Impressions*, in Vol. IV, p. 99.
3. *Winter Notes Upon Summer Impressions*, in Vol. IV, pp. 92–5.
4. See D. Fanger, *Dostoevsky and Romantic Realism*, Oxford, 1965.
5. See above, Chapter Three, note 8.
6. A. Bely, *St Petersburg*, Berlin, 1923 edition, pp. 30–1.
7. *Encyclopaedia Britannica*, 9th edition, Vol. IX, p. 193.
8. *The Adolescent*, in Vol. VIII, pp. 150–1.
9. *Crime and Punishment*, in Vol. V, p. 487.
10. *Ibid.*, in Vol. V, p. 6.
11. *Ibid.*
12. *The Eternal Husband*, in Vol. IV, p. 433.
13. *The Humiliated and the Injured*, in Vol. III, p. 66.
14. *Ibid.*, p. 186.
15. *Crime and Punishment*, in Vol. V, p. 180.
16. *The Idiot*, in Vol. VI, p. 454.
17. *The Adolescent*, in Vol. VIII, p. 184.

Five   The New Ideologies

1. *The Idiot*, in Vol. VI, p. 347.
2. *Ibid.*, p. 422.
3. Baudelaire, see above, Chapter Three, note 5.
4. Correspondence, in Dostoevsky, *Pisma*, Moscow, 1928–59, Vol. II, p. 212–13.
5. *The Devils*, in Vol. VII, p. 265.
6. *The Idiot*, in Vol. VI, p. 243.
7. *Crime and Punishment*, in Vol. V, p. 40.
8. *Ibid.*, pp. 155–6.
9. *The Brothers Karamazov*, in Vol. X, pp. 101–2.
10. A. de Tocqueville, *Correspondence*, pp. 201–2.
11. *Notes from Underground*, in Vol. IV, pp. 162–3.

12. *The Brothers Karamazov*, in Vol. IX, pp. 392–3.

13. In the midst of the shadowy future one can already make out three very distinct truths. The first is that all men today are swept along by a force they can hope to moderate and slow down, but not to master, which pushes them sometimes gently, sometimes violently, towards the destruction of the aristocracy. The second, that amongst all the societies of the world, those which will always find it hardest to escape absolutism for long will be precisely those in which there is and can no longer be an aristocracy; the third, finally, that despotism will never be so harmful as in such societies, because more than any other form of government it will encourage there the development of all the vices to which such societies are particularly prone, and thus it will push them in the direction in which, following their natural disposition, they were already inclined (A. de Tocqueville, *L'Ancien Régime*, p. 74).

14. Absolute equality, the destruction of all social hierarchies leaving no other distinctions but those of wealth, creates extraordinary greed, an insatiable thirst for gold; whether one likes it or not, men will wish to advance themselves, that is to say to classify themselves; and since wealth itself participates in the instability of government and of society as a whole, it becomes corrupting in the highest degree. Limitless and uncontrolled desires precipitate themselves towards all that gold holds out, gold the only nobility henceforward, the only honour, the only source of prestige, and in this headlong movement, since there is no time to teach people how to be wealthy, everyone abandons himself to pleasure in a kind of frenzy. In the universal disorder, everyone looks anxiously for a situation worthy of him and his services, to suit his needs or his appetite. Hence the countless demands, murmurings, complaints, passionate hate, a universal basis of bitterness and discontent which is ever growing (F. de Lamennais, *De la religion dans ses rapports avec l'ordre politique et civile*, Part I, pp. 36–7).

Six From the Banker to the Psychopath
1. *The Idiot*, in Vol. VI, p. 228.
2. *The Adolescent*, in Vol. VIII, p. 86.
3. *Ibid.*, p. 97.
4. *The Insulted and the Injured*, in Vol. III, pp. 276–7.
5. *The Adolescent*, in Vol. VIII, pp. 622–3.
6. *Winter Notes Upon Summer Impressions*, in Vol. IV, p. 102.
7. *The Idiot*, in Vol. VI, p. 200.
8. *The Brothers Karamazov*, in Vol. IX, pp. 29–30.
9. *Ibid.*, p. 137.
10. *Ibid.*, p. 611.
11. *Ibid.*, p. 609.
12. *Ibid.*, p. 602.
13. *The Brothers Karamazov*, in Vol. X, p. 272.
14. *Crime and Punishment*, in Vol. V, p. 265.
15. *Diary of a Writer*, January 1873.
16. *Crime and Punishment*, in Vol. V, p. 475.
17. Correspondence, in Vol. I, p. 418.
18. *Crime and Punishment*, in Vol. V, p. 158.
19. *The Idiot*, in Vol. VI, p. 479.
20. *Ibid.*, p. 383.

Seven The Dawn of Chaos
1. *Notes from Underground*, in Vol. IV, p. 151.
2. *The Devils*, in Vol. VII, pp. 439–40.
3. *Crime and Punishment*, in Vol. V, p. 503.
4. *The Devils*, in Vol. VII, p. 481.

5. *Ibid.*

6. *The Adolescent*, in Vol. VIII, p. 70.

7. *The Idiot*, in Vol. VI, p. 523.

8. *Crime and Punishment*, in Vol. V, p. 378.

9. *Ibid.*, p. 382.

10. *The Devils*, in Vol. VII, p. 505–6.

11. *The Adolescent*, in Vol. VIII, p. 514.

12. *The Brothers Karamazov*, in Vol. IX, p. 394.

13. *The Devils*, in Vol. VII, pp. 509–10.

Eight   The Terror to Come

1. *The Idiot*, in Vol. VI, pp. 617–8.

2. *Diary of a Writer*, July-August 1876.

3. *Diary of a Writer*, January 1877.

4. Take my liberty – I'm not selling it to you, I'm giving it to you, on condition that you make my life happy and peaceful (H. de Balzac, 'Le peuple après la révolution de juillet', *Lettres sur Paris*, Vol. II, p. 83).

5. *The Brothers Karamazov*, in Vol. IX, p. 318.

6. *The Idiot*, in Vol. VI, p. 616.

7. *The Devils*, in Vol. VII, p. 421–2.

8. *Ibid.*, pp. 436–8.

9. *The Adolescent*, in Vol. VII, p. 622.

10. *The Brothers Karamazov*, in Vol. IX, p. 515.

11. *Ibid.*, p. 538.

12. *Ibid.*, p. 288.

13. *Ibid.*, p. 320.

Nine   The Individual: Pressures and Responses

1. *Diary of a Writer*, April 1877.

2. *Diary of a Writer*, July-August 1877.

3. *Diary of a Writer*, August 1877.

4. *Diary of a Writer*, January 1881.

5. *The Adolescent*, in Vol. VIII, p. 133.

6. *Ibid.*, p. 624–5.

7. *Crime and Punishment*, in Vol. V, p. 545.

8. *Ibid.*, p. 32.

9. *Ibid.*, p. 435.

10. *Diary of a Writer*, March 1879.

11. *Diary of a Writer*, March 1877.

12. A discord in the divine symphony (Baudelaire, *op. cit.*).

13. *The Idiot*, in Vol. VI, p. 481.

14. *The Idiot*, in Vol. VI, p. 591.

15. *The Adolescent*, in Vol. VIII, p. 420.

16. *The Brothers Karamazov*, in Vol. IX, p. 138.

17. *The Adolescent*, in Vol. VIII, pp. 559–60.

18. *Ibid.*, pp. 611–12.

19. *The Idiot*, in Vol. VI, pp. 486–7.

20. *Notes from Underground*, in Vol. IV, p. 136.

21. *The Adolescent*, in Vol. VIII, p. 424.

22. *The Devils*, in Vol. VII, p. 704.

23. *Crime and Punishment*, in Vol. V, p. 554.

24. *The Brothers Karamazov*, in Vol. X, p. 236.

25. *Diary of a Writer*, January 1877.

26. Walter Benjamin, *Charles Baudelaire*, Frankfurt, 1969, pp. 81–2.
27. *The Devils*, in Vol. VII, p. 124.
28. *The Adolescent*, in Vol. VIII, p. 182.
29. *The Adolescent*, in Vol. VIII, p. 202.
30. *Diary of a Writer*, January 1877.
31. *The Dream of a Curious Fellow*, in Vol. X, p. 421.

Ten   The Anatomy of Intensity

1. But what does eternal damnation matter to him who has found, in a second, infinite pleasure (Baudelaire, *op. cit.*).
2. *The Brothers Karamazov*, in Vol. IX, p. 546.
3. Baudelaire, *op. cit.*, p. 246.
4. *The Devils*, in Vol. VII, p. 218.
5. *The Devils*, in Vol. VII, pp. 219–20.
6. *The Gambler*, in Vol. IV, p. 401.
7. *Ibid.*, p. 383.
8. *The Idiot*, in Vol. VI, p. 617.
9. *Ibid.*, p. 5.
10. *The Brothers Karamazov*, in Vol. X, p. 152.
11. *The Adolescent*, in Vol. VIII, p. 50.
12. *The Brothers Karamazov*, in Vol. IX, p. 134.
13. *Ibid.*, p. 137.
14. *Ibid.*, p. 197.
15. *Diary of a Writer*, January 1877.
16. Do you come from the depths of heaven or from the abyss, Beauty? Your expression, infernal and divine, projects, in confusion, good deeds and crime (Baudelaire, 'Hymne à la Beauté' from *Les Fleurs du Mal*, *op. cit.*, p. 240).
17. *Ibid.*
18. *The Idiot*, in Vol. VI, p. 433.
19. *Ibid.*, p. 89.
20. *The Brothers Karamazov*, in Vol. IX, p. 138–9.

Eleven   Intensity and Time

1. There are moments in life when time and space are more profound, and the awareness of existence immeasurably increased (Baudelaire, *op. cit.*, p. 1256).
2. *The Idiot*, in Vol. VI, pp. 255–7.
3. *Ibid.*, p. 70.
4. *The Brothers Karamazov*, in Vol. X, p. 232.
5. *The Adolescent*, in Vol. VIII, p. 600.
6. *The Brothers Karamazov*, in Vol. IX, p. 146.
7. *Ibid.*, p. 546.
8. *The Gentle One*, in Vol. X, p. 401.
9. *The Gambler*, in Vol. IV, p. 383.
10. *The Devils*, in Vol. VII, p. 160.
11. *The Brothers Karamazov*, in Vol. IX, p. 421.
12. *The Devils*, in Vol. VII, p. 217.
13. *The Idiot*, in Vol. VI, p. 435.
14. *The Devils*, in Vol. VII, pp. 250–1, my italics.
15. Baudelaire, 'Le Voyage' from *Les Fleurs du Mal*, *op. cit.*, p. 127.

Twelve   Modes of Intensity: Gambling

1. And my heart took fright at its envy of many a poor man, running feverishly towards the gaping gulf, who, drunk on his own blood, essentially preferred pain to

death, and hell to nothingness (Baudelaire, 'Le Jeu' from *Les Fleurs du Mal, op. cit.,* p. 92).

2. See Walter Benjamin, *Charles Baudelaire,* Frankfurt, 1969.
3. Ludwig Borne, *Gesammelte Werke,* Vol. III, Hamburg, 1862, p. 38.
4. Benjamin, *op. cit.,* p. 145.
5. *Ibid.*
6. Correspondence, in Vol. I, p. 333.
7. Correspondence, in Vol. II, pp. 9–11.
8. *Ibid.,* pp. 14–15.
9. Correspondence, in Vol. I, p. 411.
10. *The Gambler,* in Vol. IV, p. 398.
11. *Ibid.,* p. 432.
12. *Ibid.,* p. 401.
13. *The Adolescent,* in Vol. VIII, 341.
14. *The Gambler,* in Vol. IV, p. 304.
15. *Ibid.,* p. 396–7.
16. *Ibid.,* pp. 361–2.
17. *Ibid.,* pp. 398–9.
18. *Ibid.,* pp. 304–5.
19. *Ibid.,* p. 293.
20. *Crime and Punishment,* in Vol. V, p. 33.
21. *The Brothers Karamazov,* in Vol. IX, p. 36.
22. *The Gambler,* in Vol. IV, pp. 306–7.
23. *Ibid.,* p. 373.

Thirteen   Modes of Intensity: Masochism

1. It might be agreeable to take it in turns to be victim and executioner (Baudelaire, *op. cit.,* p. 1271).
2. May you be blessed, my God, who gives suffering as a divine remedy to our impurities, and as the best and the purest essence, which prepares the strong for saintly delights (Baudelaire, 'Bénédiction' from *Les Fleurs du Mal, op. cit.,* p. 9).
3. I am the wound and the knife! I am the cheek and the blow! I am the limbs and the wheel, the victim and the executioner! (Baudelaire, 'L'Héautontimorouménos' from *Les Fleurs du Mal,* op. cit., p. 74).
4. *The Gambler,* in Vol. IV, p. 312.
5. *Netochka Nezvanova,* in Vol. II, p. 105.
6. *Notes from Underground,* in Vol. IV, p. 180.
7. *Notes from Underground,* in Vol. IV, p. 203.
8. *The Idiot,* in Vol. VI, p. 452.
9. *Crime and Punishment,* in Vol. V, p. 18.
10. *Ibid.,* p. 26.
11. Anyone who doesn't accept the conditions of life sells his soul (Baudelaire, *op. cit.,* p. 384).
12. The Russian word *oskorblena* literally means insulted, but the sense is far stronger than the English equivalent.
13. *The Insulted and the Injured,* in Vol. III, p. 306.

Fourteen   Modes of Intensity: Libertinage

1. Notes from Underground, in Vol. IV, p. 151.
2. As for torture, it is born of the vilest part of man's heart, thirsty for sensual pleasures. Cruelty and sensuality are identical sensations like extreme heat and extreme cold (Baudelaire, *op. cit.,* p. 1278).
3. I believe I have already said in my notes that love is remarkably like torture or a surgical operation. But this idea can be developed in the bitterest way. Even when

the lovers are really involved with one another, really filled with mutual desire, one of them will always be calmer, less carried away than the other. He, or she, is the surgeon or executioner; the other, the patient or victim (Baudelaire, *op. cit.*, p. 1249).

4. Turgenev, *Complete Works*, Moscow, 1958, Vol. XII, p. 559.

5. N. N. Strakhov to L. Tolstoy, 28 November 1893 quoted in A. G. Dostoevskaya, *Memoirs*, Moscow, 1971, pp. 396–7.

6. Dare I admit that my heart contains the most cruel fancies – I remember that at a very early age I derived a bitter pleasure from beating the animals I loved ... Their cries rent my heart, providing some kind of sensual pity which I craved. If I were a Roman emperor I might well have my friends tortured out of a longing to feel sorry for them (Maurice de Guérin to Barbey D'Aurevilly, quoted in *Nouvelle Revue Française*, 1957, pp. 168–9).

7. *The Christmas Tree and the Wedding*, in Vol. I, pp. 582–3.

8. *The Insulted and the Injured*, in Vol. III, p. 153.

9. *The Brothers Karamazov*, in Vol. IX, p. 303.

10. *The Insulted and the Injured*, in Vol. III, p. 52.

11. *The Devils*, in Vol. VII, p. 701.

12. The adorable Springtime has lost its smell (Baudelaire, 'Le Goût du Néant' from *Les Fleurs du Mal*, *op. cit.*, p. 72).

13. *Crime and Punishment*, in Vol. V, p. 490.

14. *Ibid.*, p. 520.

Fifteen   The Aesthetics of Intensity

1. Walter Benjamin, *op. cit.*

2. Correspondence, in Vol. II, p. 171.

3. Correspondence, in Vol. III, p. 20.

4. Baudelaire, *op. cit.*, p. 952.

5. Correspondence, in Vol. I, p. 359.

6. *Netochka Nezvanova*, in Vol. II, pp. 108–9.

7. *The Idiot*, in Vol. VI, p. 457.

8. *Crime and Punishment*, in Vol. V, pp. 39–40.

9. A. Alvarez, *The Savage God: A Study of Suicide*, London, 1971.

Sixteen   The Public Synthesis

1. *Diary of a Writer*, January 1881.

2. *Diary of a Writer*, May-June 1877.

3. *The Brothers Karamazov*, in Vol. IX, p. 85.

4. *The Adolescent*, in Vol. VIII, pp. 241–2.

5. *Ibid.*, p. 140.

6. *Diary of a Writer*, July-August 1877.

7. *The Idiot*, in Vol. VI, p. 696.

8. *Diary of a Writer*,

9. *The Idiot*, in Vol. VI, p. 379.

10. Correspondence, in Vol. III, p. 50.

11. *The Adolescent*, in Vol. VIII, p. 420.

12. *The Brothers Karamazov*, in Vol. X, p. 243.

13. See above, Chapter Three, note 4.

14. Richard Peace, *Dostoevsky*, Cambridge, 1971.

Seventeen   The Living Life

1. Richard Peace, *Dostoevsky*, Cambridge, 1971.

2. *Notes from Underground*, in Vol. IV, p. 243.

3. *The Adolescent*, in Vol. VIII, p. 243.

4. *Ibid.*, p. 396.

5. *The Brothers Karamazov*, in Vol. IX, p. 137.

6. *Ibid.*, in Vol. X, p. 106.

7. Richard Peace, *op. cit.*

8. Philip Rahv, 'Dostoevsky in *Crime and Punishment*' in *Dostoevsky: A Collection of Critical Essays*, 1962.

9. Richard Peace, *op. cit.*

10. Correspondence, in Vol. II, p. 71.

Eighteen   The Heritage of Intensity

1. Anton Ehrenzweig, *The Hidden Order of Art*, London, 1967.

Select Bibliography

General

Abrams, M. H. *The Mirror and the Lamp*, New York and Oxford, 1953 (references are to the New York 1958 edition).

Béguin, A. *L'âme romantique et le rêve*, Paris, 1937.

Benjamin, W. *Charles Baudelaire*, Frankfurt, 1969.

de Tocqueville, A. *L'Ancien Régime*, 1904 edition.

Furst, L. *Romanticism in Perspective*, London, 1969.

Girard, R. *Mensonge romantique et vérité romanesque*, Paris, 1961.

Lukács, G. *The Theory of the Novel*, London, 1971 edition.

Mauzi, R. *L'idée du bonheur au 18-ème siècle*, Paris, 1960.

Schenk, H. G. *The Mind of the European Romantics*, London, 1966.

Williams, R. *Culture and Society*, 1780–1850, New York, 1958.

Rather than provide a Dostoevsky bibliography it was thought preferable to list the works that were found to be of particular relevance to this book:

Antisferov, N. P. *Peterburg Dostoevskogo*, Petersburg, 1923.

Grossman, L. P. *Poetika Dostoevskogo*, Moscow, 1925.

Ivask, Y. 'Bodler i Dostoevsky' in *Novy Zhurnal* No. 60, 1960, pp. 138–52.

Peace, R. *Dostoevsky*, Cambridge, 1971.

Rahv, P. *Dostoevsky: A Collection of Critical Essays*, Englewood Cliffs, N.J., 1962.

Index

Addiction: 129–130, 173

Adolescent, The: 58, 63, 106, 111–12, 147, 160, 176, 185, 214; Dolgoruky 77, 112, 116, 122, 135, 219; Versilov 94, 96, 118–19, 210–12; Kraft 125

Alvarez A.: *The Savage God* 202

Ambiguity: in beauty 41, 137–39; in love of life 220; moral 220; in suffering 177–78; of Russian character 214

Apathy: 131

Art and society: 18–19

Authenticity: 28, 221, 222

Authoritarianism: 102–4, 108

Bacon, Francis: 67

Balzac, Honoré de: 19, 20, 22, 37, 61, 64

Baudelaire, Charles: 33–48, 145; Romanticism 9, 34, 46, 110, 191; concept of the city 20, 37–40; Romantic anguish 24; function of the artist 33–4; materialism 35, 36; *ennui* 36, 39, 40–42, 119, 141, 185; Gothic 37, 38, 46; beauty 41; sex 39–40, 42, 44, 45, 84, 179; intensity 41–4, 47, 84; experience 42; time 42–3, 141–2; pain and masochism 43–4, 45, 85, 170, 176; compared with Dostoevsky 46, 47–8, 55, 59, 61, 67, 74, 84–5, 116, 126, 129–30, 137–8, 139–40, 143; lyricism 150; gambling 153, 160, 168; *Le Peintre de la Vie Moderne* 33; *Les Fleurs du Mal* 34, 36–7, 38–40, 41, 45, 84, 129–30, 136, 145, 150, 160, 165, 170, 185; *Correspondances* 145

Beauty: 41, 137–9

Bely, Andrey: 57

Behaviourism: 71–2

Bernard, Dr Claude: *Introduction à la physiologie expérimentale* 71

Blake, William: 24, 141

Brothers Karamazov, The: 52, 71, 112, 135, 139, 149, 182, 209, 210, 213, 215; Father Zosima 73–4, 96–7, 219; Dmitri Karamazov 81, 82–4, 106, 116–17, 121, 123, 135–6, 117, 219; Alyosha Karamazov 82, 165; Grand Inquisitor 100–2, 107, 122; Ivan Karamazov 107–8, 183–4, 219; Fedor Pavlovich Karamazov 133–4; Katerina Ivanovna 146–7; Liza Khokhlakova 185; Smerdyakov 112, 122

Byron, Alfred, Lord: 22

Camus, Albert: *L'Homme Révolté* 102; *Caligula* 102; *L'Etranger* 188, 222

Capitalism: 69

Chaos: 90–8, 106–7, 112

Chance: 161–3

Characterisation: 117–18, 222–3

Chateaubriand, François-René de: 14, 15, 22, 24, 27, 114

Children: 182–4, 185

Christianity: 177

Christmas Tree and the Wedding, The: 182–3

City, the: 20–1, 37–40, 51–65, 66, 194–5; *see also* St Petersburg *and* London

Coincidence: 193

Coleridge, Samuel Taylor: 26

Commonsense: 67, 68, 69, 73

Confession: 175–6

Crime and Punishment: 19, 58, 59–60, 62, 85, 112–13, 213; Raskolnikov 59, 60, 62, 81, 86–7, 112–13, 114, 165, 177, 185, 187, 199–200; Porfiry 59; Luzhin 70; Razumikhin 85; Zametov 87, 122; Svidrigailov 65, 92, 121, 122, 126, 183, 187–90; Lebezyatnikov 94–5; Marmeladov 64, 82, 158, 173–4, 197–8; Madame Raskolnikova 198–9

Crowd, the: 20–1

Cultural collapse: 15, 68–9, 90–1, 106

Dandy, the: 31